# PRAISE FOR
# MICHAEL ALLEN'S GUIDE TO E-LEARNING

Every subject area has its Bible. This is it for e-learning. This is the how-to book for both instructional designers and executives responsible for corporate e-learning programs. Especially well done and unique to this book are the chapters on learner motivation and how effective instructional interactivities are created. The bottom line, from our experience working with Michael Allen and his team, is the methods and principles defined in this book work—and work well.

> —MIKE GROSZKO
> *Manager, DaimlerChrysler Quality Institute*

Michael Allen has done it all: He has designed and developed huge amounts of effective e-learning material. He has built several very successful businesses providing programs to sophisticated clients. He has managed development. He personally led the creation of Authorware, the benchmark authoring system used throughout the world. He has lectured. He has written. He has taught. His opinions and perspective are sought by many. But mostly, he thinks. And the results of that thinking are to the benefit of us all. I am glad he wrote down what he thinks.

> —GLORIA GERY
> *Gery Associates*

Never boring, often insightful, I see this as the definitive e-learning guide for everyone in the field who wants to do e-learning right.

> —TED LEHNE
> *Manager, Training Technology Learning Services, Delta Air Lines*

Most e-learning today is an antidote for insomnia! Michael Allen, however, provides a road map to the design of engaging, interactive instructional materials. Any person who designs or purchases e-learning applications should read this book.

> —DR. MARTIN SIEGEL
> *Professor of Informatics and Instructional Systems Technology,*
> *Indiana University*
> *Founder and Chief Learning Officer, WisdomTools*

Michael Allen is the master of designing great, interactive e-learning applications. Flip to any page in this book and you will see practical, powerful ways to create better online courses.

—Dr. Brandon Hall
*CEO, brandon-hall.com*

It must be kismet. We had been trying to figure out how to educate developers about e-learning on an enterprise level. I started reading *Michael Allen's Guide to e-Learning* the day after our meetings concluded. I soon realized this book was exactly what we were looking for.

—Dan Bonicatto
*Senior Training Consultant, American Express*

I've been looking for a way to help businesses understand what it takes to make e-learning the tool for successful performance that it can be. *Michael Allen's Guide to e-Learning* brings the critical issues to light with clearly defined solutions and examples. Business leaders and instructional designers alike need to read this book cover to cover.

—Julie Groshens
*Conference Program Director, VNU Business Media*

I found the book not only to be readable (no surprise), but also to be a work that will be highly useful to a wide range of practitioners and managers. I heartily recommend this book to anyone who is involved in e-learning or its derivatives.

—Dr. Eugene G. Kerr
*President and CEO, Savant, Inc.*

# Michael Allen's

## *Guide to*

# e -Learning

# Michael Allen's

## *Guide to*

# e-Learning

## Building Interactive, Fun, and Effective Learning Programs for Any Company

### MICHAEL W. ALLEN

John Wiley & Sons, Inc.

Published by John Wiley & Sons, Inc., Hoboken, New Jersey
Published simultaneously in Canada

For general information on our other products and services, or technical support, please
contact our Customer Care Department within the United States at 800-762-2974, outside
the United States at 317-572-3993 or fax 317-572-4002.

Wiley also publishes its books in a variety of electronic formats. Some content that appears in
print may not be available in electronic books. For more information about Wiley products,
visit our Web site at www.wiley.com.

Library of Congress Cataloging-in-Publication Data
Allen, Michael W., 1946–
Michael Allen's guide to e-learning / Michael Allen.
        p.   cm.
    Includes bibliographical references and index.
    ISBN 0-471-20302-5 (CLOTH : alk. paper)
    1. Employees—Training of.   2. Employees—Training of—
Computer-assisted instruction.   I. Title.
HF5549.5.T7   A4686   2003
658.3'12404'0285—dc21                                                  2002014447

Printed in the United States of America

10 9 8 7 6 5 4 3 2

# Considerations

### Should you buy this book?

Yes. Neither my publisher nor I are biased on this point. As objective and independent thinkers we've come to a unanimous agreement. You should buy it.

### Why?

e-Learning represents an opportunity for everyone. Good e-learning is powerful and very much worthwhile, and when design and development expenses are amortized over a number of learners, it can be very inexpensive. If e-learning gets on the right path:

- We'll have widespread access to learning opportunities that will allow us to pursue activities, interests, careers, and avocations.

- Corporations will have the means to achieve high-quality customer service, increased business flexibility, lower-cost greater-benefit employee support, lower attrition, and improvement everywhere human performance is a key factor.

- World peace? Possibly. It's tempting to add it to the list, because peace is dependent on understanding, and understanding is a product of learning. There is real potential here, though it's admittedly a stretch.

You could, of course, claim such objectives for any system of learning you favored, but e-learning has so much potential, practicality, and power, it deserves special attention. Saving training time, cutting instructional costs, ensuring top quality and consistency for all learners in all locations, and offering high-impact instruction in a fun and entertaining manner is the lot of e-learning. This potential isn't achieved every time, of course—hence this book—but the potential is there, proven, and without question.

With all there is to gain, we shouldn't waste a minute perfecting the ability of e-learning to do the good things it can for us. With all there is at risk, and the question of whether tomorrow's instruction will be delivered via the Internet having been decisively answered in the affirmative, for whatever reason, we had better get hopping to be sure we get the good and not the bad—because whatever it is, it will stick around longer than it should. With all hands on deck, we can get there.

That's why.

## Who is it written for?

I have attempted to address two primary audiences—audiences that usually read from very separate libraries:

- *Executives, managers, superintendents,* and all *decision makers* who fund (or should fund) the design and development of learning applications and need to make smart decisions about learning and instruction
- *Designers* and *developers* of learning applications, whether novice or experienced, degreed or not

There are strategic issues at stake here, as well as tactical ones. Neither group is going to do as well without the input and support of the other. In fact, it can be quite a struggle without frequent, meaningful communication between the two, as is often the case. As a start, each group *really* needs to understand the perspectives of the other. For example, regarding design and development issues, decision makers need to:

- Understand what's possible in e-learning.
- Know how to avoid wasting money on e-learning.
- Know how to achieve a strong ROI on e-learning.
- Know what to demand in e-learning.
- Know how to evaluate e-learning project proposals.
- Know how to evaluate e-learning solutions and applications.

Regarding business issues, e-learning designers and developers need to:

- Apply the organization's vision as a set of value guidelines for choosing among alternatives.
- Understand the business needs being addressed in e-learning initiatives.
- Design learning applications to address performance needs.
- Understand and meet the criteria for an acceptable ROI.

Of course, each group needs expertise in its respective areas of responsibility. To this end, as this is a book about e-learning, I've tried to do something unusual. I've tried to address for *both* audiences, in plain, reasoned talk, those critical principles of instructional design that I feel are often misconstrued—even frequently by seasoned instructional designers. For e-learning to succeed, decision makers and designers need to work as team members who can communicate with each other, understand what's at stake, and appreciate the options.

I am knowingly taking a risk with the design audience, because I counter so much conventional wisdom and skip over tons of basics and nuances. I have not taken pains to be politically correct. Some might argue that I'm simply being obstinate and argumentative, but I hope they'll give me some space.

My rule of thumb on design principles is, if it doesn't work or it turns out boring learning activities, there is something wrong with the principle, our understanding of it, or the application of it. In most cases, the principles are fine but understood incompletely or out of context. Because they have been misunderstood, they are misapplied, but nevertheless are offered up as justification for a decision. Whatever the cause, politically correct or not, we shouldn't take boring or ineffective e-learning as an acceptable norm—principled or not.

I hope the discussions of critical design principles and their effective application will be understandable and useful to both decision makers and designers. If so, they should contribute to a common ground for discussion about what's really important—developing learning applications that are good investments—and lead to meaningful successes.

## Who is it written by?

I'm Michael Allen, and I have been creating computer-assisted learning applications, tools, and development processes since the late 1960s. The field allows me to address all at once a number of things about which I'm passionate: user-interface design, graphic and architectural design, staging and drama, and, most of all, teaching. As a result of being totally, 100 percent hooked by all this stuff:

- I have many, many years of experience in designing, building, and using numerous forms of technology-assisted instruction.

- I have a PhD in educational psychology with an interdisciplinary specialization in user-interface design.

- I have developed and taught instructional design methodologies over the years that seem to turn out quite a few more effective learning experiences than is typical.

- I have led, instigated, or supervised funded research efforts on topics ranging from issues in learning theory to human perception to intelligent tutoring systems.

- I led the design and managed the construction of two of the most widely used learning and content management systems of their day, long before their rise to corporate interest.

- I have researched and led the creation of many design and development tools, including Authorware, about which I will be forever proud—and consternated.

- I have managed both small and large programming efforts as well as content development activities of almost every size.

- I have been active in professional organizations, twice serving as president of the former Association for the Development of Computer-Based Instructional systems and holding a variety of other positions.

- I was the founding editor and later editor emeritus of the *Journal of Computer-Based Instructional Systems*.

- I worked with IBM to enhance its foundational Coursewriter system, providing advanced capabilities used worldwide, while also documenting the system and lecturing internationally on instructional breakthroughs accomplished with this system.

- As director of the Advanced Educational Systems Research and Development division and a member of an outstanding team of brilliant engineers, researchers, and programmers at Control Data Corporation, I had a privileged opportunity to work on the famous PLATO system and learn from the broad array of instructional approaches pioneered on that system.

- I have worked in both large and small companies, started my own several times—going public with one—had large numbers of people reporting to me, and taken positions responsible for strategic advice needed by top corporate leaders.

- And finally, although in truth I'm very shy and prefer working away quietly with a few esteemed colleagues, I have given perhaps far too many lectures and presentations hither and yon about both the invaluable possibilities and deplorable realities of learning by computer. It's been a great life, being the guest of heads of state, featured speaker at royal symposia, an ambassador of learning technology behind the Iron Curtain, when it was still up, flown fully halfway around the world without any advance notice from keynoting at Windows World Japan to fill in for a suddenly incapacitated celebrity speaker in Brussels, and so on.

As chairman and CEO of Allen Interactions Inc., a consulting and training company offering advice, training, and e-learning development services through its distributed professional studios, I am working with many talented people dedicated to demonstrating the frequently untapped potential of e-learning to make a major difference in the lives of both individuals and organizations.

With all this, and it has been grand, neither you nor I should think I know it all. As usual, the more I learn, the more I realize is yet to be learned. I have learned a lot about what not to do, however. And I have gathered quite a few insights that, I hope you will agree, are worthy of sharing.

But enough about me. Really. I'm running out of pages already.

## What's in it?

This is a two-part book, combining a discussion of why e-learning is often so poor and the problems of breaking out of this tradition with a section on design, geared to addressing some of the most powerful paradigms that seem to work over and over again.

*Part 1* presents an observation that the real costs of poor training are frequently overlooked. Not recognizing them doesn't mean organizations escape payment for this failure. Indeed, they pay handsomely in lost productivity, injuries, inflexibility, poor customer service, quality fluctuation, and so on. The problem is that no one wants to identify the failures and the costs associated with them. As a result, those funds paid out over and over again, year after year, aren't collected and used for an investment in effective training that reaps business benefits over and over again, year after year. They are simply wasted.

This cycle must change for organizations to become unbound from the traditions of lackluster training and take advantage of what e-learning really can do for them. We propose that projects must not accept content presentation as an inescapable prime responsibility. If necessary, very inexpensive transmission of information, such as electronic documents, may have to suffice. Projects should often be reduced in scope so that real interactivity—meaningful, memorable interactivity—can take place to demonstrate its power. Once done, organizations will see the alternatives and begin a positive cycle of high-ROI investments in training. The old alternatives will no longer be acceptable.

Part 1 continues with a review of the components of excellent e-learning and the processes that can be used to ensure a quality outcome. While some people are just naturally gifted in the art of good instructional experience design, there are reliable principles and procedures all of us can use to confidently produce an effective learning application.

*Part 2* turns to design and application of previously presented principles in more detail. Decision makers might too quickly decide this section is not for them, but if you are a decision maker, please consider spending some time here. I've tried to write this in a way that's easy to read and demonstrates a number of very interesting possibilities. It will be very helpful to those who are trying to meet your requirements if you can talk with them about alternatives at this level. Further, this will give you criteria you should expect your designers and developers to meet. If you don't have some familiarity with what's possible and what the alternatives are, how effective can you be as a client, and how can you effectively handle the responsibility of putting good solutions in place?

For designers, I've often advocated reuse of successful designs. It's not necessary to invent original instructional paradigms for each need. It's probably not even possible to do so. But it sure is possible to spend a lot of money programming the same solutions over and over again, not even recognizing how similar the solutions are to others already used. What's the worst of the worst is repeatedly building interactions that were never very good to begin with.

What I've tried to do is chart out some specific designs that cover a host of instructional needs. Not every need, to be sure, but enough of them to impart a pattern of thought you can run with. The need here is to always keep your head not in the clouds, but high enough to get a learner's perspective on what's going on. As a designer or developer, the challenges you are overcoming might lead you to imagine a lot more of interest than learners will see. If what you're doing is boring to learners, it doesn't matter how triumphant the technical solutions are, how correct the design is on some professor's checklist, or where the interactivity falls on a theoretical continuum. Boring is boring, and it's poison. Not too many theories talk about the boredom factor, but it's a real-world thing. So we'll talk about it a lot, with plenty of examples of non-boring designs.

## What's not in it?

This book is not like other books on e-learning. It's neither a primer nor a master compendium. It's not exactly a how-to book, although it definitely has a lot of examples and specific principles. It's not a theory book.

It doesn't go on in detail about how to write good true/false questions. (The real question is who wants a true/false question anyway? Why is it that you should be trying to perfect true/false questions?) Nor does it even talk about how to construct accurate assessments. In fact, there are many important things about instructional design it doesn't talk about. This isn't because they aren't important; rather, they are *too* important to treat lightly and are major topics in and of themselves. This book isn't intended to take nondesigners to the level of expert designers, although it may work quite well for this for those having just enough aptitude.

No, this book is intended to fill a gap—a gap identified for me by a person whose name I've lost. After I had completed a presentation to a large audience at an online learning conference, an attendee came up to me and said, "I've been an instructional designer for 18 years. I have a master's degree and experience in hundreds of projects. What you said today was the most valuable message I've heard about instructional design in all this time. I'd like to redo almost every one of the projects I've completed. Although I can't do that, what I will do going forward will be much different and much better.

"By the way, don't you feel obligated to write a book on this? This has been so helpful to me, and I know many others here today feel the same way. You might get hit by a bus, you know. Then where would we be?"

Question is, where would *I* be, but I guess that's another matter—a matter that didn't seem to concern him, actually. . . .

Anyway, here's the requested book. It doesn't cover the many important things this most-supportive designer had learned from all his classes, books, and years of experience. I'm not trying to retrace all that. Many others are doing it, and new books reorganizing this material seem to come out monthly. This book is intended to provide the other stuff—the stuff they didn't tell you in design school—plus some fundamental things everyone seems to be forgetting.

Also neglected, by the way, are details on such hot topics as blended learning, collaborative learning, reusable learning objects, and standards. These would make excellent material for a companion book, as would the whole subject of managing effective e-learning development. But it seems appropriate to get some critical foundations in proper perspective first. While standards, for example, are fun to talk about, we certainly wouldn't want to standardize around the often less-than-mediocre instructional technology perpetrated on innocent learning victims today. In the haste to make big business out of technology-based instruction, it seems that talking about the necessary attributes of effective learning experiences has become too bothersome and time-consuming. Somehow, I can't subscribe to the notion of "let's get everything organized, modular, and reconfigurable—and later on, we'll worry about whether any of it is really useful."

There is an industry here and enormous future opportunities. But in the race to be first, biggest, and dominant, I'd like to see some deference given to quality and desirability. Wouldn't you? It does take a little time, effort, and thought. Perhaps some patience and values-based leadership, too. I'm all for that.

## Can a book help?

Not if it isn't read. (I'm not constraining my eagerness to sell you on this book very well.)

My hope is that you'll have an opportunity to read through at least some sections, look at the illustrations, and dream about what e-learning could do for you, your friends and family, your coworkers, your organization. Then find a way you can help this technology develop for the best, not for mundane, trivial, ineffective, or boring wastes of time.

My view is that computers represent an opportunity to amplify our humanity, not to control it or restrict it to the lowest common denominator. Technology gives us a way to look at ourselves objectively, to assert our values, and to share the best of our insights with others. This won't happen with our eyes closed or on automatic pilot. It won't happen without vigilance, energy, and commitment. And it won't happen without vision—not just my vision or yours, but with *ours*. Let's do this thing.

Can a book help? It will if it:

- Exposes weaknesses in current approaches

- Verifies that alternatives exist

- Suggests practical ways to improve

- Pulls us together in a motivated campaign to make e-learning all it can be

Perhaps this book will, at least in some small but genuine way, accomplish parts and pieces of these goals. It if does, it will all have been quite worthwhile.

Thanks for your time.

# FREE CD-ROM

**Demo on CD** Whenever you see this icon, a portion of the application being discussed is provided on the free *Guide to e-Learning* CD-ROM, available on request. (The CD-ROM is PC-compatible.)

In some ways, describing an e-learning application is like describing a good movie. Just as there's no substitute for seeing the photography, witnessing the acting, and hearing the music and sound effects all combined, *experiencing* the e-learning examples discussed in the book will make some of my points clearer than any written description can.

Intrigued? I hope so! Here's how to get your *Guide to e-Learning* CD-ROM.

## What we need from you
Please communicate the following information to us:

Your Name
The name of your company or organization (if applicable)
Your mailing address, including zip code (or postal code)
Your telephone number (in case we can't read your address!)
Your e-mail address (in case you don't answer your telephone!)

## Request your free CD-ROM by mail, e-mail, or Internet
By mail, please write to:

*Guide to e-Learning* CD-ROM Offer
Allen Interactions Inc.
8000 West 78th Street, Suite 450
Minneapolis, MN 55439

By e-mail, address your message to:

books@alleni.com

Through the Internet, go to our Web site:

www.alleninteractions.com/books

# Contents

## PART 1   THE BUSINESS PERSPECTIVE     1

Part 1 discusses the value of good e-learning and the indispensable role it can play in your organization's competitiveness. It discusses the essential components and characteristics you must demand. At the same time, it is hoped that this discussion will encourage instructional designers and e-learning developers to adopt your perspective—the business perspective. It isn't complicated, but it is much different from what many organizations are doing with this powerful technology.

## Chapter 1   Plain Talk     3

The legitimate intent of e-learning is not to get a good-looking training program in place, but to achieve important and often elusive business goals. Chapter 1 introduces the notion that business success always depends on getting people to do the right thing at the right time.

Unfortunately, many executives do not see the power of e-learning as a competitive tool. Many look only at the expense of training or at poor examples of e-learning that betray its real potential. Inadequate support both in funding and in executive involvement leads to poor e-learning applications, which then tend to prove the case that e-learning isn't a strategic weapon. Advice is given on how to break free from this self-defeating circular trap.

## Chapter 2    Context—The Possibility of Success    29

e-Learning succeeds only when it addresses problems it can solve and only when essential resources, including leaders and learners, are involved in the process. Once a good e-learning application has been built, it will have disappointing results unless the performance environment is supportive and conducive to the behaviors being trained.

## Chapter 3  The Essence of Good Design  **57**

This chapter discusses the design of effective e-learning applications at a high level. It's intended to give executives the background they need to be informed buyers and to think more strategically about how e-learning can help. It intends to help them see that the poor e-learning applications they may have seen do not represent its true prospects.

This chapter is also intended to help all designers, even experienced designers, think about things that often get too little attention, such as learner motivation and avoiding boredom at all costs. It outlines design discussions to be taken up in much greater detail in Part 2.

## Chapter 4  Getting There through Successive Approximation  **99**

Chapter 4 covers the iterative process of working from a quick analysis and rapid prototyping to modelized production. It's a team process because gifted people who can do it all are too rare, and persistence by people with less talent just takes too long. The chapter discusses being both very pragmatic yet insistent on doing something meaningful (or not doing anything at all).

## PART 2  Design   143

Part 2 returns to the design issues raised in Part 1, but in much greater detail. The hope is that some decision makers will have developed enough interest and curiosity from Part 1 that they will pick out a few issues to explore in more detail. They can thereby improve their ability to specify the characteristics they want to see in e-learning solutions and become more savvy buyers of e-learning applications.

For designers, this material should prove valuable as a source of ideas and guidebook for creating the kind of impressive, engaging e-learning that succeeds from every point of view.

## Chapter 5   Learner Motivation   149

After making the case that motivation is essential for learning, this chapter explores seven specific ways to heighten motivation through good interactivity design.

## Chapter 6   Navigation      229

While navigation is much different from instructional interactivity, it can provide learners an important utility for accessing information and training when
they need it. The difficulty of designing and building good navigation aids is
often underestimated. While a whole book could easily be devoted exclusively to the issues and principles of navigation, this chapter keys into the
most important guidelines for building navigation aids into e-learning applications.

## Chapter 7   Instructional Interactivity      253

This chapter attempts to get at the essence of *interactivity*—a term frequently
bantered about, but meaning many different things to different people. Arche-
types of interactivity are presented with analyses. Frequent interactivity impos-

tors are identified, then a list of specific interactive models that have had robust success in multiple content areas are presented, with detailed examples.

# Foreword

Between us, Michael Allen and I have more than 62 years in the interactive learning business. That's probably more collective hands-on experience in designing, developing, and managing interactive learning than any other two people in the field. About 20 of those 62 years overlap. And we became *friends of the road* the first time we met and found that we shared a passion for learning and performance—and an excitement about using technology to achieve it. Over the years we have become *friends of the heart* as we have gotten to know and like each other. Our professional and personal relationship is largely anchored in a shared point of view, personal values, and a deep commitment to making a difference in the worlds we live in. Michael's commitment to making such a difference is why he wrote this book—and his knowledge and experience will matter to all its readers. I am honored to introduce the book and Michael Allen's thinking to you.

Michael Allen has done it all: He has designed and developed huge amounts of effective e-learning material. He has built several very successful businesses providing programs to sophisticated clients. He has managed development. He personally led the creation of Authorware, the benchmark authoring system used throughout the world. He has lectured. He has written. He has taught. His opinions and perspective are sought by many. But mostly, he *thinks*. And the results of that thinking are to the benefit of us all. I am glad he wrote down what he thinks.

I am a consultant in e-learning and performance support. I work with major organizations and vendors worldwide. I write: I work to articulate strategy, concepts, and possibilities. I also see a *lot* of e-learning. One of the things I do often is review and evaluate courseware. Just days before reading *Guide to e-Learning* I finished reviewing a commercial Web-based learning program. I was told the products were "enormously expensive" to create and that "no expense was spared to wow learners." I was excited about seeing the result. The graphics and animations were almost Disney-quality; the videos were professional and the story lines slick. Sadly, within minutes, I was lost—out of control and frustrated.

The program's structure was unclear. Navigation controls didn't make sense or align with the course structure. I kept winding up in the wrong place and had to derive my own mental model of the program structure to gain control. But I was always a bit off. The visual effects and product values were most impressive, but the program basically was a linear sequential storyline with a bit of content thrown in with text overlays. Frankly, I was bored. I learned nothing. I paid no attention to content because I was being amazed by the visuals. I leaned back in my chair and watched. The only things with any interaction were the pre- and posttests. I was *immensely* disappointed and kept thinking: After all these years, couldn't huge amounts of money buy excellence?

The answer is a resounding *no!* And in this book, Michael Allen tells us why. It's not money that makes a difference, although money is always nice to have. It's the *thinking, process, focus on the learner and learning outcomes,* and *design* that engage and sustain learner involvement and participation. In *Guide to e-Learning,* Michael Allen tells us how to do it.

When I wrote *Making CBT Happen* (Gery Performance Press, 1987—originally published by Weingarten Publications), I used the phrase, *the Law of Diminishing Astonishment.* This law states that any new technology, tool, visual effect, or software trick quickly becomes the baseline. What initially amazes people quickly becomes the new expectation. The Law of Diminishing Astonishment requires that we continue to up the ante to keep people attentive and involved. Many people think it's gee-whiz features. I disagree. If I have learned nothing else during my 26 years in the e-learning field, I have learned what matters. It's *creating motivation, sound instructional strategies and design, significant and almost constant interaction—*combined with *learner feelings of control, progress, and power.* Interactivity—what it is, and how to create it—is a major focus of this book.

As Michael explains throughout this book, buyers and designer/developers of e-learning programs must develop shared expectations and quality standards, and work jointly using proven processes to create the best result. Surely, *someone* must have noticed how inadequate and frustrating the learning program I described above was *during* the development process! But nobody did. And why? Because there was not an integrated development team focused on learning. Rather, the team was a *collection* of graphics designers, visual effects artists, programmers, and Hollywood types with a goal of doing cool things. Clearly, there was not a shared goal of significant and accelerated learning. Content and process were obviously ignored in favor of creative and rich visual efforts.

The reason *Guide to e-Learning* is significant is that Michael Allen:

- Carefully builds the case for good design—and describes the price of failure to achieve it

- Defines, describes, and prescribes the methods to achieve it

- Provides significant and practical examples of good interactive e-learning that have been developed using these sound methods

- Advocates shared understanding, point of view, and goals by all involved

- Raises to high levels of consciousness the specific variables that must be built into e-learning programs—and tells us how to do it

- Provides practical, usable, experience-based frameworks, models, and techniques that enrich the reader

- Generates confidence that good work can be done by normal people without fantasy budgets and resources

## My Favorite Things

Sometimes deep experience in a field can be frustrating. The frustration arises from the increasing difficulty in learning new things. You feel you've seen it all, or the effort associated with incremental learning is so great that you are tempted not to bother. I learned many things from Michael Allen in this book—a turn of phrase, another point of view, an articulation of something that was just below the surface or that I hadn't expressed quite right. Let me share some of my favorite things from this book in hopes that it will frame some of your thinking in reading it.

- *Simplicity is good.*   There's a great quote from Niklaus Wirth, a professor of computer science: "People seem to misinterpret complexity as sophistication." Michael Allen advocates a minimalist approach to design with a focus on the experience outcomes, not on virtuoso technique or trivial, gratuitous use of media and other tricks.

- *Successive approximation as a primary approach to achieving quality.* It's obvious when it's described. And it's obvious after designers and developers use prototyping, iteration, and successive approximation (or continuous improvement) to get closer and closer to a powerful result. But it's not used as often or as well as it should be. Michael hits the nail on the head.

- *The Seven Magic Keys to motivating e-learning.*   I don't believe in cookbooks for design. But I do believe in sound ingredients that can be combined and recombined in many ways to turn out a simple— or elegant—meal. The difference in outcomes is not typically grounded in the ingredients, but rather in the particular combinations used and the sophistication of the chef. Sometimes these ingredients turn out "biscuits," and other times "croissants." Same starting elements, just more steps to do and more skill required. Michael's Seven Magic Keys are fundamental and should be posted on the wall of every designer—and every client. They are clearly articulated and, as important, illustrated and described in sufficient detail to enable even the most inexperienced author to turn out an adequate and involving learning program.

There are many others—but I've said enough. Read this book. Mark it up. Put yellow sticky-notes on it. Use it till you wear it out. Don't pass the book on. It's too important a resource. But do pass the word: As Michael says, "Boring is bad."

*Gloria Gery*
*Gery Associates*
*Tolland, Massachusetts*
*www.gloriagery.com*

# Acknowledgments

I often browse through book acknowledgments, amazed that so many people are typically involved in the production. At first, I didn't think that would happen in this project. Wrong. Way wrong. I am so indebted to so many people, my fear now is that I have forgotten to acknowledge someone. If I have, I pray for your forgiveness. This book wouldn't exist without the gracious contributions of so many friends and colleagues.

All the examples are real, functional e-learning applications. This is a rarity in publications such as this, because obtaining rights to show applications is a daunting and complex undertaking. I was extremely fortunate to get the support of many organizations who have developed leading-edge e-learning applications and were willing to share them. Among those providing support (and willing to accept acknowledgement) are Corning, Inc.; DaimlerChrysler Corporation; Fallon Worldwide; Iconos, Inc.; Macromedia, Inc., National Foods Services Management Institute; and Twin Cities Public Television, Inc. Thanks to all of you. I hope your contributions herein will encourage others to raise their expectations for e-learning.

Examples master Ethan Edwards did an heroic job in harvesting examples and contributed thoughtful descriptions. Sharilyn Fehr led our internal editing efforts with patience, professionalism, and creativity. Corey Stern contributed masterful illustrations. Mary Breslin organized and managed us all. Bob Russell helped with screen captures and document assembly. Andy Pace helped us through the last-minute crunch.

I held chapter review meetings with professional instructional designers and producers. Their comments and suggestions were invaluable. I can only hope I did them justice. Thank you all: Scott Colehour, Keith Craig, Paul Howe, Mary-Scott Hunter, Joy Kopp, John Lenker, Murray Levitt, Ted Manning, Tim Martin, Bill Mills, Laura Nedved, Laurie Squillace, Nan Thornton, Shannon Turner, Jeff Weinberg, and Jason Zeaman.

My business partner, Marty Lipshutz, contributed in countless ways, kept our business running during both my physical and mental absences, and encouraged me even at my most frustrated moments. We have assembled an extraordinary team of e-learning professionals who inspire us and teach us every day. If it weren't for the extraordinary value of their works, many of the e-learning insights shared in this book would still be hidden from view.

My sincere thanks to Matt Holt for his vision in initiating the project and for his resolute encouragement, patience, and advice throughout. I shall always be grateful to him. Thanks to M. R. Carey for his long hours, talented editing assistance, tolerance of my determination to break rules, and ability to reflect my thoughts more clearly than I could reveal them. Thanks to Virginia Carroll for writing a valuable, professional index. Thanks to Courtney Platt, Cayman Islands resident, whose spectacular photographs appear in such prestigious works as *National Geographic,* for capturing my humble likeness. And very special thanks to luminary and warm-hearted friend Gloria Gery for reviewing rough manuscripts and writing such an expressive and substantive foreword.

My wife and partner in life encouraged me to undertake this project shortly after advising me that I needed to learn the freeing power of the word *no.* She spent many hours reading and critiquing at the most inconvenient times. At other times, she parented, hosted, and coordinated our lives while Dad was sequestered somewhere amongst piles of notes, papers, books, and computers.

**P A R T   1**

# THE BUSINESS

# PERSPECTIVE

Executives, you cannot be expected to have in-depth knowledge of training systems, human learning processes, instructional design, or instructional technology, but your support is essential to the success of your e-learning program. You can see that electronic transmission of information is now easy and inexpensive, but simple availability of information does not mean that your business performance needs have been solved.

Part 1 discusses the value of good e-learning, the role it can play in making your business more competitive, and the components and characteristics that must be included in a robust, effective e-learning application.

# PLAIN TALK

**Success is getting people to do the right thing at the right time!**

Did I shout loudly enough? e-Learning is about success, both individual and organizational. It's about behavioral change—again, both individual and organizational. It's also about inspiration, competency, and fun with technology. It's where I've lived for well over 30 years, and I invite you to join me in reviewing the state of e-learning from a very personal perspective.

I'd like to show you the often untapped potential I see in e-learning and share with you some lessons I've learned about how to make e-learning a valuable competitive investment for any success-oriented organization.

There is a reason for e-learning. Actually, there are many reasons for e-learning, ranging from practical to idealistic. Pundits note that in our information-based economy and society, e-learning may be the missing integration that will most dramatically change our lives. It will allow us to learn what, where, and when we want to learn. It will provide choices in how we learn. It will make hard things easy and fun to learn. It will wrestle our intellectual laziness to the ground while helping each of us use more of our untapped capabilities. Life will be grand.

Sure. And, with knowledge and skills readily acquired when the spirit moves us, we will blissfully pursue alternate careers on a whim.

# The e-Learning Myth

Organizations sit down to study their primary goals and performance needs. They look at the products and services they want to provide; the fidelity of service or manufacturing that will be competitive, marketable, and profitable; and their current abilities to provide them. If they are not already performing at a sufficient level, questions of staffing, process, and management are reviewed. (See Figure 1.1.)

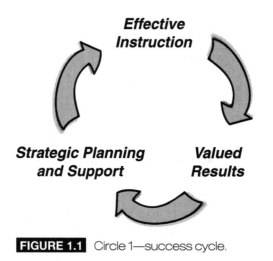

**FIGURE 1.1** Circle 1—success cycle.

A strategic program is put into place, which likely includes training as a cornerstone. With excellent results systematically achieved, those responsible for the training take an honored seat at the executive table to help plan the next strategic advancement.

Right. Wake me when the dream is over.

## Who's Kidding Whom?

To me, a long-term (many would simply say *old*) proponent, researcher, observer, and developer of technology-based learning applications, this goose-bump-generating hyperbole brings frustration and impatience. It's very nice to hear of such confidence in the future of our field. It's a future I've believed in for some decades now. The possibilities keep opportunities alive and cash flowing.

My high blood pressure results from a personal realization that prognostications of learning technologies and their applications continue to lollygag as futuristic fantasies. It doesn't seem to matter how much technologies for the delivery of effective interactive instruction evolve or how much we have learned about effective instructional design.

Boring instruction is not effective instruction. Minds wander, attention wanes, learners muddle through, maybe. When learners are through, they're through—relieved it is over and ready to escape to something else as quickly as possible. Little is retained. Needed behaviors have not been established. Rich associations do not exist for learners to remember key points. It's a waste. It's bad.

What is happening today is a lot of boring stuff. Boring instruction is being developed for electronic distribution in ever-increasing quantities. It is getting to more and more people more and more efficiently every day. The applications may have been designed following structures validated by research on human learning (although probably not), and they may be totally correct from a content accuracy point of view. They may be totally proper in terms of graphic design, typography, and grammar. But they are boring. Boring is bad. (See Figure 1.2.)

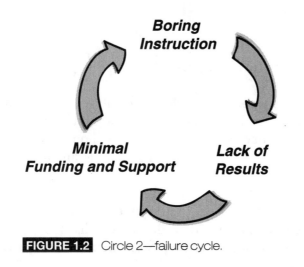

**FIGURE 1.2** Circle 2—failure cycle.

"Oh," you're thinking. "Everyone knows boring instruction is bad!"

Do they? Would people deliberately put out bad instruction? No, but they would and do put out *boring* instruction, so they see some difference. Bad isn't acceptable, but boring is.

When budgets are tight (and when aren't they?), an unwitting experiment ensues. Training has to get by on less. It isn't likely to become less boring on a reduced budget. So, if any development is done, more boring stuff is produced.

"Guess what?" one executive says to another. "Training did just fine with their reduced budget. I don't see any difference, really. Of course, they're complaining that they didn't have enough resources to do it right, but it seems we're getting by just as well as before. Maybe we can cut training a little more! It doesn't seem to matter."

## Entertaining Doesn't Mean Good

Of course, avoidance of boredom doesn't equate to good instruction either. In fact, many instructor-led training events get outstanding "smile-sheet" ratings because trainees have a great time. They enjoy lots of laughs and take home some little-known facts that are great for image enhancement, but nothing significantly changes behaviors, improves processes, or otherwise enhances functionality.

Providing a lively experience is a worthy goal. Boring is bad in the instruction business. Bored learners don't learn. *Boring* and *effective* are mutually exclusive attributes in learning. You can't be effective if your training is boring.

# Effective versus Boring—Pick a Circle

Nobody consciously opts for Circle 2, the failure cycle (Figure 1.2), but if initial efforts at e-learning produce no meaningful, observable results of value, it's easy to believe that there are no good options here—that Circle 1, the success cycle (Figure 1.1), is a fantasy or is suited only to the very rich. At that point, Circle 2 becomes the functional road map and an entrapment that is difficult to break free from.

The failure of so many e-learning applications to produce recognized results (beyond the rapture of their developers) has led to some very wrong conclusions about e-learning. Some popular but misleading conclusions are:

- e-Learning is boring by nature. The only interesting e-learning is that developed by a few creative people with generous funding and loose timelines.

- e-Learning can't be developed quickly or responsively.

- e-Learning can't be cost-justified.

## This Just In: Good e-Learning Is Possible and Practical

Even if you haven't yet seen it done well, you need to know that e-learning can provide extraordinary performance enhancements. It can be cost-effective and very popular among learners. e-Learning can address some of the innumerable performance problems organizations face, while it can work at an individual level to help us all achieve more of our potential and a better quality of life. It doesn't do this often enough, of course, but it's possible.

Some of the things we know about good e-learning are very impressive, as noted in Table 1.1. Of course, not all e-learning has all of these attributes, as not all e-learning is alike and not all of it is good. In fact, too much of it is deplorably bad—needlessly bad, as is discussed throughout this book. But look again at the list of attainable e-learning attributes and benefits. It's an honest and impressive list.

While there is an undeniable upfront investment, the positive return on this investment can make e-learning one of the least expensive means of accomplishing critical organizational performance. With the right process, tools, and models, it can even be developed with amazing speed. It is the intent of this book, in fact, to reveal some of the secrets of accomplishing all these goals.

## Ineffective Training Is Costly

Ineffective training is bad for more than just the obvious reasons. You may be thinking, "Of course it's bad. Who doesn't know that?" Well, a lot of ineffective training is being offered. Either managers don't think ineffective training is a problem, or they don't recognize bad training when they have it. Somewhere along the line, if people thought bad training was truly bad, wouldn't someone terminate those projects or at least prevent ongoing dissemination and use of poor learning applications? Instead, organizations become trapped in a downward spiral, dying within Circle 2.

I must point out that the business cost of ineffective e-learning goes far beyond simply losing all the money spent on it. The total cost can be many, many times the direct cost of e-learning and may easily soar to multiples of the combined costs of the poor e-learning and on-the-job training fix being provided. The final bill is a sizeable sum comprised of these tangible costs, plus all the costs of poor performance and missed opportunities.

**TABLE 1.1  Good e-Learning**

| Attribute | Benefit |
|---|---|
| Shorter learning time, often much shorter | Less time away from productive work. Lower training costs. |
| Adapts to learner needs (i.e., learning mastery is fixed but individual learning times may vary) | Minimized time away from productive work (people return to work as quickly as individually able). No waiting for those needing extra time. Extra attention for those needing more help. |
| Actively involves learners; frequent activity | In-depth learning experiences for each learner, not just for selected learners or those volunteering. |
| Ensures learning | No sliding by. Each learner must achieve and demonstrate competency. |
| Generates positive learner attitudes (When done well, learners often rate e-learning activities as preferable to alternatives.) | More enthusiastic participation. More receptivity. Greater likelihood learning will be applied to on-the-job performance. |
| Provides consistent quality | e-Learning doesn't have bad hair days, headaches, or late nights out. |
| Allows instant, world-wide updates | Through networked services, corrections, improvements, and new information can be made available to all learners instantly. |
| Is available 24/7/365 | Learning can start any day employees are hired or immediately upon assignment to new responsibilities. Learning can be worked in and around higher-priority activities. Learner-managed schedules—learners can work late into the night, in short sessions distributed throughout the day, or in long blocks of time; whatever works best for them. |
| Is patient and treats all learners objectively and fairly | Same options and same performance criteria for all learners. Blind to racial, cultural, and sexual differences. Offers no more or less learning support to any individual. |
| Is highly amenable to systematic improvement | Easily provides data necessary for the evaluation of each and every component. |
| Saves money through low-cost delivery (no or mini-mized travel; fewer or no instructors; automated administration; no classrooms, supplies, whiteboards, etc.) | Big savings have resulted from many applications of e-learning. Even taking full account of development costs, e-learning has a big advantage in cost savings. |
| Allows options for more in-depth study or review whenever needed | Support for learners with special interests or needs to go beyond the bounds of classes. Material used for instruction can be accessed for later use as reference material in a well-designed application. |

# What You Don't Know Can Kill Your e-Learning

One cause of the frequent failures is that the real reasons for undertaking e-learning projects are not defined, are not relayed, get lost, or become misinterpreted. Instead of guiding projects through to the end, the success-related goals of enabling new behaviors are cashed in for the pragmatic goals of simply putting in place something that appears to be a training program. Because executives are not sufficiently attuned to the criteria against which their e-learning solutions should be evaluated, the focus of development teams turns to what will be assessed: mastering the technology, overcoming production hurdles, and just getting something that looks good up and running—within budget and on schedule, of course. The budget and schedule become much more the focus than the original goals.

Surely operational *success* is the primary reason most e-learning projects are undertaken. Success comes from more responsive customer service, increased throughput, reduced accidents and errors, better-engineered designs, and consistent sales. It comes from good decision making, careful listening, skillful performance. Remember: *Success for organizations and individuals alike requires doing the right things at the right times.*

How do things run amok so easily? Two reasons: counterfeit successes (a.k.a. to-do list projects) and undercover operations (a.k.a. on-the-job training [OJT]).

## To-Do List Projects

Unfortunately, many e-learning projects are *to-do list* projects. The typical scenario: People aren't doing what they need to be doing. Someone in the organization is given the assignment to get training in place. A budget is set (based on what, who knows?), and the clock starts ticking down to the target rollout date. The objective is set: Get something done—and, by all means, get it done on time and within budget. Announce the availability of training, cross the assignment off the to-do list, and move on to something else. Goal accomplished.

For the project manager given the assignment, the real reason for implementing e-learning easily transforms from the instigating business need of getting people to do the right things at the right times to the pressing challenge of getting the training project done. Since expenditures for training development and delivery are calculated easily, but training effectiveness is not quantified easily and rarely is measured, the project manager knows how the success of the project will be assessed. It will be measured by timeliness and cost control and probably also by whether learners like it and report positive things about it. It will be measured by how good it looks, how quickly it performs, and whether it's easy enough to use. Complaints aren't good, so safeguards are taken to make sure the training isn't too challenging and doesn't generate a lot of extra work for administrative staff or others. *The absence of complaints is a win.*

Again, the original, purposeful goal of the project is no longer the operating goal. The project quickly becomes somebody's assignment to get done (a to-do list project), and it will be a success—a "success," however, that will most likely fail to contribute significantly to the organization.

## Nobody Checks

Indeed, many of the e-learning developers I know commiserate that no assessment of behavior change is likely to be assessed seriously and no assessment of the return on investment (ROI) is likely to be performed. In one recent study, for example (Bonk 2002), nearly 60 percent of more than 200 survey respondents noted that their organizations did not conduct formal evaluations of their e-learning. It would be very surprising if even 10 percent of organizations using e-learning actually conducted well-structured and executed evaluations. Most organizations use any training funds they can earmark for training for the development of additional courseware, rather than for evaluation of completed programs.

## The Real Project

What does this say about the *real* reason the project is being done? You have to wonder: If people think it's so unlikely that *any* training program is going to be effective, perhaps the learning outcomes aren't the real reasons for offering them. Unspoken, covert, and perhaps subliminal rationales may include thoughts that some sort of formal training, regardless of its effectiveness, will be better than nothing. That is, the *real* reason for implementing the training program might actually be to have the *appearance* of providing training. Otherwise, employees would complain and even have cause to do so. By offering a training program—*any* training program—the burden shifts to the employee.

"What? You don't know how? Didn't you learn anything in the class we sent you to? You must not have been paying attention. We go to all the expense of providing you training and you're still not getting it? Better get on board fast!"

The likelihood of hearing such a comment may be low in actuality, because an employee would have to be caught not knowing what to do or voluntarily admit not knowing what to do even after taking the training provided. There are many reasons for employees to avoid such exposure, of course. So instead of speaking up, admitting lack of readiness, and enduring the consequences, they duck observation, quietly observe others, and, if experimentation and all else fails, surreptitiously interrupt coworkers to learn what's necessary—just enough, at least, to get by and avoid censure.

## Unplanned On-the-Job Training: A Toxic Elixir for Poor Training

Formal training is delivered, observation suggests employees are able to perform, and no one is complaining. Success! Or maybe not. What's working may actually be unplanned on-the-job training, not the gratuitous, impotent, and probably boring e-learning that's been put in place primarily to demonstrate the company's recognition of techno trends.

Who's more anxious to learn than people trying to perform a skill, finding they can't do it, and fearing exposure? Nobody. The helpful guidance of coworkers gratefully received in this ominous situation is often effective, at least in terms of assisting in the specific task at hand. Unfortunately, providing poor e-learning and then invisibly dealing with its ineffectiveness through haphazard knowledge sharing is very expensive, slow, and potentially counterproductive—even dangerous. Let's see why this is so:

### It's Expensive

It's expensive because you have the costs of two training systems—the e-learning system and the ad hoc, clandestine, on-the-job training system. While the costs of e-learning are rather easily identified and include design, development, distribution, and learner time, only the distribution costs and learner time are continuing, recurring costs (Table 1.2). Providing access to e-learning has become inexpensive and quite practical in many settings, whether it's done through CD-ROMs, local area networks, or the Internet.

Unplanned, unstructured on-the-job training doesn't cost anything for design and development, but it carries high and continuing costs that include coworker disruption and resulting loss of productivity. The learning worker probably receives an incomplete tutorial, as well, and will have to continue to interrupt others as additional incompetencies become

**TABLE 1.2   Cost Comparison**

| Parameter | Good e-Learning | Training Approach Unplanned On-the-Job Training (OJT) | Poor e-Learning Plus Ad Hoc OJT |
|---|---|---|---|
| Design cost | Sizeable, one-time | None | Sizeable, one-time |
| Development cost | Sizeable, one-time | None | Sizeable, one-time |
| Distribution cost | Small, recurring | High, recurring | Higher, recurring |
| Effectiveness | High, dependable, consistent | Variable, depending on source, current demands | Variable, depending on source, current demands |
| Risks | Potentially high if enabled performance is not supported within the organization | Potentially high, such as when live, dangerous apparatus is used, business opportunities weigh in the balance, or deadlines need to be met | Potentially high, such as when live, dangerous apparatus is used, business opportunities weigh in the balance, or deadlines need to be met |
| Employee morale | Appreciates recognition of needs | Realizes must fend for self | Realizes must fend for self |
| Total | | | Negatives of both poor e-learning and OJT |

apparent. Performance errors and employee frustration are likely. They contribute to the high costs of this strategy and can cause domino effects of unhappy customers, missed business opportunities, disrespect for management, and so on. (See Figure 1.3.)

### It's Slow

Serendipitous on-the-job training can be timely, but it often is not timely and almost always is slow. It could be that the knowledgeable individual needs to finish a task before providing help on another. Perhaps a machine has to be shut down and restarted each time a procedure is demonstrated. The learner stands and waits, perhaps even being distracted by something to be done elsewhere and then being detained when the aid becomes available. The coworker then stands and waits. It's easy to imagine a multitude of realistic, probable causes of scheduling difficulties and inefficiency. Even when on-the-job training is planned, many companies look for alternatives

Etc.

Missed business
opportunities

Recovery
through OJT

Errors, accidents,
low productivity

e-Learning
development costs

**FIGURE 1.3** Stacked costs of poor
e-learning.

because of the inherent scheduling difficulties, costs, quality-control problems, lack of scalability, delays in
updating, and other problems inherent
in on-the-job training.

### It's Risky

If all these problems weren't bad
enough, there are dangers in some situations that could be devastating. It
could be that the learner doesn't realize
help is needed or doesn't want to admit
it, which could allow problems to reach
an unmistakable or indisguisable sever-
ity. You don't want doctors making
decisions on hunches and then discovering their need for training while
treating you, for example. You don't
want a first-time Bobcat operator
working next to your house.

Trial and error may be a good teacher, but there are costs. If errors are
necessary before a user of an ineffective e-learning program (or any training program) gets needed help, errors will be made. Even further, if the
consulted worker misunderstands the procedure, it's quite possible that
misconceptions will be perpetuated, compounding error upon error. It's a
risky path to take.

## Good Training Is Possible

Training can work. e-Learning can work. Of course it can, and it does
work beautifully for growing numbers of people every day. Well-designed
e-learning can be extraordinarily effective, be efficient with time, and pay
for itself over and over again. It can put your organization in a more competitive position by:

- Improving customer service
- Getting new processes up and running faster
- Reducing employee turnover
- Improving morale

- Increasing production
- Decreasing errors
- Improving product quality
- Improving efficiency

Study after study has demonstrated the potential effectiveness of e-learning. An extensive list of studies appears in Horton (2000). Of course, e-learning isn't more effective than other forms of instruction just because it's delivered via computer. The quality of e-learning is specific to each application, just as the quality of books, television, and film varies with the particular content, program, or movie. e-Learning can be very good, very bad, or anything in between. The *way* in which e-learning capabilities are used makes all the difference.

## Example

Here is a quick example showing that the value of good e-learning instruction can be instantly apparent while its use is fun. This example may be far different from what you need to teach, but consider it for a second. Suppose you were teaching the fundamentals of finding the epicenter of an earthquake with seismographs. This topic could be taught through some pages of text and graphics, as shown in Figure 1.4. Add a question as in Figure 1.5 and it's interactive, right? Wrong.

**Demo
on CD**

# Locating an earthquake's epicenter

The three dots are three different seismograph stations. Each station registers how far away the earthquake occurred. The circles represent the distance from each station. The epicenter is the point where all three circles intersect.

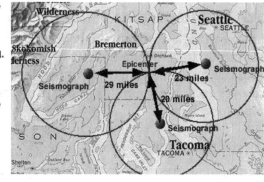

3 of 4

**FIGURE 1.4**  Page turner.

# Locating an earthquake's epicenter

How many seismographs are needed to find the epicenter of an earthquake?

▶

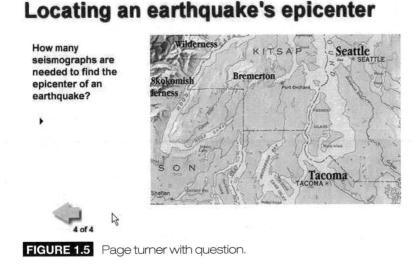

4 of 4

**FIGURE 1.5**  Page turner with question.

Truly interactive learning builds an experience that facilitates both deeper understanding and easier recall. In the design shown in Figures 1.6 to 1.8, learners place seismographic stations one at a time, take a reading, and see from the radius distance how necessary it is to have more than one reading. Wouldn't this be a lot better?

# Locating an earthquake's epicenter

Seismologists identify the center of an earthquake by measuring its strength at different points. A seismograph can determine the distance from the center of a quake, but it can't tell the direction. If you have readings from three different stations, though, you can find the center. Try it.

These dots represent seismographic stations. Drag each dot to the map; then draw the circle to match the measured distance from the quake.

Double click the map at the epicenter when you have located it.

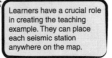

Learners have a crucial role in creating the teaching example. They can place each seismic station anywhere on the map.

**FIGURE 1.6**  Pique the learner's interest.

# Locating an earthquake's epicenter

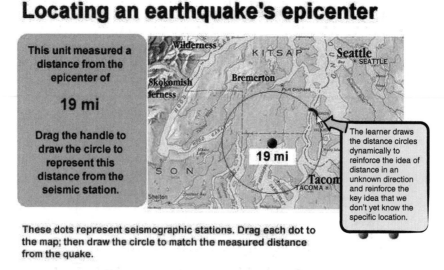

This unit measured a distance from the epicenter of

**19 mi**

Drag the handle to draw the circle to represent this distance from the seismic station.

19 mi

The learner draws the distance circles dynamically to reinforce the idea of distance in an unknown direction and reinforce the key idea that we don't yet know the specific location.

These dots represent seismographic stations. Drag each dot to the map; then draw the circle to match the measured distance from the quake.

Double click the map at the epicenter when you have located it.

**FIGURE 1.7**   Let the learner play.

It shouldn't be surprising that the most common learner action after completing this sequence is to try it again. It fosters no end of curiosity: What if I put the stations really close together? What if I put them in a straight line? What if I place one exactly on the distance circle of another station? The interface allows all these questions to be explored, each answer developing a richer understanding in the learner's mind.

# Locating an earthquake's epicenter

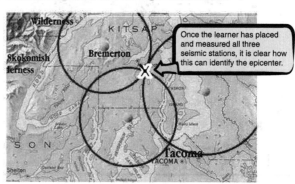

Correct! The three seismograph readings pinpoint a single spot that is the center of the quake.

Once the learner has placed and measured all three seismic stations, it is clear how this can identify the epicenter.

**FIGURE 1.8**   Confirming feedback is almost unnecessary.

# Where Does e-Learning Fit?

Almost everywhere. Whatever business you're in, whatever content and outcome behaviors you're dealing with, e-learning can probably make a valuable contribution.

## Cognitive Skills

Procedures, facts, and conceptual knowledge are all natural types of content for e-learning. These are vital components of learning almost anything. From food preparation to accounting, from aircraft navigation to marketing techniques, from quality manufacturing to drug abuse prevention, e-learning can help.

## Soft Skills

Sometimes it's thought that "soft skills" such as management, leadership, interpersonal relationships, client management, and dealing with upset customers are beyond the reach of e-learning, yet experienced e-learning program designers know that these are, in fact, areas in which e-learning has been singularly effective. Pioneering work done by the Internal Revenue Service to teach agents to deal with upset taxpayers and work done at Carnegie Mellon University (Andersen, Cavalier, and Covey 1996) to teach ethics has demonstrated how uniquely powerful computer-supported learning environments can be for learning soft skills. We'll examine some sample applications later.

## Psychomotor Skills

There are, of course, skills that need practice. e-Learning is probably not the best way to learn to play the drums or hit a baseball, yet these activities have critical knowledge components, such as knowing how to read a musical score or knowing when to bunt. Knowledge components can be taught through e-learning very effectively, of course, as can various mental imaging techniques that are known to improve performance (Korn and Sheikh 1994). Don't overlook the opportunity to use e-learning as an appropriate and effective part of a training program for behaviors that are primarily based on motor skills.

Interface devices and sensors are now being developed for application in various simulators and virtual reality systems and to assist disabled persons and recovering medical patients. Striving for perfection, some golfers and Olympic athletes already analyze their performance using such technologies (Sandweiss and Wolf 1985). These devices are rapidly becoming available for use with e-learning applications designed to teach a great variety of psychomotor skills. It's clear that the applicability of e-learning will expand ever wider as our experience grows and technologies develop.

# You Have Choices

You don't have to live with e-learning programs that don't work. You don't have to pretend your e-learning application is good when you know it isn't. You have options. Because a good e-learning program is a cost-effective way to get people to do the right things at the right times, it can help achieve vital business goals. Cloaking poor training with an on-the-job training coverup (whether it's done consciously or not) neither fixes the problem nor achieves the many positive competitive outcomes possible. And it costs plenty. This shouldn't be a difficult choice.

## Smart e-Learning

There are some critical and often overlooked elements to being smart about e-learning (Table 1.3). When the goal is not just to get some training in place but to change behavior, you're off to a good start. Then, you have to accept that good e-learning applications, while far less expensive than poor e-learning applications, are an investment. Good training isn't cheap in absolute dollars, and the major expense for e-learning is up front. This is why the rich can get richer and the poor do get poorer. The rich don't have to merely dabble in e-learning, strangling its success potential through inadequate funding and support (although they frequently *do* dabble). But neither the rich nor the poor benefit from just doing something, from just going through the motions. If you merely go through the motions, rather than focusing intently on changing behaviors, there will be no winners, and e-learning will look like an impotent technology. Even if you have little to spend, you can spend it effectively on key behaviors that can make all the difference. And especially if you have little to spend, you can ill afford to waste what you have.

It is estimated that in 2004, over $23 billion will be spent just on corporate e-learning programs, not including academic e-learning programs (IDC 2001). The likelihood is great that $22.5 billion of that will be wasted. If money is available, it will be spent, but it will achieve little of importance if we stay on the same path most are on today with their e-learning applications. You don't have to take that path, rich or poor.

## TABLE 1.3  A Smart Approach to e-Learning

| Critical Elements | Critical Because |
| --- | --- |
| Goal is to change behavior | It's easy to assume that e-learning is only about teaching things, but success isn't the result when people know the right things to do, yet continue to do the wrong things. Both the e-learning system and the environment in which it is applied must be designed to enable, facilitate, and reward good performance in order to achieve maximum success. |
| Adequate financial investment | While the return on an investment in a good e-learning program can be incredible, it takes an up-front investment in design and development. Inadequate investment can severely reduce the ROI, even making it strongly negative. (Don't go with the lowest-price option unless you're sure that what you'll get will meet your success criteria.) |
| Partnership between business managers and e-learning developers | If business managers abdicate their critical role in the process of achieving needed human performance, it's much less likely that e-learning will succeed. Training designers need a continuing partnership with management to know exactly what behaviors are needed, to understand the challenges trainees will face on the job, and to influence posttraining support and incentives. |
| Partnership with subject-matter experts | There are many ways to inadequately fund e-learning projects and ensure their failure. One is to provide inadequate access to subject-matter experts—the people who really know what behaviors are needed and what must be learned to enable people to perform them. Almost continuous availability is often required to ensure success in the investment. Note that subject-matter experts include not only the people who may teach courses and write manuals, but also the people who supervise operations and know exactly what their teams need to do. |
| Partnership with learners | Learners should not be the blind victims of whatever instructional approaches experts think would be helpful. Learners can be helpful throughout the entire development process, from definition of what needs to be taught, through the design process, and into the final evaluation. |

## Partnerships

It takes careful planning, organization, and support to build and deliver good training solutions, regardless of the medium used. Design of successful e-learning systems can be done in-house or contracted to outside developers, but neither approach is often successful enough to justify the costs without the involvement of management, subject-matter experts, and learners *throughout the process*. Many projects fail to reach much of their potential because these support groups are not available enough or are not asked to participate. If you're planning e-learning development for your organization, be sure arrangements are made for adequate participation by each group.

## Management Participation

Organizational leaders can provide the financing for training development and assume their involvement is done, but this is often a severely handicapping mistake. Management needs to provide not only the financial support but also continuing help to clarify the vision, define success criteria, and provide a performance-centric environment.

Achieving an organization's vision nearly always depends on human performance. If everyone understands the goal, including those developing the training and support systems expected to help deliver critical performance, the probability of reaching the goal is much higher.

The criteria for success translate portions of the overall vision into specific performance requirements. Clearly relating these criteria to the larger vision gives designers a vital context within which to work and to motivate learning. Everyone needs to be clear that success won't be achieved if the e-learning program doesn't result in specific behavioral changes, and that this is what the effort is all about.

Finally, financial support is only one kind of support that management needs to provide. While financing is critical, it's insufficient to ensure success. Behavioral patterns are established in response to instructions, rewards, effort, available resources, perceived risk, observed behavior in others, team values, and so on. Being *able* to perform as management would prefer does not guarantee that it will *happen*. Management must understand that change is difficult, that there is inertia behind existing behavior patterns, and that change will not be accomplished unless management provides a strongly supportive context.

Management is responsible for one of the pillars needed for a successful e-learning program, but it needs the skills of an on-target design and

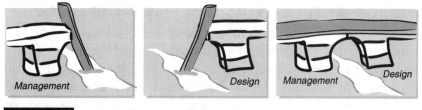

**FIGURE 1.9**  Success requires support at both ends.

development team to turn the vision, criteria, and support into a successful investment in e-learning (Figure 1.9).

The design team's challenge is to provide a strong matching pillar. After defining appropriate behaviors to enable, designers begin by creating ways to ensure high levels of learning motivation. They then make sure that the enabling instructional content is clear and accurate, as a base on which to evolve meaningful and memorable learning experiences (Figure 1.10).

Both pillars are needed to achieve success in e-learning, although designers often struggle for success without much support from management. What they achieve is often commendable under the circumstances. Management, in turn, needs designers who will strongly resist building superficial solutions, provide needed insights, and lead development through a participative process that effectively involves all needed people and resources.

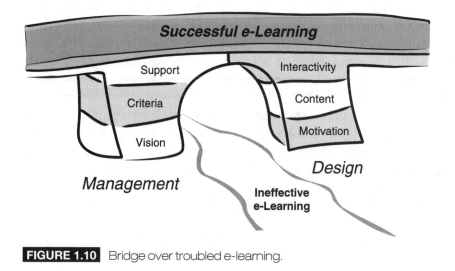

**FIGURE 1.10**  Bridge over troubled e-learning.

## Subject-Matter Expert Participation

Obviously, subject-matter expertise is important, but what is surprising to many is that this expertise isn't just needed at the beginning of an e-learning development project; it is needed throughout. As application prototypes are built and reviewed, for example, needs and opportunities arise for additional content and revisions. If experts aren't available, or aren't available without considerable advance notice and scheduling, projects suffer—sometimes fatally.

Interactivity can be viewed as a dialog between the learner and the e-learning application. The e-learning application represents the combined subject-matter, instructional, and media expertise of the design and development team. The application becomes, if you will, an expert mentor with whom the learner communicates.

Interactive events evolve through the process of design and development (see Chapter 4 for details on the process). As they evolve, the design team looks for ways to make the learning experience as beneficial as possible. This frequently involves searching for ways learners can be allowed to make instructive mistakes. As this occurs, many possible learner behaviors are identified, quite often including a number that were not originally anticipated. These behaviors can be accepted and reinforced as instructional events only if subject-matter experts are available to specify appropriate consequences and feedback.

## Learner Paticipation

Many e-learning application development efforts seek the participation of learners only near the end of the project. Learners are invited to use the application so that functional problems can be observed, ambiguities and unintelligible elements can be identified, and learning effectiveness can be measured. Unfortunately, this is too late in the process to use learner participation for insight on structuring learning events and shaping the experience as a whole.

All too often, organizations are ready to speak for their employees—to make assumptions about what they will find interesting, what they do and do not understand, where their learning problems will be, and so on. When learners are put in a situation where they can respond to such issues meaningfully, many assumptions are frequently disproved. Just asking potential and recent learners some basic questions often reveals important information for design.

Beyond answering initial questions, learners can make vital contributions when asked to review prototypes and interact with evolving e-learning applications, even if quite rough, long before they are completed.

Developing optimal e-learning applications involves sensitivity to many perspectives and values. It involves the interplay of knowledge, technology, art, and design. It's not at all like sending out for a pizza—listing a few parameters and getting a hot product delivered to your door. The effectiveness of the involvement and partnership of all key players will determine the ultimate success of any project. Unfortunately, this means being available and much more.

# How This Book Can Help

If e-learning systems typically failed for only one reason, there wouldn't be so much confusion, and this could be a very short book. We could attack the root of the problem and be done with it. Unfortunately, there are many causes of e-learning failures and much confusion about what constitutes good e-learning methods.

## Part 1 Overview

Chapter 2 tracks down and describes some of the all too common and frequently unrecognized causes of e-learning failures at an overview level.

### Management Issues

If you're an executive considering a new investment in e-learning or wondering why your current e-learning program isn't working out better, the next chapter is especially for you—as are, in fact, the remaining chapters in Part 1. Chapter 2 talks about how many principles that could work don't work as they're often applied. Chapter 3 lays out design criteria you can use to specify criteria for the e-learning solutions you would be willing to fund, and Chapter 4 talks more about the design process to help you feel comfortable with your participation in the process.

### Design Issues

If you're a designer, Part 1 should help you communicate about the essential concepts of successful e-learning with your clients. Chapter 2 may help you work with organizations to create an environment in which e-learning can achieve the performance success needed, while Chapter 3 may give you some ammunition for fighting off failed traditions in instructional design so you can focus on what's really important. Chapter 4 discusses an iterative process so essential to developing creative products of complexity. If you're stuck in a linear, waterfall process, this chapter may give you the confidence to try something that many of us now feel is indispensable.

## Part 2 Overview

Part 2 makes a second pass through design issues, although at a much more detailed level. It shows a collection of examples—or at least screen captures of examples—that are from real applications and demonstrate how vibrant and effective good e-learning can be.

You might be thinking that Part 2 isn't for you because you are not an instructional designer. Although it is indeed written to help project leaders and designers avoid the tempting mistakes so many of us have made in e-learning, it is written just as much for business leaders. Executives must become informed buyers—able to make smart investment decisions, on guard against alluring but inconsequential applications of technology, and ready to assess whether e-learning solutions rise to their expected and needed levels of quality. In other words, you need to know something about instructional design. I've tried to make the coverage of critical principles quick and easy to read and understand.

## My Mission

The purpose of this book is to show that pursuit of a productive, beneficial path doesn't happen without attentiveness, leadership, and expertise. It takes awareness of the alternatives and the predictable results of choosing each alternative. It requires questioning and making some smart decisions. Experience helps. Duh.

In many ways, I'm surprised this book is needed. I meet so many intelligent and dedicated people in the field of designing and developing e-learning applications. We commiserate over the same topics (year after year) and talk about the exciting possibilities of interactivity. I rarely meet with anyone who disagrees with me about the importance of engaging the learner, building a meaningful context, providing valuable opportunities for performance failure coupled with excellent, intrinsic, corrective feedback, and so on. Then when I see their work, I wonder what we were agreeing about. It's clear that one can talk a good game and still not really get it.

# Get It Here

There are challenges to creating good training, granted—but it's not that hard, either. It's not the sheer difficulty of creating good e-learning programs that's keeping us locked in this unproductive trench, it's:

- Lack of awareness that poor decisions can and often do look reasonable
- Lack of knowledge that intuition in the design of instructional interactions is often a poor guide
- Lack of effective teamwork between business leaders and e-learning designers
- Lack of realization that instructional design is a complex undertaking and that to create good designs requires specialized knowledge and skill—not just enthusiasm and creativity

As Tom Werner writes in his direct and insightful publication, *Getting up to Speed on E-Learning* (Sunnyvale, CA: Brandon Hall, 2001):

> Today e-learning could come from anywhere. Management consultants, technology vendors, enterprise system implementers, and outside content providers may drive e-learning without the input or collaboration of the traditional training department. If you want to participate in e-learning, to guide the changes and to have a satisfying and useful role in e-learning, you must be literate about the issues, options, and tools. (Werner 2001, p. 2)

But there's a problem here, too. It's not easy to be functionally "literate about the issues, options, and tools" involved in successful e-learning. It's not as easy as getting an advanced degree, for example, although getting an advanced degree is a smart thing to do. And, of course, it is far from easy to earn an advanced degree. But is a degree enough?

# Knowing versus Succeeding

Unfortunately, many who have advanced degrees, and sometimes years and years of experience, aren't getting it either. They can follow principles they've been taught, discuss research findings in depth, and be compliant with all applicable guidelines and standards without producing anything close to optimal learning applications. In fact, some of the worst e-learning applications I've seen have been built by some of the most educated and knowledgeable individuals in the field. (If you're one of my friends or colleagues, make no mistake about it—we're talking about somebody else.)

On the other hand, I've seen people with no formal education or training in instructional design produce brilliantly effective applications. These people are the rare exceptions, but they really get it. They may not know why they've made the design decisions they have, nor what's really important about them, but they instinctively reject what may, in fact, be very traditional and widely accepted axioms of good design in favor of doing smart, interesting, and effective things.

Of course, this book isn't intended to substitute for a graduate degree in human learning or instructional design. Knowing the things taught in formal courses on human learning, tests and measures, curriculum development, perception, educational psychology, graphic design, communications, and so on can be very, very helpful. I strongly endorse such programs, while recognizing that many of them need considerable improvement and don't go nearly far enough into what makes an effective adult learning experience. What you can't be assured of is that these formal programs will help you *get it*—the *essence of effective instructional interactivity*. And this makes all the difference.

My hope in this book is to help all my readers get it; at the very least, to recognize approaches and designs that have high prospects of success—of getting people to do the right things at the right times. To recognize designs that don't work. To identify some possible remedies. And to enjoy the benefits of great e-learning design.

# Summary

Through some frank plain talk, I've tried to clear up some misconceptions about e-learning. When done well, e-learning saves money, provides effective and consistent training, is available at all hours, and offers many other benefits. I listed the attributes and benefits as clearly as I could in Table 1.1, finding even as I wrote them down that, indeed, there is a very long list of benefits to be realized.

Many of the potential e-learning benefits are not realized often, however. There are many reasons for this. One is that management is often

# What Exactly Is e-Learning?

Simple question.

There should be a simple answer. It helps a lot if definitions can be simple and clear-cut. But with e-learning, a very new term relative to the decades of research on the use of computers in support of learning, there are differing opinions about which types of applications fit within the concept and which do not.

It is popular to use an all-inclusive definition, such as this one:

**e-learning**   A structured, purposeful use of electronic systems or computers in support of the learning process.

The American Society for Training and Development (ASTD), a worldwide association for workplace learning and performance professionals, offers the following definition of e-learning in its Web-published glossary. The all-inclusive nature of the term is made explicit by the listing of example technologies and applications included:

**e-learning**   Covers a wide set of applications and processes, such as Web-based learning, computer-based learning, virtual classrooms, and digital collaboration. It includes the delivery of content via Internet, intranet/extranet (LAN/WAN), audio- and videotape, satellite broadcast, interactive TV, and CD-ROM. (American Society for Training and Development 2001)

Some argue that only *Internet-delivered* applications in support of learning should be included—that the vital role the Internet plays in certain applications makes it important to distinguish these applications. Others note that there are many excellent Internet-delivered learning applications that do not use any capabilities that are in any way different from those of instruction delivered via CD-ROM. Many applications simply use the Internet as a means of distribution. They do not: invoke communication among learners or between learners and instructors; access changing databases; involve searching Web sites. This doesn't make them good or bad necessarily; they simply are not using unique Internet capabilities and so could be delivered by other means.

Indeed, it would be good if there were a term to differentiate those learning applications that take advantage of the Internet's unique capabilities. Unfortunately, the differentiation hasn't taken root even with the alternate term, *WBT* (Web-based training). Perhaps those learning applications in which the Internet plays a vital and essential role should be called *I-learning.*

For better or worse, all computer-delivered instructional applications are frequently grouped under the general heading of *e-learning,* while those specifically delivered over the Internet are called *WBT.* Neither term specifies the most critical characteristics of applications—the instructional paradigms employed—nor even what specific technologies are tapped.

Interactive multimedia comprise the primary technologies upon which e-learning applications are built. Students see text, graphics, and animation on their screens. They sometimes also see video and hear sounds. Problems are posed and students respond through the keyboard, the mouse, or sometimes the microphone. Input gestures are recognized, and the software responds through one of the presentation media. Instructional paradigms vary widely, ranging from simple multiple-choice questions with corrective feedback to high-fidelity simulations to group role playing.

not in a position to see the correlation between the support given for e-learning application development, the quality of e-learning applications put in place, and the benefits achieved. Management often makes unfortunate decisions regarding e-learning program support (and we're not talking about just money here) as a result.

By the same token, e-learning application developers are often not included in the creation of business plans and are unable to help create success strategies. They therefore strive to complete projects on time and within budget, knowing they will be judged more on this than on actual effectiveness—which is often hard to observe and frequently goes unmeasured anyway. Designers rarely have the time or support they need to learn how to create truly powerful e-learning experiences that are also cost-effective. As a result, e-learning applications fail to become part of an effectively designed, complete solution that includes ongoing support and incentives for behavioral change and improvement.

The primary justification for e-learning is that it can, with great efficiency, help organizations achieve success by enabling people to do the right thing at the right time. The mission of this book is to bring both management and e-learning application designers to a common point of understanding about good e-learning—its attributes and development processes that can work to help any organization succeed.

# CONTEXT—THE POSSIBILITY OF SUCCESS

It is surprising how many training solutions have no chance of success. The reason might surprise you. Although poor e-learning design is rampant, the most pervasive inhibitor to success may be the failure to scrutinize the training and performance context and take it fully into account.

The many factors that determine training and performance success include:

- Who participates in the design of the training
- What resources are available for training design and development
- Who is being trained and for what reason
- The instructional delivery media and instructional paradigms used
- The learning support available during training
- The performance support and guidance available after training
- Rewards and penalties for good and poor performance, respectively

This chapter considers the importance of context. It starts by examining the prerequisites for success, then discusses the role of good design as the means to success.

# Unrecognized Context Factors

Failed training programs can often be chalked up to a number of contextual conditions. The barrier can be an environment that inhibits desired performance. It can be poor training solutions developed without the essential participation of key individuals. And it can easily be a combination of both.

Costly failures may not be recognized for some time, of course. All who are responsible for getting training programs up and in operation revel at the achievement and announcement of the programs' availability. They most probably receive congratulations from those who can easily imagine that the development and deployment of a new training program is a considerable undertaking. News that trainees like the new programs and are giving positive feedback validates the cause for celebration. All is well. . . . Not necessarily.

Learning failures will be recognized eventually. Even though trainees may appreciate the excuse to escape the usual work routine and to enjoy the donuts provided in the learning center and the good humor of the instructors and staff, organizations do typically come to realize that people are not performing as well as is needed, that new employees take a long time to get up to speed, that complaint levels haven't dropped, or that throughput continues to deteriorate significantly when additional staff is added. Chapter 1 discusses how effectively organizations, wittingly or not, cover up the ineffectiveness of their training programs and how easily they may come to believe training programs can't be effective solutions.

# Change Is Necessary

"If you continue training the same way you've always trained, don't expect to get better results," says DaimlerChrysler Corporate Quality Training Specialist Jim Crapko. There are many reasons e-learning or any training solution can fail. An objective assessment of the context for a learning solution is essential to identify some of the real barriers to success, and it is very likely that some changes will prove critical to success.

If we're talking about employee training, for example, employees may not be doing what management wants because doing something else is easier and seems to be accepted. In this context, training focused on teaching how to do what management wants done may have absolutely no positive effect. It's quite possible that employees already know full well how to perform the tasks in the manner desired, but they simply choose not to do so. The performance context needs to change.

# Prerequisites to Success

An exhaustive list of e-learning success prerequisites is probably not possible, because so many factors can undermine an otherwise excellent and thoughtful plan. The items in the following list seem to be rather obvious requirements; yet, inaccurate assessments are often made about them:

- Performer competency is the problem.
- Good performance is possible.
- Incentives exist for good performance.
- There are no penalties for good performance.
- Essential resources for e-learning solutions are available.

It is not rational to ignore any one of these prerequisites and still hope for success, so let's look closely at each one.

## Performer Competency Is the Problem

It is crucial to understand business problems and define them clearly, if any proposed solutions are likely to address and solve them. Unfortunately, problems are often hard to identify. Perhaps this is because decision makers are too close to see them, or problems and their suspected causes are too hard to face. When pseudoproblems are mistakenly targeted, the real problems persist, ill-defined and unsolved.

### Throw Some Training at It

It can be comfortable, even reassuring, to conclude that training is needed in the face of a wide range of problems. No one needs to be culpable for the problem. The prospect of a new training effort can paint enthusiastic pictures of problem-free performance. With high expectations, training programs are launched that have very little, if any, prospect of solving the real problem.

The error, however, is probably not what you're thinking. It may actu-

One client asked us to build a program to teach flight attendants how to perform preflight safety checks. This seemed like a very appropriate use of e-learning. We began analyzing the performance context and found some unexpected facts.

The objective of the training was really not to teach people how to perform safety checks (which is an easy process of following the instructions in the flight manual)—it was to get people to do them.

You see, manuals with comprehensive checklists are provided to flight attendants. Even without training, almost everyone could use the manual and perform well. But the manual is thick and heavy as a result of covering many aircraft configurations and providing specific checklists for each attendant's assigned position.

When experienced flight attendants aren't seen carrying their manuals, less experienced attendants are eager to shed theirs as well. As a result, the checklists were not always readily available, and preflight safety procedures were not properly performed.

Performer competency wasn't really the problem at all. Everyone could use the manual and perform the safety checks with 100 percent proficiency. Trying to teach these skills again was not the solution.

Together, we worked out what I think was an ingenious solution. But that's another story.

ally be quite correct that people *do* need training for the ill-defined problems. Because the preponderance of business challenges involve human performance, a blind guess that training is needed will be correct more often than not.

The error is likely to be in deciding who needs training on what. For example, it may well be that *supervisors* of ineffective performers need training so they can more successfully draw out the desired performance from their already capable teams.

## Nonperformance Problems

Businesses face many problems, of course, as I know from having started and run a number of them myself. There is a new challenge every day: higher costs than expected, slow receipts, telecommunication breakdowns, and so on.

**FIGURE 2.1** Misdirected training.

*A question:* You can solve business problems not emanating from employee performance with training. True or false?

Sorry, you're wrong. Actually, this is a trick question. The correct answer is "sometimes."

Here are two reasons:

- Most "nonperformance" problems, on closer inspection, include some performance problems.

- Not all performance problems can be solved with training.

The main point here is that training is a more broadly applicable solution than it may appear. Of course, training isn't a good solution when there are no performance issues or when all players are fully capable of the desired performance. But think carefully. Are *all* players capable of the desired performance? Who are all the players? Training sometimes needs to be offered to suppliers, customers, buyers, and others. Think through the whole process. Again, it's very important to accurately assess the situation—the *whole* situation (Table 2.1). Different answers may emerge.

**TABLE 2.1   e-Learning Opportunities**

| Performer Competence | Performance Problem | Nonperformance Problem | |
| | | No Internal Performance Issues (really) | Hidden Performance Issues |
| --- | --- | --- | --- |
| Competent performers | Consider supervisor training | Consider customer, client, or vendor training | Consider supervisor, customer, client, or vendor training |
| Incompetent performers | Performer training | Consider customer, client, or vendor training | Consider performer, customer, client, or vendor training |

On one hand, I often have clients planning a training solution when the problem doesn't appear to be a performance problem at all. They aren't aware of the true source of their problem, and the training solution they seek will be for naught. If the training proposed doesn't address the source of the performance problem, it will be ineffective, no matter how good the instructional design and implementation are.

On the other hand, *nearly all business problems are performance problems*, at least in part. You must carefully examine performance problems to determine the root cause, or more likely, the root causes. It is likely that part of a good solution will be training. Generally, the questions are whose performance is the problem, and who needs training?

### Go Ahead—It's Easy

Easy to go wrong, that is. A sweeping order to put a new training program in place may yield welcome expectations that, as soon as it kicks in, problems will vanish. However, those receiving the order to go forth and train are set up to misunderstand what's really important. Most likely, they will build a good-looking training program that trains the wrong people or trains the right people to do things that won't actually help much with the identified problem. They were on the wrong path from the beginning.

### Disguised Competency Problems

Many business problems not obviously amenable to training solutions can actually be addressed through e-learning, at least in part. Consider such significant problems as undercapitalized operations, outdated product designs, unreliable manufacturing equipment, noisy work environments, poor morale, bad reputation, and so on. Is training a fix? The somewhat surprising answer is that training should not be ruled out too quickly.

Although many factors determine the possible success of an enterprise, what people do and when they do it is the primary factor. If training can help change what people do and when they do it, then one component of almost every solution might well be training. Consider the following possibilities:

*Undercapitalized operations.*    Finding more money might not be the only solution nor the best solution. Achieving new levels of efficiency, offering better service, or redefining the business model to match available resources may be better solutions with or without new money, and all of these solutions probably require people to change what they're doing.

If squeaking by without additional funding is the chosen route, it often means having fewer people covering more bases. To be successful, they need to learn how to handle a greater variety of tasks; just as important, they also must understand why they need to take on so much responsibility and what can be achieved if they manage well. Successfully squeaking by can be a business triumph if customer service is strong and customer loyalty is maintained. Could effective training separate the winners from the losers in your field when times are tough?

*Outdated product designs.* How did this happen? Were people not tracking technologies, markets, or competitors? Did they know they were supposed to? Did they know how? Are they able to design better products? Perhaps some training is needed—the sooner the better.

*Unreliable equipment or tools.* Is equipment purchasing ongoing? If so, do buyers know enough about your processes, needs, and cost structures to know the difference between a smart buy and a low price tag? If you're stuck with the equipment you currently have, are there effective tricks or precautions known only by a few, maybe only by those on the night shift or by a few silent employees, that could be learned by others to make the most of your equipment's capabilities? This could be a training opportunity.

*Poor morale.* Poor morale isn't just a condition, it's a response. It can stem from a wide variety of problems or perceptions. At the heart is often lack of understanding, lack of communication, lack of trust, or conflicting agendas. Some good coaching and team-building exercises are probably needed. e-Learning may be helpful in some of these situations as an antidote to an acute problem, but it's more likely to be helpful in ongoing measures that energize the workforce and safeguard against chronic morale problems. For example, the corporate mission can be communicated in ways that lead not only to knowledge of the mission, but also to energetic participation and endorsement of the vision. e-Learning can help management learn more effective ways of encouraging spirited contributions through listening, feedback, and appreciated incentives. Often improperly and narrowly viewed as a vehicle limited to the transfer of knowledge and skills, e-learning might overcome a lack of insight and nourish a sense of pride that restores or helps maintain the essential health of your entire organization.

*Turnover and absenteeism.*    People don't feel good about themselves when they aren't proud of their performance. They may be getting by, perhaps skillfully hiding their mistakes and passing more difficult tasks to others, but it's hard to feel good about yourself when you can't do well. As a result, it's hard to get to work, and you're constantly on the lookout for a more satisfying job. With the ability e-learning has to privately adapt the level of instruction to each learner's need, it might just be a solution to problems of turnover and absenteeism.

*Tarnished reputation.*    Why does the organization or product have a bad reputation? Are deliveries slow, communications poor, or errors frequent? In the outstanding book *Moments of Truth* (New York: Harper & Row, 1987), Jan Carlzon shows how successful companies focus on the customer, the front line employees, and the interactions between them that define their respective companies through "moments of truth." In an effective organization, "no one has the authority to interfere during a moment of truth. Seizing these golden opportunities to serve the customer is the responsibility of the front line. Enabling them to do so is the responsibility of middle managers" (Carlzon 1987, p. 68). But how do those on the front line know how to serve the customer? How do middle managers know how to support and guide the front line? Through e-learning? It's a possibility.

Until a problem is identified and framed as a competency problem, e-learning is not the solution. The types of problems just listed are not the ubiquitous problems for which training is an obvious solution. They are listed to underscore the widespread, multifaceted nature of competency problems and the often unsuspected value e-learning can bring to corporations and organizations of all kinds.

Few problems are devoid of human performance difficulties, and, generally, few solutions without a high-impact training component will be as effective as those with it. Still, identifying the real problem is a prerequisite. Guessing about the problem is unlikely to lead to effective solutions. If e-learning is going to work, it's necessary to determine quite clearly what the performance factors are and what is preventing the needed performance from happening. The problem may well lie in one of the other contextual inhibitors in our list.

## Good Performance Is Possible

It doesn't make sense to train people to do things they can't do. It doesn't matter whether people can't perform because there's never a case where trained skills are actually allowed or appropriate, or because it would take too long to complete a process if it were done by the book, or because appropriate situations occur so infrequently that it's unrealistic to expect any trainee to retain learned skills between them.

I know that it seems too obvious to be included in this list of essential preconditions for successful e-learning, but there have been many times our consultants have looked at each other, shaking their heads in frustration, because they have realized that no matter how good the proposed training may come to be, trainees *will not* be able to live up to management's expectations. Without changing the performance context, the desired behavior is not going to happen.

We once had a client, a major U.S. corporation, wanting us to train the company's many account reps on the details of more than 100 insurance plans. The problem was that each agent generally stuck to selling only about six different plans—the plans with which they were very familiar.

Although agents could remember the details of a half-dozen plans and could therefore answer questions correctly, place orders quickly, and show at least some flexibility, there was also a good possibility that other plans were a better fit for clients' needs. To be more competitive and more profitable, the company needed to have its agents consider the full range of products. The solution? "Train our agents to know all of our products."

Who could possibly remember just the major characteristics of more than 100 different insurance plans, let alone the details of each? Well, *nobody* could—at least nobody with less than a decade or so of experience. It wasn't realistic to solve this problem through training alone.

The solution? We developed a performance support system to help agents work with all plans by prompting agents in real time to ask clients selected questions. This could be done when agents were talking on the phone with clients. When on site, clients and agents could work together to answer questions on laptop computers.

After agents narrowed the possible fit to a small number of policies, they could access training on the appropriate class of policies. Agents were eager to learn at this point, and the tasks taught were possible to perform.

Training does not make the impossible possible or the impractical practical. Good performance needs to be a realistic possibility before e-learning has the potential to help. It's common sense, but it needs to be mentioned.

## Incentives Exist for Good Performance

Although the reasons aren't always obvious, behavior happens for a reason. People turn up at work for a variety of reasons, but it's safe to assume that most would not continue to appear if they were not paid.

Many people receive a fixed amount for the hours they work. They will not make more money immediately if they do a better job, and they will not receive less, unless they are fired, for doing a poorer job. So, for these people, pay is an incentive for being present and for doing a minimally acceptable job—and not much more than that.

Fortunately for employers, other incentives exist:

- Approval and compliments
- Respect and trust
- Access to valued resources (tools, people, a window with a sunny view)
- Awards
- Increased power and authority
- More desirable or interesting assignments

Because these incentives are consequences of desired behavior and are usually offered in a timely, reinforcing manner, they can and do affect behavior in profound ways. If valued incentives exist for desired behavior, training that enables such behavior is likely to be successful as well.

**FIGURE 2.2** Ineffective incentives.

**Management**    **Training**

**Willing** **&** **Able**

**FIGURE 2.3**  Partnership of responsibilities.

A partnership between management and training is critical for success (Figure 2.3). Management's role is to provide a learning and performance context that results in a workforce willing to do what needs to be done, how it needs to be done, when it needs to be done. Training is responsible for enabling willing workers to do the right thing at the right time, to see opportunities, and to be effective and productive. The outcome is a win through a willing and able workforce.

When incentives do not exist or rewards are given regardless of behavior evaluation, personal goals take precedence. For many—certainly and thankfully not all—behavior-determining goals may become:

- Reserved effort (doing nothing or as little as possible)
- Increased free or social time
- Avoided responsibility
- Avoided accountability

Management may complain that employees are uncooperative, unprofessional, or in some other aspect the cause of operational failures. Seeing this as a performance capability problem, management might jump quickly to ordering up new training. Unfortunately, *skill training for employees who lack incentive makes little, if any, impact.*

## Use Training to Fix the Performance Environment

By the way, e-learning may offer a means of improving the performance environment when positive incentives are absent:

- Consider training managers on how to motivate employees, seek input, build teams, or provide effective reinforcement.
- Consider providing meaningful and memorable experiences through interactive multimedia to help employees see how the impact of their work determines the success of the group and ultimately

affects their employment. (Please refer to Chapter 5 to better understand how e-learning design can affect motivation.)

These solutions may be the most cost-effective means of getting the performance you need, and they will dramatically increase the effectiveness of training you subsequently provide performers working in the improved environment. Remember, of course, that you will still need to provide incentives for the people who receive training on providing incentives, or this training will also fail.

## Blended Training Solutions

Consider these, also. Blended training solutions mix e-learning with classroom instruction, field trips, laboratory work, or whatever else can be made available. They can provide face-to-face interaction and the nurturing environment of colearners. Many believe the learning process is fundamentally a social process. Observing others, explaining, and questioning can all be very helpful experiences when other learners are working close by and at similar levels, have time scheduled for learning together, and are as concerned with depth of knowledge as developing proficiency as quickly as possible. In general, however, this is more of an educational model than a training model.

Nevertheless, just as it is important to provide incentives and guidance for job performance, it is also important to provide encouragement and support for learning. A well-nurtured learner is going to do much better with e-learning or any other learning experience than an isolated, ignored learner. Learning is work, too (although with well-designed learning experiences, people don't mind the work—even if they should happen to notice it). Incentives, rewards, and recognition facilitate better learning just as they do any other performance.

Blended learning used to be more necessary than it is today, because computers and other instructional media were expensive and difficult to provide. Good interactivity was difficult to build, and media were often slow and of low fidelity.

Blended training solutions are once again in vogue. The reason, in many cases, seems to be that e-learning is not working as well as was hoped. Adding more human interaction to the experience is a quick and easy way to overcome some of the failure. It is perhaps too often argued in hindsight that e-learning just isn't up to the challenge.

e-Learning isn't the best solution for all learning needs. Few would argue that human interaction isn't highly desirable in support of learning, but it is unfortunate to turn to blended learning as a coverup for poor e-learning. Many of the advantages of e-learning are lost in blended solutions, including scheduling flexibility, individualization of instruction, and low-cost delivery.

Blended solutions can be great. When done well, they can accomplish what no single form of instructional delivery can achieve. When done poorly, they stack e-learning failures on top of the disadvantages of other forms of instruction—and that's not a win.

## There Are No Penalties for Good Performance

We haven't discussed avoidance of penalties as an incentive for good performance, although it is a technique many organizations rely on, even if subconsciously. Penalties are more effective in preventing unwanted behaviors than in promoting desired ones; but, over the long haul, they are weak even in doing this. Further, the burden of penalty avoidance (hiding out) saps energy and creates a negative atmosphere.

Although combined use of penalties (even if just verbal penalties) and positive incentives (even if just words of encouragement) is generally considered the most effective means of controlling behavior, employees will be drawn to work environments in which positive rewards are the primary means of defining desired behavior. They will tend to escape environments where censure is prevalent, whether deserved or not.

The worst case, of course, is one in which there are penalties for desired performance. While it may seem absurd that any work environment would be contrived to penalize desired performance, it does happen. In fact, I can—and, unfortunately, feel I must—admit to having created just such an environment at least twice myself. I offer an account here as both evidence that this is easier to do than one might think and as a small atonement for past errors.

I was privileged to lead efforts at Control Data Corporation, where major e-learning tool development was undertaken (including the invention of PCD3 and PLATO Learning Management systems) and the research that led to Authorware was conducted. I had some of the most talented and capable researchers and engineers reporting to me. I'm very proud of the achievements of these people. As we worked together, I felt that we were truly accomplishing some pioneering efforts that would have worldwide impact.

The feeling that we were doing something very important, if not actually noble, motivated us to work long hours and at the top of our abilities. People contributed fantastic ideas. So many of them led to other ideas, and I was almost euphoric with all of them swimming in my head.

One day, one of my most valued employees made an appointment to talk with me at lunch. While it was customary to conduct business over lunch, the formalism in making the appointment and the unstated topic indicated something was up. With a nervousness I had never seen in him, he hesitatingly told me that I was penalizing people for their good ideas. Because I saw each idea as a gateway to another idea, I immediately wanted explore all the things we might build on the original insight. He needed to help me see how people thought I didn't appreciate their contributions—that it appeared I wasn't happy with what they contributed, and that the ultimate goal would have to be even beyond what they had envisioned.

I was unwittingly punishing the very performance I felt blessed with. I couldn't have been happier with what everyone was doing. I appreciated every idea. In truth, I *did* see many of them as stepping stones and hastily appraised them in that context. As a result, my teams wanted to contribute less, although that was thankfully in conflict with their personal and professional goals, and they didn't hold back despite their feelings. We needed a better working environment—one that didn't *penalize desired performance.*

The people on my team didn't lack skills, but if they had, training them wouldn't have fixed the problem. Training me might have. I unfortunately received similar feedback some years later during the development of Authorware. It has taken me a long time to develop better teaming skills, and I'm sure many of my employees would suggest I've still a long way to go. They're right. But I hope I'm doing more these days to reward great performance and less to punish it. In any case, if great performance is punished, even if in seemingly subtle ways, it will counteract the benefits of e-learning. This is an important message to take to heart.

## Essential Resources for e-Learning Solutions Are Available

Design and development of good e-learning is a complex undertaking. It requires content knowledge and expertise in a wide range of areas including text composition, illustration, testing, instruction, interactivity design, user-interface design, authoring or programming, and graphic design. It's rare to find a single person with all these skills, and even when such a person is available, training needs can rarely wait long enough for an individual to do all the necessary tasks sequentially. Forming design and development teams is the common solution, although teaming introduces its own challenges. (Chapter 4 identifies those and presents some process solutions.) What is essential in teaming approaches, however, is that all necessary skill and knowledge domains be included and be available when they are needed.

## Not the Usual Suspects

Making sure all the needed participants are available and involved is not only a coordination problem, but also a problem of understanding who needs to be involved. For example, while everyone understands that subject-matter expertise is required, few executives see themselves involved in e-learning projects beyond sanctioning proposed budgets. But executives are presumably owners of the vision from which organizational goals and priorities are derived. e-Learning provides the means for executives to communicate important messages in a personal way that can also ensure full appreciation of the organization's vision, direction, and needs, so it's a major missed opportunity when executives have no involvement. e-Learning can truly help all members of any organization understand not only what they need to do, but also why it is important. Check Table 2.2 for suggestions on who needs to be involved when.

The more sophisticated the instructional design, the more likely it is that great amounts of time and money will be wasted if the creators lack a full understanding of the following elements:

- Content
- Characteristics of the learners
- Behavioral outcomes that are really necessary to achieve success
- Specific aspects of the performance environment that will challenge or aid performance
- Organizational values, priorities, and policies

In short, a lot of knowledge and information must guide design and development.

## "Watson—Come Here—I Want You"

People must be available, not just documents. Other than having a too-shallow understanding of instructional interactivity, perhaps the biggest

**TABLE 2.2   Human Resources Needed for e-Learning Design**

## Executives

| Why | When |
| --- | --- |
| The vision and business need must guide development. As projects are designed, opportunities arise to question and more fully define the vision—always strengthening, sometimes expanding the contribution of the training. Executives also need to see that posttraining support is provided. | At project definition to set goals. At proposal evaluation to weigh suggestions and alternatives. During project design for questions and selection of alternatives and priorities. During the specification of criteria and methods for project evaluation. |

## Performance Supervisors

| Why | When |
| --- | --- |
| The people to whom learners will be responsible need to share not only their observations of performance difficulties and needs, but also help identify the interests and disinterests of learners and prepare posttraining incentives and support. | At project definition to propose alternative goals. During project design for questions and selection of alternatives and priorities. During the specification of criteria and methods for project evaluation. |

## Subject-Matter Experts

| Why | When |
| --- | --- |
| Unless the instructional designers are also subject-matter experts, designers must have articulate experts to help define what is to be taught and to ensure its validity. | Throughout the instructional design process, beginning with prototypes and later for content scope determination and reviews. |

## Experienced Teachers

| Why | When |
| --- | --- |
| If the content has been taught previously, those who have taught it will have valuable insights to share. They will know what was difficult for students to learn, what activities or explanations helped or didn't help, and what topic sequencing appears to be best. | Throughout the instruction design process to help sequence content and suggest interactive events. |

## Recent Learners

| Why | When |
| --- | --- |
| Recent learners are often the most valuable resource to instructional designers. Unlike experts, recent learners can remember not knowing the content, where the hurdles to understanding were, and what helped them get it. | During rapid prototyping, content sequencing, interactive event conceptualization, and early evaluation of design specifications. |

**TABLE 2.2** *Continued*

## Untrained Performers

| Why | When |
|---|---|
| It's very important to test design ideas before e-learning applications have been fully built and the resources to make extensive changes have been spent. Since you can only be a first time learner once, it's important to have a number of untrained individuals for the evaluation of alternate instructional ideas as they are being considered. | During evaluation of second- and later-round prototypes through to final delivery. To add fresh perspectives, different performers will need to be added to the evaluation team as designs evolve. |

problem corporate teams have in producing high-impact e-learning applications is the lack of sufficient access to key people.

## "Now!"

It is important not only to have the right people available but also to have them available at the right time. Otherwise, the project will suffer. A great many interdependent tasks are scheduled for the development of e-learning applications. They are far more complex than you can imagine if you haven't yet been part of the process. If people are not available for needed input or reviews, it can be very disruptive, expensive, and damaging to the quality of the final product.

## "Never Mind—We Have the Manual"

*Repurposing* is a term used to put a positive spin on some wishful thinking. It's the notion that existing materials, designed for another purpose or medium, can be used in lieu of having more in-depth resources available for e-learning development. It sounds like an efficient if not expedient process to take existing material and turn it into an e-learning application, like turning a toad into a prince. It seems particularly attractive because key human resources, people who are always in high demand, should not be needed very much. The team members can just get the information they need from the documents, videos, instructor notes, and other materials.

Sorry. It's a fairy tale.

Noninteractive materials are far too shallow to supply sufficient knowledge for e-learning design. You've heard the adage, "To really learn a topic you should teach it." Preparation for teaching a subject requires much more in-depth knowledge and understanding than even the best students can gain from just taking a class. e-Learning approaches vary from timely e-mailed messages to fully interactive experiences incorporating dynamic simulations, but even the simplest form of interactivity tends to reveal weaknesses in the author's understanding.

*Repurposing* is essentially a euphemism, because without additional content, in-depth knowledge, and design work necessary to create appropriate interactivity, repurposed material turns efficiently into ineffective electronic page turning. Any plan, for example, to take a manual and turn it into an effective e-learning application without the involvement of people knowledgeable in the subject, experience teaching the subject, and guidance from managers of the target audience is, if not doomed to failure, going to be far less effective than it could be. And, perhaps worse, the faulty applications produced may lead to the erroneous conclusion that

**TABLE 2.3    e-Learning Alternatives**

| Parameter | Alternative | |
| | Repurposing | Designing for Interactivity |
| --- | --- | --- |
| Base | Existing materials | Existing materials plus additional content and instructional experience |
| Design focus | Clear content presentation | Learner needs |
| Product potential | Page-turning application, possibly with shallow interactions | Highly interactive e-learning adaptive to learner abilities and readiness |
| Subject-matter human resources needed | None or little, depending on quality of existing materials | Extensive |
| Materials to be created | Content presentations structured for computer screen presentation and for transmission compatibility via chosen medium (intranet, Internet, CD-ROM, etc.) | Motivational material to prepare learners to learn<br>Carefully structured learning events made up of learning contexts, performance challenges, activities, and feedback<br>Logic to select appropriate events for each learner, given their individual readiness and needs<br>Logic to judge the appropriateness of student responses<br>Assessment events to measure the learner's increasing level of proficiency |

effective e-learning solutions don't exist, are too expensive, or are too difficult to build.

As you can see from Table 2.3, the materials to be created for effective instructional interactivity reach far beyond the information available in noninteractive resources. Much of this work requires in-depth content knowledge—more than can be gained from careful study of materials designed for declaration-based instruction.

In listing essential resources, it may indeed sound as though all e-learning applications are tedious and expensive. This isn't true, but just as any organizational initiative should be guided by people in the know and with experience, it would be an error to attempt e-learning without the expertise needed to direct the effort.

 Advisory

Although common sense would dictate the need for strong knowledge of content, learners, environment, and needed outcomes, the number of clients we see who have sincere hopes of getting the e-learning applications they need without significant involvement of their organization and key people warrants this advisory: *Don't suffocate the potential success of e-learning solutions by making essential resources unavailable.*

# Why Do We Do Things That We Know Are Wrong?

In outlining the contextual prerequisites in the preceding section, I worry that I've made an important mistake. I think the reasoning is logical, yet organizations repeatedly do things to suppress the success of their investments. My mistake may be twofold: (1) assuming that organizations will change their behavior if a better path is identified and (2) assuming that the overall success of the organization is the primary goal of individual decision makers.

The reality may be more like this:

- *We like to fool ourselves.* "We don't like the costs we're hearing for good e-learning applications. If we can get a project going with minimal investment, at least we won't be completely behind the times—and who knows, maybe something really good will come out of it. I love getting a real bargain."

- *Our people are smarter than everyone else.* "We don't need to baby our people with all this learning rigmarole. Just get the information out to them, and they'll do the rest."

- *It's not really this complex.* "I was a student once, and sure, some teachers were better than others. But pretty much anybody with a few smarts can put a course together."

- *Being conservative makes me look good.* "I play it conservative. We don't need Cadillac training, and I sure don't want to be seen as throwing money around. I save a little, and we get some training. It might be pretty mediocre. But who knows? Everybody argues about training anyway, no matter how much we spend. So I look interested, and keep the costs to a minimum."

It's tough to fight such mentalities. The truth remains, however, that astute use of e-learning provides a competitive advantage. Many companies have completely changed their views of training. Whereas they once saw it as an unfortunate burden, they now see it as a strategic opportunity. They hope their competitors won't catch on for a long time.

# How to Do the Right Thing

It's easier to point out errors than it is to prescribe failsafe procedures. There's no alternative I know of to strong, insightful management. A short checklist with respect to e-learning would include:

- ❑ Define performance needs clearly and specifically.
- ❑ Measure current levels of proficiency.
- ❑ Determine what is motivating current behaviors.
- ❑ Make sure desired behavior is possible and reasonable.
- ❑ If appropriate, launch a training development effort:
  - Make all needed knowledge resources available.
  - Determine what's most important to achieve and what the benefits will be.
  - Look at ROI, not just expense, in determining your budget.
  - Use designers and developers who have portfolios of excellent work.

- Define changes to the work environment that will build on learning experiences.
- Keep involved.

❑ Develop a supportive environment that recognizes and rewards good performance.

❑ Keep alert for the kind of rationale that supports doing the wrong things.

# Design—the Means to Success

We've seen the importance of the design context for achieving training success and performance goals. Some errors are made by not using e-learning when it really could be of help. In other cases, training could not solve the problem, regardless of the approach taken. Finally, e-learning development, if it could otherwise be successful, is often held back by lack of access to critical resources.

When all the external factors are in place, we're just getting ready to start. The challenge ahead is that of designing and developing a high-impact e-learning application. This is where the return on the investment of resources will be determined. The design, if you will, is yet one more element of the context that determines whether e-learning fails or succeeds.

In a process something like peeling away the layers of an onion, we will work down to the nitty-gritty details of design. We start first with questions of how good design happens.

# e-Learning or Bust

There is an undeniable rush toward e-learning. The pioneering efforts in computer-based instruction of the 1960s have demonstrated the feasibility of outstanding education and training success, whereas e-commerce has fostered today's expectation that electronic systems will be a primary component of nearly all learning programs in the future. People no longer wonder whether e-learning is viable, but rather wonder how to convert to e-learning most expeditiously.

There probably isn't enough concern or healthy skepticism. It's good if you are concerned about all this e-learning commotion. I'm there with you. I think it is good to be concerned because much (probably most) e-learning is nearly worthless. Just because training is delivered via computer doesn't make it good. Just because it has pretty graphics doesn't make it good. Just because it has animation, sound, or video doesn't make it good. Just because it has buttons to click doesn't make it good.

Excellent design is required to integrate the many media and technologies together into an effective learning experience. Excellent design isn't easy.

## Quick and Easy

Multiple approaches have been advocated over the years, and elaborate systems have been developed. Some have tried laying out more simplified cookbook approaches and providing step-by-step recipes for design and development of learning applications. Although all of them have provided many good ideas, the task continues to prove complex, as evidenced by the plethora of short-lived and little-used applications. Paint-by-numbers solutions just don't hack it, although you wouldn't know that from the number of people who continue trying to invent them.

There is an undying optimism that just around the corner is an easy way to create meaningful and memorable learning experiences that swiftly change human behavior, build skills, and construct knowledge. I am firmly in the camp that doesn't think so. We don't have automated systems producing best-selling novels or even hit movies. Developing engaging interactivity is no less of a challenge. In some senses, I see it as a greater challenge.

Clearly, tools will advance, and we will have more flexibility to try out more alternative designs faster. Our knowledge will advance, so first-attempt designs will be more successful than our first attempts are now. More powerful tools will help us evolve initial ideas into very successful applications. And perhaps, way down the line, computers will be able to create imaginative learning experiences on command. We'll just access a database of knowledge, provide information about ourselves (if the computer doesn't already have it), and indicate whether we want to study alone, with others nearby, or with others on the network. The computer will configure a learning experience for us, and voilà—there it will be! But not today.

## Learning Objects

In the excitement of both e-learning's popularity and our compelling visions of the future, many have been working to create approaches, if not enterprises, that expeditiously solve today's problems and meet foreseeable needs. They hope to develop the primary catalyst that will bring it all together.

One instance of this is the concept of *reusable learning objects* (RLOs). An RLO (Table 2.4) is a small "chunk" of training that can be reused in a number of different training settings. RLOs are a speculative technical solution to reduce development costs. They address the technical issues of e-learning development and maintenance, but applying objects to all training situations can make designing quality training much more difficult. There are some unfortunate difficulties with RLOs that put their utility in question. For example, very small RLOs would seemingly allow the greatest flexibility, but because they are small, they carry minimal context and are therefore instructionally weak. As we've discussed, a strong context is needed for maximum performance impact. Context-neutral objects are generally undesirable learning objects, regardless of the number of times they might be reused. Larger RLOs, conversely, can provide essential context, but therefore need considerable revision when used in alternative contexts. Large RLOs tend to work against the fundamental purpose of RLOs.

Is lowering the quality of e-learning a fair trade-off to ease maintenance? In some situations where content is changing rapidly and out-of-date materials are of little use, an approach that repurposes content is worth investigating. But poorly designed training that is easy to maintain is of little value.

Intrigue, challenge, surprise, and suspense are valuable in creating effective learning experiences. The drama of learning events is not to be overlooked when seeking to make a lasting impression on learners. Just as

**TABLE 2.4  Reusable Learning Objects**

| Characteristic | Pros | Cons |
| --- | --- | --- |
| Reusability | They can be reused in different training situations. | Difficult to design training that will have the desired impact in several different training situations. |
| Standard structure | They are easier to use and lead to more rapid development. | Less flexible; instructional design must use an existing template. |
| Maintainability | Using templates and databases to store objects makes content easier to update and maintain. | Designers should not have to be limited to repurposed content; they should be able to create content that matches the context of that specific training situation. |

we have not yet seen automated ways to create such elements in other media, it will be a while before e-learning evolves to fulfill its potential. We still need to develop a greater understanding of interactive learning before we attempt to make courses by either automation or assembly-line production.

## Art or Science?

A fascinating debate has been carried on among our industry's most knowledgeable and respected leaders and researchers. The debate concerns whether instructional design is, or should be, approached as an art or a science. If based on science, then it should be possible to specify precise principles and procedures which, when followed properly, would produce highly effective e-learning applications every time. If instructional design is an art, then procedures remain uncertain, effective in the hands of some, who add their unique insights, and ineffective when used by others. It's a lively debate in my mind, and I find myself in the frustrating position of agreeing with both sides wholeheartedly on many of their respective arguments.

I come out centered securely on the fence. It seems clear today that a combination of science and art is required and that neither is sufficient without the other. I believe the advocates of each position actually accept this centrist position in their practice.

No one can produce optimal meaningful and memorable learning experiences in a single pass of analysis, design, and development. Certainly experienced and talented people will do a better job than those with little experience or background. Although scientific methods are appropriate for the investigation of alternative instructional approaches, the sci-

### WHAT IS CREATIVITY ANYWAY?

Creativity is often considered to be nothing more than originality or unusualness, but, on second thought, it's clear that divergence alone is not enough. For example, I may decide to cut my lawn with a pair of scissors. This would be generally considered more odd than creative. It would be unusual and unexpected, but very inefficient. If I were able to find an unusual way to cut my lawn easily and quickly, then the solution would be considered creative. Therefore, creative acts are also measured by their *utility*—that is, their ability to accomplish a defined task with acceptable effectiveness.

ence of instructional design is not yet sufficiently articulate to prescribe designs matching the impact of those devised by talented and, yes, artful instructional designers.

It seems that no matter how complex some theories may be—and some are bewilderingly complex—dealing with the complexity of human behavior overwhelms the generalizations of many research findings. By the same token, we need to draw heavily on research foundations to teach people the art of instructional design. Without the rudder of research, creative design results in applications that are simply different and unusual, but not effective.

## Art + Science = Creative Experiments

Within each e-learning project, we are looking for ways to achieve behavioral changes at the lowest possible cost and in the shortest amount of learner time. Creativity helps us achieve these goals with just the right blend of content, media, interactivity, individualization, sequencing, interface, learning environment, needed outcomes, valued outcomes, and learners. Each of these components is complex, and the integration of them with others brings yet another layer of complexity. Each e-learning application is therefore something of an experiment—a research project in its own right—and creativity is needed to find an effective solution as quickly as possible.

This is not to say that each new application must be developed from a blank slate. Far from it; there is much more research and experience to draw upon than seems to be considered by most teams. An excellent compendium with interpretations for practical application can be found in Alessi and Trollip (2001).

## Problems Applying Research Results

When research is considered, its message is often misunderstood and misapplied. Most problematic is the designer's tendency to overgeneralize research findings. The temptation is to hastily apply theories without carefully considering whether the findings in one context apply to the present context.

When I have asked graduate students to justify various peculiarities in their designs, they could frequently and proudly cite published research findings. But in nearly every case, with a bit more analysis, one could see how the referenced findings can be valid and yet not support the graduate students' design decisions. In many cases, one could go on to cite other findings that would suggest doing quite contradictory things.

Scientists are careful to address the applicability of their findings and to caution against overgeneralization. Researchers are continuing to look for principles that are broadly applicable and less dependent on detailed contextual nuances. While many advances are being made—most promisingly, in my view, through a collection of theories known as *constructivism* (Duffy and Jonassen 1992)—it is very important to realize that many appealing principles are far from universal truisms. It's easy to make mistakes.

Valuable as scientific findings should be, it's perplexing to me that so many who know research literature well cannot or at least do not design appealing and effective e-learning applications. If a pill tastes too awful to swallow, it will remain in the jar, benefiting no one. Such is the case with many e-learning applications too awful to swallow.

The problems appear to lie in two major areas. First, it's important to keep not only the *intent* of an experience in mind, but also the likely *assessment* the learner will make of the experience. Is it meaningful, frustrating, interesting, intriguing, painful, confusing, humorous, or enlightening? Learners are emotional, just as they are intellectual, and emotions have much effect on our perceptions and what we do. In addition, adult learners are zealous guardians of their time. If they perceive a learning experience to be wasteful of their time, it is likely to become in short order exactly what they perceive—wasteful and quite ineffective. Irritation and resentment will build, attention will shift away as engagement fades, and the motivation to escape will take command.

It's often noted that a high percentage of learners do not complete e-learning courses. Optimists say attrition occurs because learners quit when they have gotten all they need from a course. Because e-learning offerings are intended to assist people individually, learners should, in fact, opt out when they've gotten all they need. Of course, the more likely explanation for not finishing is that learners have had enough. Not all they need, but all they can stand. In their judgment, the benefits of completing the course do not justify the time expense or the pain of sticking it out. Harsh? I suppose. Reality? I think so.

Second, many common design processes actually prohibit successful creativity. In general, they crush inspired design ideas, rip them apart, and gravitate toward the mundane—all with an explicit rationale and justification to present to management and concerned stakeholders. It's amazing how readily organizations complain about their lack of empowering training and yet find themselves structurally, mentally, and even culturally defiant against change and approaches necessary to get them to their beleaguered goals.

Chapter 4 discusses an effective process called *successive approximation*. It requires a dramatically different approach to application design and development, even though nearly all of the basic steps and procedures are found in every other formalized development process. It requires change, a new group dynamic, and managerial flexibility, but it's worth it. It can make all the difference as to whether winning ideas will be discovered and incorporated in applications, or whether practicality will pronounce powerful insights dead on arrival.

# A Pragmatic Approach

So if creativity requires guidance, and current scientific findings are helpful but insufficient, and the processes typically employed don't get us the solutions we need, what can we do? We can take a pragmatic approach that depends on some creativity, intuition, and talent, to be sure, but also depends on experience as much as published research, intelligence, and an iterative process that includes experimentation and evaluation as fundamental activities. These foundations work well, but they work well only for those who are prepared and armed with the knowledge of how they work together.

The approach I advocate and will present shortly doesn't drag you through a lot of research; there are plenty of available sources if you want that. What you'll find here instead is:

- A frank, outspoken, impassioned, and blunt critique of what doesn't work

- A list of conditions and resources essential for success

- A process that promotes error identification and rectification as a manageable approach to achieving excellence

- Examples of good design you can use

Get ready; all this is coming up next.

# Summary

This chapter reviews a range of multifaceted situations in which e-learning might be a powerful component of a mission-critical solution, including some unexpected situations in which e-learning might be very helpful. It also presents a list of essential conditions for success:

- Performer competency is the problem.
- Good performance is possible.
- Incentives exist for good performance.
- There are no penalties for good performance.
- Essential resources for e-learning solutions are available.

Finally, this chapter shows that for e-learning, or any training solution, to succeed, it is essential that it be designed well—much better designed than what is typically seen—and this requires an investment of human resources going all the way up to the key visionary. If you are that visionary, you must be on guard, because people will let you down for many reasons (some of which are identified in this chapter), while doing what they think is best for the organization. You will need to invest the necessary time and resources to achieve your objectives, regardless of what the purveyors of technomagic would like you to believe.

The next two chapters address in detail the case for a systematic, iterative, exploratory approach to the design of e-learning solutions.

# THE ESSENCE OF GOOD DESIGN

Excellent e-learning is a treasure that pays for itself over and over again. Each positive experience energizes, focuses, and enables yet another learner to be both more individually successful and more able to contribute to the organization.

Many traditional instructional design principles are either misapplied or used in justification of designs that simply do not work. They should be abandoned. It's not my intent to start a religious war. I only hope to help free designers from a widespread bondage to some design principles that are frequently adhered to with something akin to religious fervor.

When we find that some things work over and over again, we should use them even if we don't understand all the reasons why they work. Designers shouldn't be hesitant to take nontraditional directions if they can see a possible benefit for learners. In other words, it is best to abandon traditional principles and methods in order not to abandon the primary goal of creating truly effective learning experiences. We should be guided by *values*, not habits.

I am somewhat irreverent in my treatment of many design practices and vote strongly in favor of on-target pragmatic approaches. What I value is learning experiences that are interesting, meaningful, and memorable, because they have the best chance of enabling people to do what they want and need to do. I hope you already share these values; if not, I hope to convince you that these values are most likely to return the success you're looking for.

This chapter covers key design concepts at a high level, but in sufficient detail so that you will be able to specify criteria to be met by any e-learning application developed or purchased by your organization. It will also help you to judge whether a proposed design properly considers all the key issues and to recognize good and poor designs.

# Design versus Technology

Excellence in e-learning comes not from the fact that it employs technology for delivery, but rather from how e-learning uses available media and the purposes to which it applies them. In other words, it's instructional design that determines the excellence of any instructional experience, not the use of delivery technologies or lack thereof.

WHIZHEAD:  Hey! Look at how I got that graphic to spin around!

YOU:  That's great, Whiz, but um, why is that spinning around, Whiz? Doesn't all that commotion make it harder to concentrate on the key principles listed?

WHIZHEAD:  We couldn't do this spinning effect over networks until just now. I love these new software tools. Learners will think this is really cool.

YOU:  Wouldn't learners find it more useful to zoom in and inspect details?

WHIZHEAD:  I don't have time to do that. It took a while to get this thing to spin, and I think it's cool! Don't worry. They'll love it.

Don't mistake the appeal of new delivery technologies for good e-learning design. Good design, not the latest delivery technology, is essential to success. Good e-learning design is good because it effectively uses available technologies to make learning happen. It's the design that will make the experience boring or inspirational, exhausting or energizing, meaningful or meaningless. It's the design that creates value from the potential technology offers.

# The Three Priorities for Training Success

Instructional design work provides many opportunities for designers to lose focus. This is especially true in e-learning, because its multimedia nature provides an endless array of opportunities for invention and artistic expression. The success of any training effort depends on keeping priorities straight and focusing efforts on those things that will really make a difference.

This is one topic within the great complexity of successful instructional design that is really quite simple and straightforward. Design success comes from doing just three things, and doing them well.

## Ensuring That Learners Are Highly Motivated to Learn

Motivation is essential to learning because it energizes learner attention, persistence, and participation in learning activities. The concept is certainly not new to the literature of learning and instructional design (Keller and Suzuki 1988; Malone 1981), but, unfortunately, explicit treatment of motivation seems to be creeping into e-learning design plans only recently.

I've seen the wonderful effects of stimulating learner motivation, but there's still much work to do before designers feel they can devote enough attention to this issue. Buyers of e-learning applications find it much easier to specify content coverage than to specify even a minimum treatment of motivation. As a result, explicit efforts to ensure sufficient learner motivation are often given only superficial attention, if any attention at all.

*Spend wisely!* In contrast to traditional thinking, I would suggest that if you have a very small budget, it may be appropriate to spend nearly the entire budget to heighten motivation. Highly motivated learners will find a way to learn. They will even be creative, if necessary, to find sources of information, best practices, and so on. They will support each other, exchanging information and teaming up to find any missing pieces. If your training program gets you only this far, you've probably already won the toughest battle. Now you can go on to make your performance solution more cost-effective by addressing the remaining two priorities.

## Guiding Learners to Appropriate Content

Highly motivated learners are eager to get their hands on anything that will help them learn. In response to this motivation, it is important to provide appropriate material in a timely manner, before the motivation wanes.

There's much more to this than meets the eye, and it's not just the challenge of creating clear, understandable content—which does take expertise, make no mistake about that. Making sure content is appropriate for an individual learner means either providing excellent indexing (navigation) to help learners identify appropriate material, or applying an assessment that will determine what each learner needs and is ready to use. In either case, e-learning is often a cost-effective means of providing content access.

## Providing Meaningful and Memorable Learning Experiences

Motivation and good materials are sometimes not enough to enable people to perform at the necessary level or to ready them fast enough. In many cases, there is a wide chasm between building motivation and providing good resource materials and achieving sustained performance competencies. Preparing effective learning experiences is then essential.

One can read extensively about delivering good speeches, handling a difficult customer, or managing a complex project, for example, but guidance and practice will still be necessary to reach needed levels of proficiency. In many cases, it is preferable for learners to make mistakes in a learning environment, where guidance is available and errors are harmless, rather than on the job, where thorough guidance may be more difficult to provide and errors could be damaging to people, equipment, materials, or business.

 Advisory

*Make no mistake!* It is critical that learning experiences have two characteristics: They must be *meaningful* and *memorable.* If a learner can't understand the learning experience, or the experience seems irrelevant, it is obviously a waste of time for that individual. If a learner can't remember what was learned, the experience is similarly unproductive.

## e-Learning—A Tool for All Three

It's important to see e-learning as a means to an end, not as the ultimate goal. The three priorities just listed suggest a prioritized approach for effective e-learning application. First, e-learning provides the multimedia experience that can stimulate emotions, set expectations of success, and help learners visualize the meaning of success and the rewards that can accompany success. Second, e-learning similarly provides the multimedia and navigation components for communicating content to learners clearly and on demand. Finally, the interactivity and multimedia capabilities provide the essential ingredients for meaningful and memorable experiences.

 Let me emphasize the importance of meaningful and memorable (M&M) qualities of learning experiences before we go on to specific design requirements within each of the components of e-learning.

## Meaningful Experience

If a learner doesn't understand, then that learner will not gain from the experience. This is instructional failure. Designers of single-channel deliveries for multiple learners, such as classroom presentations, must decide whether to speak to the *least able* learners (in hopes that other learners will tune in at the appropriate points) or target the *average* learner (in hopes that unprepared learners will catch up and others will wait patiently for something of value). The approach often results in many learning casualties.

Further, if learners don't see the meaningful implications of learning prescribed tasks, such as the tasks' applicability to the work they do or the advantages of new processes over the ones they currently use, the learning experience is also likely to be of little avail. When different learners perform different functions, it is important to help learners see the relevance of the training to their respective responsibilities. You shouldn't just assume that they'll see it.

Well-designed e-learning has the means to be continuously meaningful for each learner. It can be sensitive to learner performance, identify levels of need and readiness, select appropriate activities, and engage learners in experiences that are likely to be meaningful.

## Memorable Experience

If meaningful experiences and the knowledge they convey are easily forgotten (as in a day or two after a posttest), or if learners don't think to apply them in appropriate on-the-job situations, they might as well not have occurred. Time spent in training is expensive to employers. It is not usually the goal of training to simply give workers some enjoyable time off, only to return to the job with no improved abilities. Thankfully, e-learning has many ways to make experiences memorable, such as using:

- Interesting contexts and novel situations
- Real-world or authentic environments

- Problem-solving scenarios
- Simulations
- Risk and consequences
- Engaging themes
- Engaging media and interface elements
- Drill and practice
- Humor

# Primary Components of e-Learning Applications

Good design is comprised of good decisions made both during the design of each primary component of the e-learning application and later as all the components are integrated to create the overall learning experience.

The primary components of e-learning applications to be designed are:

- Learner motivation
- Learner interface
- Content structure and sequencing
- Navigation
- Interactivity

We will review the critical role each component plays in creating effective learning experiences and cover the primary design principles applicable. To ensure success in e-learning and a positive return on investment (ROI), everyone, from responsible executives and purchasing agents to designers and graphic artists, should be aware of the issues involved and their importance for effective e-learning.

I hope the perspective given here will increase your ability to see design issues and options more clearly. I hope also that it will provide a useful perspective for assimilating the more detailed principles presented in Part 2, which revisits learner motivation, navigation, and interactivity design in finer detail. The many examples provided there suggest ways of achieving a wide array of learning outcomes. You might use these designs as a starting point for new application design.

# My Guarantee

I guarantee that proper treatment of these essential design elements will make a difference in your success with e-learning, no matter how familiar or unfamiliar you are with research on human learning or instructional design. The approaches suggested here might be sufficient to help you produce much better than average e-learning applications even if you have no formal in-depth knowledge of the literature, although I truly don't want to discourage you from knowing all you can about learning, perception, and assessment. Get into the literature if at all possible, but whatever you do, don't overlook what I'm sharing with you here. These points are very important and ignored far too often.

# Learner Motivation

You cannot learn someone. The challenge isn't a grammatical one; it's a logistical one. Perhaps, in fact, our language requires verb substitution—you can *teach* someone, but you can't *learn* someone—in recognition of the fact that learning is an internal, personal, and ultimately individual act. It takes energy to learn—one's own energy. Someone else's energy can't be used instead. Personal energy fuels essential activities of perception, recall, analysis, creation of meaningful associations, and storage of information.

With no fuel, it doesn't matter how streamlined the design of your car is, how beautifully appointed the interior, nor how spacious the trunk. The car isn't going to transport you very far. (Well, okay, maybe downhill for a short distance, but that's it.) Similarly, it doesn't matter how stunning your presentation slides are, how beautifully appointed the learning environment is, nor how easy it is to access great volumes of information. We don't learn without focusing energy and activity on the task.

From observations of highly motivated learners, one can conclude that learning motivation:

- Releases the energy necessary to undertake learning activities
- Energizes the learner for learning
- Helps to filter out irrelevant stimuli that can hamper the learning
- Fosters recall of knowledge

- Encourages synthesis of new information
- Causes potential relationships to be considered and evaluated
- Builds and reinforces meaningful new relationships that will be stored in long-term memory

## How Does Knowing about Motivation Help?

### Think Backwards

We evaluate teaching efforts by the level of their success in stimulating learning and achieving valued *behavioral abilities*. So let's start with the outcome of desired abilities and see what is needed to achieve it (Figure 3.1).

EXAMPLE: **CHANGE AN AIRCRAFT TIRE**

**FIGURE 3.1** Thinking backwards, Step 1: Behavioral abilities.

Now, think what creates behavioral abilities. Teaching? Well, not directly. Remember that you can't learn someone. If learning does indeed result, it isn't because the teaching "learned" the learners. It results because learners do something; they do the things necessary to learn. So *learner activity* must precede the development of behavioral abilities (Figure 3.2).

We assume, by the way, that learning activity precedes changes in ability, regardless of whether the activity is externally observable. Internal neurological activity without external expression may be sufficient, but regardless of whether it is discernible, energized action is necessary to cause the biochemical changes that enable new behaviors.

Now ask what causes learner activity. In order for learners to undertake any voluntary activity, whether physical or mental, motivation must exist. By definition, motivation determines what we do with our time and summons the necessary energy. *Motivation* fuels learning activities, and maximizing it strongly predisposes learners to learn (Figure 3.3).

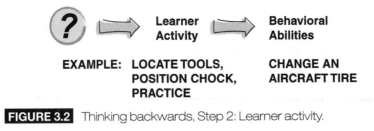

EXAMPLE: **LOCATE TOOLS, POSITION CHOCK, PRACTICE** **CHANGE AN AIRCRAFT TIRE**

**FIGURE 3.2** Thinking backwards, Step 2: Learner activity.

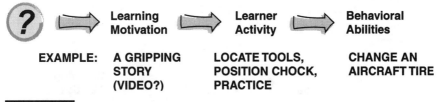

FIGURE 3.3　Thinking backwards, Step 3: Learning motivation.

Where does motivation come from? It comes from many sources, as Chapter 5, a full chapter focused on motivation, discusses. But for now, think of the voluntary intent to learn as a response to assessed needs, opportunities, and perceived rewards.

*Teaching* can influence how we perceive needs, opportunities, and potential rewards for better performance and therefore increase our motivation to learn (Figure 3.4). It can show us specific things that can happen once we've acquired certain skills. For example, a demonstration of good time management can show how just a few simple changes in daily habits can provide more quality time with our family and friends.

The most effective instructional designs therefore deal explicitly with motivation enhancement. But good teaching also *responds* to the motivations and perceived needs it helps learners construct. It guides learners into and through meaningful and memorable activities that lead to targeted goals (Figure 3.5).

It is a common but serious mistake to think of teaching as simply the presentation of information. It is a common mistake because, so often, teachers focus almost exclusively on the presentation of information. Yet teachers who are recognized as foremost in their profession are almost always cited for their creative invention of highly motivating learning experiences.

If teaching is to embrace the responsibility of building behavioral abilities, it is critically important that it center on ensuring adequate learner

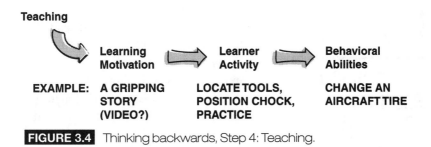

FIGURE 3.4　Thinking backwards, Step 4: Teaching.

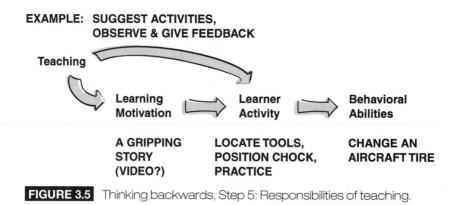

**EXAMPLE: SUGGEST ACTIVITIES, OBSERVE & GIVE FEEDBACK**

Teaching → Learning Motivation → Learner Activity → Behavioral Abilities

A GRIPPING STORY (VIDEO?) — LOCATE TOOLS, POSITION CHOCK, PRACTICE — CHANGE AN AIRCRAFT TIRE

**FIGURE 3.5** Thinking backwards, Step 5: Responsibilities of teaching.

motivation to instigate learning activity and to provide the energy needed for the learning process (Figure 3.6).

## No Mo, No Go

We can go through the traditional and expected steps of teaching, but without motivation, learners won't learn (at least not much). Although with zero motivation there is arguably no learning, the relationship between learning and motivation to learn is probably a proportional one. The more motivated to learn one is, the stronger the focus and the greater the readiness to do what's necessary to accomplish the task.

## Recursive Rewards

Once in motion, of course, learners will benefit from appropriate guidance offered at opportune times. This too is a responsibility of good instruction. Without the support of good teaching to identify appropriate learning experiences, motivation must be all the higher for learners to essentially find ways to teach themselves.

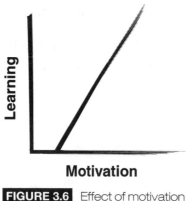

**FIGURE 3.6** Effect of motivation on learning potential.

Good instruction provides a double dose of help. It raises initial motivation levels and also makes learning easier by providing effective assistance. In turn, successful learning builds learner confidence and creates expectations of success, which increases motivation and makes subsequent learning activities more effective and easier to construct. The cycle repeats, nurturing itself and gaining strength. Getting off to a good start with maximized learner motivation has compounding advantages.

## Motivation Levels Can Be Modified

When learners begin reading a book, enter a classroom, or start interacting with an e-learning application, their motivation levels are determined primarily by their initial expectations—expectations of what they will learn, its value, and how much effort is going to be required. They have expectations of how much they are going to enjoy or dislike the experience. They have expectations of whether they will do well enough to impress the instructor and fellow learners or whether they will struggle and possibly be embarrassed. Motivation levels are set by a complex interaction of many factors that no one is ever likely to understand fully—although, introspectively, we would agree that our expectations are largely responsible for our motivations.

## It Can Go Either Way

Fortunately, there are many things you can do to pump up a learner's motivation; unfortunately, there are also many things you can do to shatter a learner's motivation (Figure 3.7). Still more unfortunate is the tendency of e-learning developers to do more of the latter than of the former. This sad situation is probably the result of so much focus on what appear to be the primary challenges—technology and content—and not on what is really the challenge—behavioral change.

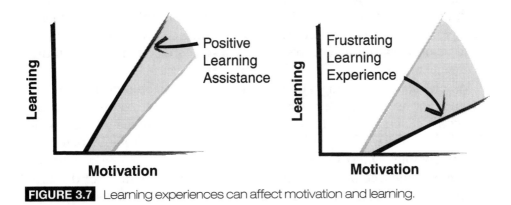

**FIGURE 3.7** Learning experiences can affect motivation and learning.

This is not to say that technology and content aren't important, of course. And it is not to belittle so many well-intended efforts. The attention both technology and content require can be exhausting, especially to newcomers who discover there's so much more to developing learning experiences than meets the eye. Many just don't have the time, money, or energy to get any further than their efforts to deal with content and technology. Ironically, when resources are limited, it's probably better to start with what many never get to: motivation-enhancing experiences.

One of the characteristics of successful e-learning is that it doesn't take motivation for granted. Rather, continued effort is made to stimulate interest, point out benefits, and confirm progress. While effort is necessary for learning, it doesn't have to be unpleasant, monotonous, and wearisome work. Perhaps the adage "Work hard, play hard!" should be extended to "Work hard, play hard, learn hard!" Just as full involvement in work and play can be exhilarating, learning can be an invigorating and even addicting experience that provides lifelong benefits. Chapter 5 provides specific dos for designing learning experiences that raise motivation and specific don'ts for ways of avoiding motivation destruction. They may be the most important keys to successful e-learning I can share.

# Learner Interface

A good user interface is difficult to achieve. Anyone who has used a computer knows that just to operate some of today's most ubiquitous software you have to accept some absurdities (like clicking the Start button to shut down or ejecting a diskette by dragging it to a trash can). Poor user interfaces persist when people don't realize how much better the interface could be or when the advantages of using a standard system outweigh the inconvenience and frustration of its poor user interface.

When I started working with computers in 1967, computers were designed for use by engineers or people formally trained to operate them, not by the general public. Programming languages assumed a mathematician's view of the world or at least a mathematician's aptitude. Articulate use of a complex syntax was necessary even for the simplest tasks. Part of the fun of being a computer programmer was being a member of the elitist group that could make computers do things most people couldn't. Specialized knowledge was indeed power.

One of the wonderful things about working at Control Data Corporation (CDC) in the 1970s, and especially working on the PLATO learning system there, was being part of a pioneering educational system that was clearly shaping the future of instructional technology. Perhaps just as exhilarating was being part of a corporate subculture with a radical view for the time: that computer resources should be accessible to all people.

We felt it shouldn't be so difficult to tell computers what to do. Instead of continuing to build more sophisticated and powerful tools usable only by advanced engineers, questions turned to whether such complex skills could actually be made obsolete.

We developed a tool known as the PLATO Courseware Design, Development, and Delivery System (PCD3) to assist in the development of instructional applications, and also for use as a design tool. Programming abilities needed were minimal, and it was a reconfirming step forward.

To get there, we analyzed some of the best available instructional programs to identify repeating structures—those structures that seemed fundamental to exemplary instructional interactivity. We then developed icons to represent each structure and to serve as visual, movable building blocks.

We went to some extremes in search of usability. For example, we had instructors with no computer skills use our icon-based system to develop instructional applications. Some of their designs, their very first designs for instructional software, were more instructionally sophisticated than most of today's e-learning designs. And the designs were instantly functional. No programming was required. We decided to call the process *authoring* as a contrast to *programming*.

For interface usability, we repeatedly tested the effectiveness of our icon images. After introducing groups of people to our icons as part of overview presentations, we would surprise them with a test two weeks later to see if they could still recall the function represented by each icon. We revised icon designs until nearly everyone could remember them with 100 percent accuracy for at least two weeks without rehearsal.

This work eventually led to the commercial authoring tool, Authorware, which happily took a commanding position in the market. I believe this happened in large part because of the underlying research on which it was based—research on user interface and the process of instructional software creation.

# The Interface Is the Computer

What people see of a computer is its external skins or interfaces—the keyboard, the mouse, and the options presented to them on the screen. Learners couldn't care much less how the computer works internally or how much effort it took to build instructional applications. Rather, they care about what they can do through reasonable effort with their computers and how interesting learning exercises are.

The lack of greater technical knowledge worries many computer users, however, and they feel a continuing risk of doing something stupid—or worse, something damaging. Interfaces provided for controlling the machine often contribute to this sense of insecurity. With many interface designs, for example, users wonder if there are unknown options that could make their work much easier or simple ways to fix problems they are having. They suspect there are features they want, but they can't find them and don't know what they are called. So they muddle along somewhat anxiously within the realm of known procedures. Help systems frequently infuriate people as much as they actually help, and users resign themselves to working within a set of familiar features.

To be more productive and comfortable, people need interfaces that relate to how and why they use a computer. They need interfaces that make options clear and understandable, rather than hidden, unintelligible, and exasperating. Product designers continuously strive to meet exactly these goals in addition to providing efficiency and ease of learning. It is more difficult than it looks, but nevertheless an extremely important endeavor. A single interface weakness, just one, can lead to widespread user anxiety and discomfort.

Why should a single weakness have a far-reaching effect? Users look for patterns or *conventions* among controls and options provided. Conventions reduce the number of unique protocols that have to be remembered and usually provide helpful expectations of how unused options also work. The assumption users make is that the options work similarly to other related options or in exactly the same way as identically named options in other places.

When the consistency of conventions is broken in even a single instance, learners become uncertain about whether other conventions are also inconsistent. Every convention becomes immediately suspect. The software seems harder to use, confidence decreases, and many users barricade themselves within a subset of options that have proven reliable and at least minimally sufficient.

## The Primary Responsibilities of Learner-Interface Design

Learner-interface design carries many responsibilities. It is not only supportive of interactivity, navigation, and information retrieval, but also integral to the success of all components of the e-learning application. It carries both the responsibilities of general user-interface design and special responsibilities to enhance the effectiveness of e-learning.

Briefly stated, the responsibilities of learner-interface design are to:

- *Minimize memory burden.*   Except in cases of simulation, we are not generally interested in teaching learners to remember the details of the e-learning interface. Instead, we want them to use their learning energy to learn target skills. Learner interfaces should therefore be meaningful without having to memorize symbols, terminology, and procedures.

- *Minimize errors.*   Good interfaces provide strong cues that help prevent errors. Learner expectations are properly set and reinforced by the interface, so that it's not necessary to think carefully and behave cautiously.

- *Minimize effort.*   Ideally, learners can perform each function with a single command, whether it's a mouse click, keystroke, spoken word, or other quick command. Although such an approach may not be possible or might negatively impact other goals such as minimizing memory burden or errors, effort should be minimized as much as possible. Where different levels of effort are necessary, greater effort should be correlated with the learners' perception of the computational task's difficulty. That is, it should take little learner effort to get the computer to do something that seems quite simple, and more learner effort to command the computer to do something that seems difficult.

- *Promote features.*   The learner-interface design has a role in reminding learners of features they can use. Hidden features obviously increase the memory burden and do nothing to promote features, but it isn't always possible to keep all features visible. Frequently used features will be remembered most easily, so it may be appropriate to use unprompted commands for them while prompting for less commonly used features. Careful choices need to be made, as there are penalties for almost every compromise.

- *Contribute to the learning process.* The learner-interface design must do all it can to facilitate an optimally effective learning experience. The challenge is great, and every component must do its part. The ways of enhancing learning experiences are often context-specific. For example, if a machine process is being simulated, controls should resemble the controls learners will use. If learners are comparing documents, then it should manage selection and viewing of documents.

Overall, learner-interface designs should keep learners in control and able to communicate comfortably with learning applications. Although a little anxiety and discomfort can actually be helpful for learning, they should come from the learners' desire to do their best and not from fear and frustration with the interface. Designers should always be concerned about learner comfort with the interface and must attend carefully to its psychological impact. We want to keep learners focused on beneficial learning activities and not on overcoming challenges in the interface.

# Interface Creativity in e-Learning

Today's development tools give e-learning designers great flexibility in designing user interfaces. Once learners have accessed an e-learning application, nearly all of what they see, hear, and can do is under control of the application. In many ways, this is great news—and quite worrisome at the same time.

## The Great News

The great news is that it's possible to create an intuitive and comfortable environment for learners, even if they have little familiarity with computers. Options can be integrated into the interactive context to appear natural and recognizable. They can reinforce the effectiveness of the context as a whole. We are now more able than ever to devise highly "transparent" interfaces—interfaces that keep the focus on content and interactivity and do not drain attention or learner energy, yet are easily found and understood when needed. With an intuitive interface, fewer instructions are needed, and learners can engage in interactivity more readily (Figure 3.8).

## The Worry

The worry comes from the same fact that e-learning applications can define the learner's interface to a great extent. The designer's power to

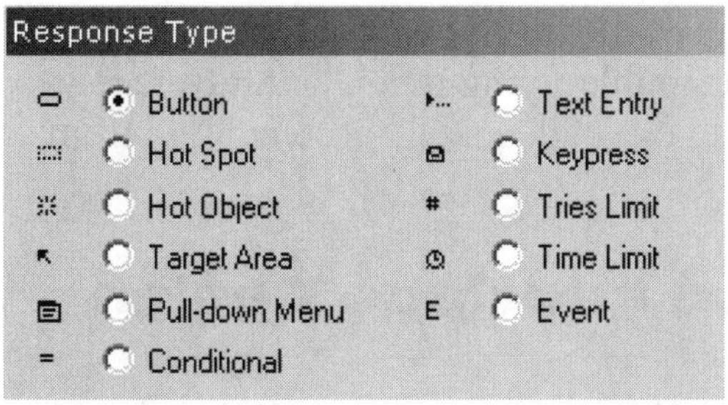

**FIGURE 3.8** Types of responses available in Authorware 6.0.

define and build interfaces goes to the head quickly. Different isn't necessarily better, and divergence leads easily to the penalties inherent in undermining conventions. Application designers sometimes do things differently as a matter of expressing personal style, but their desire to be inventive doesn't justify divergence. Interface design needs to provide utility and comfort for learners. Application interfaces should not be an unnecessary additional learning task!

## Don't Replicate Failures (Even If Everyone Else Does)

Computer environments are still not as easy to use as they could and should be. The last high point of computer–user interface may have been achieved when Apple Computer introduced its Macintosh computers with three primary software products, MacPaint, MacWrite, and MacDraw. The interface consistency, clarity, and naturalness in this trio of programs demonstrated that powerful operations could be learned quickly and easily by people having no prior familiarity with computers.

While many of the ideas introduced to the broad public through these products have been widely adopted and refined, many of them have also been compromised and perverted. As David Gelernter (1998) points out in his insightful book *Machine Beauty* (New York: Basic Books), there is a "relentless drive in the industry to complicate and featurize every piece of software until it keels over out of sheer brainless ugliness" (p. 132). We must combat this very real and present tendency in the design of e-learning applications if we are to succeed.

Jeff Johnson (2000), Ben Shneiderman (1987), Aaron Marcus (www.amanda.com), Donald Norman (1999), John Lenker (2002), and many others have shown us in their works and publications how things can be considerably better than they are. Often, when laid out clearly, principles of good user interface seem simple and obvious, yet good design is clearly not simple and obvious in practice. The evidence lies in the plethora of poorly designed software products, including major applications developed with vast resources. We've gone so far adrift that I even hear people say, "I haven't tried any of those options. I couldn't tell what they do, and I was afraid I'd get in trouble trying them." Unfortunately, even having multiple levels of Undo can't adequately protect users from the consequences of poor design.

## Importance of Good Interface Design for e-Learning

If good user interface design is important anywhere, it's critically important in e-learning. Why? It is a daunting challenge to get people to change their behavior, which may include changing habits, perceptions, and values, as well as acquiring knowledge and developing new skills. It's less of a challenge if you have instructional design education, training, experience, and talent, but even for those select pros, it's always a difficult challenge. To succeed, it's important to gain a high percentage of the user's attention.

## Effects of Poor Interface Design

There are many ways poor user interface reduces the effectiveness of e-learning. Poor user interface can:

- Repeatedly and frequently distract the user's attention
- Make text difficult to read and graphics ineffective
- Cause branching to the wrong information or exercises
- Confuse learners about their progress and their location within the application
- Make useful activities too bothersome to complete
- Obscure access to needed information
- Make comparisons difficult
- Slow interactions
- Debilitate feedback

Designs fettered by poor user interface have reduced learning impact. Learning energy is diverted to coping with uncertainty, mistakes, and frustration. Because it is a significant measure of success to achieve any behavioral change at all, few instructional applications can afford any reduction in impact due to poor interface design.

 # Advisory

Some behaviors are easy to shape. A simple demonstration, explanation, or answer to a question is sometimes sufficient. In these cases, interactions are easy to build, and the learner interface can and should be very straightforward; but it's not unusual for designers to get carried away with possibilities and build applications with far more options, controls, and elaborations than are necessary or even helpful.

It's more usual to underestimate the behavioral challenge, however, and to provide too little of a learning experience. A true/false or a multiple-choice question does not often create much of an experience. Experiences have options that parallel real-life performance and tend to build from a series of decisions and choices. The instructional and interface designs must therefore work together to provide both a workable multiplicity of options.

# Content Structure and Sequencing

Defining what happens, how it happens, and when it happens is the essence of instructional design. The focus is generally on content—what content to include, how to use it, and in what order.

## What Is Content?

*Content* is a term frequently heard in discussion of instructional design, but there are several common meanings (see Table 3.1).

## Who Cares?

Lack of a standard definition may not be a critical issue in itself, but it is clear there are many misunderstandings about e-learning—what's good, bad, possible, impractical, and so on. Varying definitions of content may cause some of the misunderstandings, since assumptions of what a person means by *content* may be quite incorrect.

MANAGER: I can't spend much on this training project. If nothing else, at least we need to be sure to present all the content as clearly as possible.

What did he say?
It depends on which definition of content is used. Those with an information-based definition would be thinking that the manager wants little spent on interactivity so that careful presentation of information can be accomplished, perhaps with good navigation controls. Those with an

**TABLE 3.1    Alternative Definitions of Content**

| | |
|---|---|
| Information-based | Content is all the information, such as facts, concepts, and procedures to be learned. A detailed outline, for example, would summarize the components. |
| Objectives-based | Content is a collection of learning objectives specifying behavioral outcomes. For example, "At the conclusion of this learning activity, students will be able to name four of the planets in our solar system." |
| Media-based | Content is all the text, graphics, videos and other multimedia components of an instructional application. |
| Experience-based | Content is the sum of all instructional components in a learning application, including the learning objectives, media, interactions, and assessment activities. |

experience-based definition might well think the manager wants to make sure interactions are well chosen to teach essential behaviors.

## Content-Centric Design

It makes intuitive sense that, if one can do no better, the content should be presented to learners as clearly as possible. Sometimes the simple presentation of information *is* sufficient to achieve needed behaviors, such as when:

- Learners are highly motivated.
- The information is readily understood.
- Skills can be learned without guidance.
- Each step can be prompted and guided as it is performed.

In other cases, however, content needs to be taught through meaningful and memorable experiences. It's important not to mistake the two very different requirements of situations—those needing only the dissemination of information and those requiring training.

There's a tendency to focus on content (information-based definition) and to judge training applications by how thoroughly they present information. The bias tends to work against objectively assessing learner needs and choosing an effective approach. This is no doubt because it is easy to judge whether information presentations are accurate, clear, and complete, whereas it seems difficult to appraise the quality of instructional design.

Content-centric design risks giving too little critical attention to essential attributes of the learner's experience. It often looks at content structuring and sequencing from the subject-matter expert's point of view, rather than from the learner's point of view. Even when the learner's point of view is considered, the design context is usually one of declaration and elucidation rather than a set of carefully sequenced activities that draw learners eagerly into skill-building exercises.

It's not just nice for learning experiences to be interesting, meaningful, and memorable; it's critical for success. Adult learners are ready to bail out as soon as they sense a waste of time, and younger learners respond similarly as soon as they lose interest. Content-centric designs can be a real turn-off for anyone.

## Learner-Centric Design

The predigested, squeaky-clean content of content-centric designs is often prized and yet sometimes provides a true disservice to learners. Well-devised imbroglios can be fascinating and anomalies can be intriguing. Think of mystery novels versus textbooks. Which one more easily attracts readers?

One of the PCD3 features (see earlier background story a few pages back) that unfortunately never made it into Authorware recognized that experts need a tool to ensure that all critical content components are identified. They need to specify content, input text, graphics, and other media, and organize it for repeated analysis, including reviews by other experts.

The expert's content compendium, however, is not an appropriate structure on which to define and sequence learning events. Considerable reorganization and structuring is necessary to fashion a learner-centric application from encyclopedic information.

So separate interfaces were built, one for subject-matter experts using an outlining tool interface and another for instructional designers using a flowcharting metaphor. Once subject matter was prepared, instructional designers needed only to reference content elements from within their learner-centric designs and the elements were dropped into the instructional interactions automatically.

We released the initial version of Authorware with the full intention of adding this component as soon as we could afford to. It's most unfortunate that such a capability has not been developed through all the years of Authorware's amazing commercial success.

Why is so much e-learning unmistakably and undeniably boring? Look to the level of design attention given to the learner's experience versus the level of attention given to making sure the content is complete, clear, logically presented, and "properly" sequenced.

Completeness is not in itself interesting. In fact, it's probably more boring than presentations that are full of gaps and require you to fill in the holes yourself. If you can and do indeed fill in the gaps and keep pace, you're actively applying a lot more of your intellectual capabilities and gaining more from the experience than when you listen passively.

Learner-centric designs focus on creating events that continuously intrigue learners as the content unfolds. By providing tasks of approachable difficulty, you challenge learners to figure things out on their own. When they can, they are rewarded. When they can't, aids are available.

After they complete tasks, learners are asked to put new skills and understandings in perspective. This might be done through a subsequent task requiring integration of multiple skills or tasks in which learners must choose appropriate procedures.

Repeatedly, learners are shown how each advance they make is a step toward realization of an important and attractive goal.

## Content-Centric versus Learner-Centric Design Examples

Any time you are presented with a training challenge, you must determine which design is most effective. Let's listen in as one of those decisions is being made right now. . . .

DECREE FROM ABOVE: We've spent a lot of money on these employee handbooks, and nobody's reading them. The folks at our Employee Assistance Program (EAP) said that in the past six months, they've only received one phone call from us—and that was a wrong number. We don't have a large budget, or a lot of time, so how can we get the message out there?

### Content-Centric: The Classic Approach

WHIZHEAD: Hey, no sweat! It's all in the book, right? So let's put the book online.

We'll start with a menu. The learner has full control! It's totally interactive. [Figure 3.9]

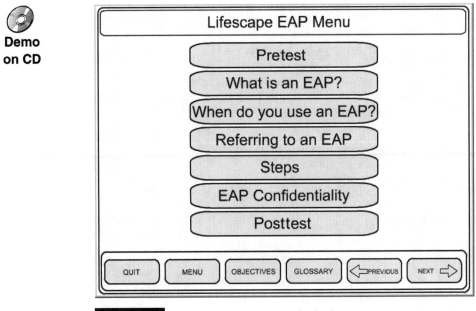

**FIGURE 3.9** A typical content-centric design.

We'll put all the handbook information in each section, and add some nice graphics to it. They'll want to scour every page. And check out that spinning logo. . . . [Figure 3.10]

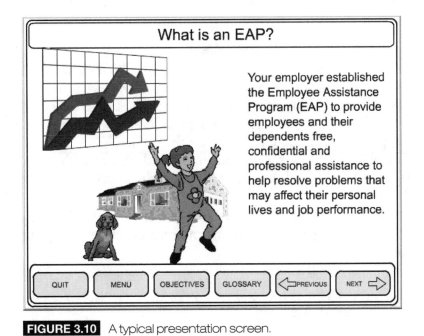

**FIGURE 3.10** A typical presentation screen.

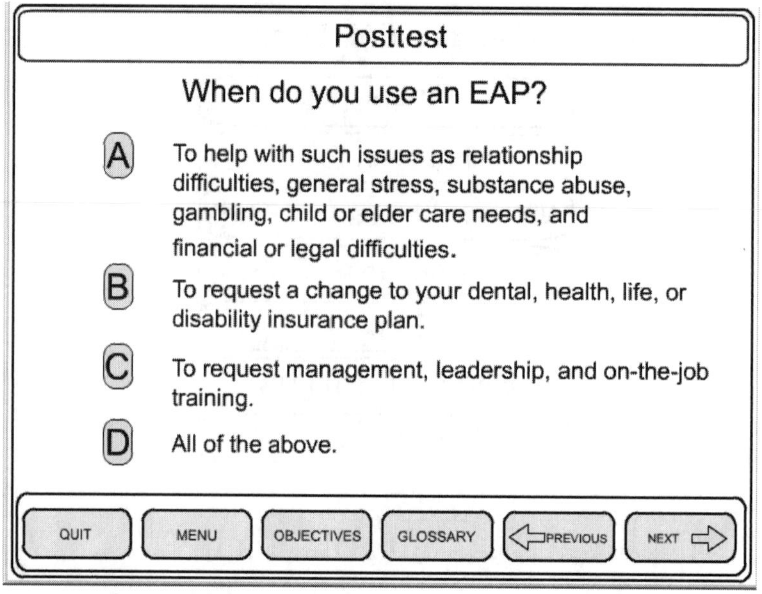

**Posttest**

**When do you use an EAP?**

A. To help with such issues as relationship difficulties, general stress, substance abuse, gambling, child or elder care needs, and financial or legal difficulties.

B. To request a change to your dental, health, life, or disability insurance plan.

C. To request management, leadership, and on-the-job training.

D. All of the above.

QUIT   MENU   OBJECTIVES   GLOSSARY   ⇦PREVIOUS   NEXT ⇨

**FIGURE 3.11**  The obligatory meaningless posttest.

YOU: Um, Whiz, how will we know the learner has actually learned anything?

WHIZHEAD: Oh, don't worry about that—we'll have a test! [Figure 3.11]

## Learner-Centric: A Better Way

DESIGNER: What if we looked at this problem in a different way? The problem is that people aren't using the services that are provided. That's probably because they don't relate to the EAP as a service they really need. No amount of reading the handbook is going to create that appreciation and intentions to use the service.

But what if managers were confronted with those tough situations first-hand? How would they react? Look at this approach. . . . [Figure 3.12]

YOU: Oh, poor Olivia. My mom died from cancer just a few years ago. I had trouble managing my emotions and responsibilities. What can we do for Olivia?

*Figures 3.9 to 3.16 from material codeveloped by Allen Interactions Inc. and the Multimedia Group at Lifescape, Sean York, director.*

**FIGURE 3.12**  Your first simulated employee request: What decisions can you make to best help Olivia?

DESIGNER:  Well, learners can talk to her coworkers to get more information. Or, they can check with Human Resources or the Employee Assistance Program to get helpful information tailored precisely to this situation. [Figure 3.13]

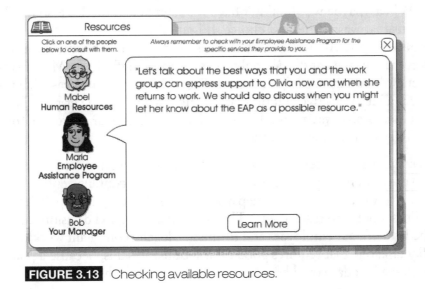

**FIGURE 3.13**  Checking available resources.

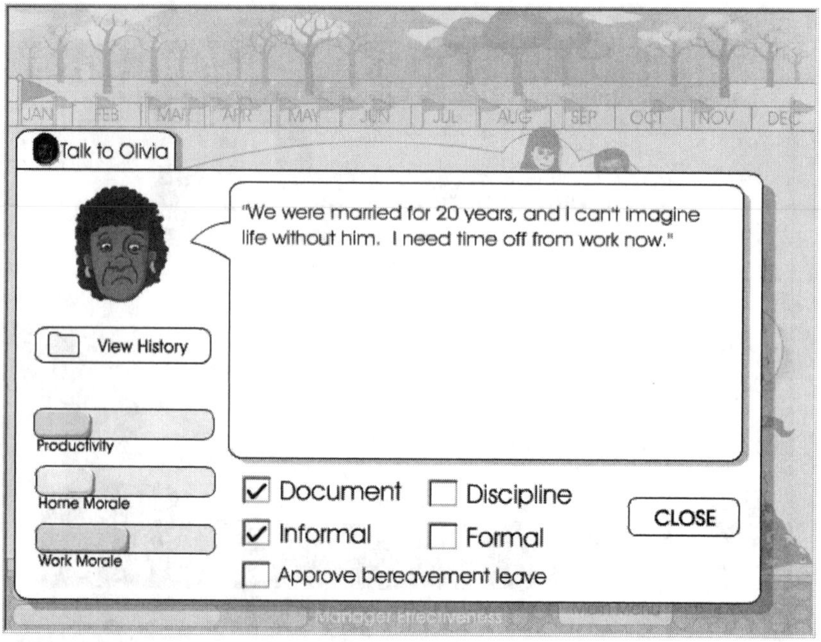

**FIGURE 3.14** Time to make some choices!

Once learners have gathered all the information they need, they make the call whether to document the issue, discipline her, or make a formal or informal referral to the EAP. They then decide whether to approve the bereavement leave. [Figure 3.14]

YOU: Whoa, maybe we shouldn't have referred her to the EAP so quickly. Seems that wasn't the best choice. [Figure 3.15]

DESIGNER: Right. All of the feedback messages include the same information that's in the handbook; only it's more meaningful here. Most managers will be surprised that an immediate EAP referral in a case like this one is a bit insensitive and premature. How would they ever pick this up in a memorable way without an experience such as this? [Figure 3.16]

YOU: This is worth the investment.

Management or interpersonal development skills (often called "soft skills") are training opportunities that defy traditional content-centric design. Every human resources department publishes employee policies and guidelines—but who reads them? The fact is, making good decisions to better the lives of your employees and maintain a legally compliant workforce is a tricky task; one that requires good critical thinking skills, because a poor decision made today could have drastic effects two months from now.

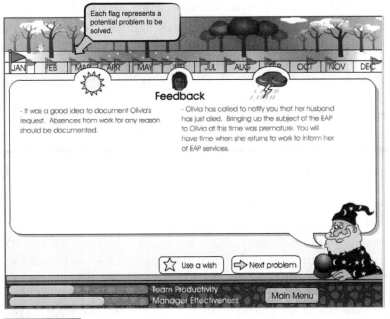

**FIGURE 3.15**  The results of your decisions—the good and the bad.

Clearly, this material could have been presented as a series of slides and a posttest, but how does that relate to your daily environment? Placing you in a real-life situation lets you more easily relate to the subject matter (meaningful experience), and you are more likely to remember the consequences of your choices (memorable experience).

In a program such as this, you might be tempted to make really, really bad decisions to see what awful things might happen. *Great!* What a wonderfully safe place to make those bonehead decisions so that you won't make such errors in real life.

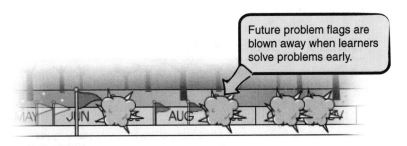

**FIGURE 3.16**  Good choices lighten your workload later on. Note the elimination of problem flags from the calendar.

### Learner-Centric Design Requires Commitment

Building great learning experiences often becomes onerous as deadlines approach and constraints seem ever more difficult to meet. Managers, designers, artists, writers, and programmers look fearfully at the constraints and scurry to provide content coverage—perhaps simply noninteractive text or some bullet slides. Many project stakeholders can be comforted knowing that all elements identified in a thorough content analysis are being presented. (After all, if the content is there, it is the learner's responsibility to get something out of it, right? All the other things we might do would just make it easier for learners to get it. Give me a break.)

Again, it's easy to determine if content is present. You just have to see it to know. It's not nearly so easy to know if experiences are effective in building skills. So, when the pinch is on, content coverage often takes precedence over building critical learning experiences. It passes judgment, but fails in the long run.

 Look for the M&Ms: *meaningful* and *memorable* experiences. You must include them. They'll keep your designs learner-centered.

## Sequencing for Learning

There is a big difference between the structures of an encyclopedia, a textbook, and a course of instruction. The differences correspond to the different purposes for which they are designed.

Content-centric design and learner-centric design lead naturally to very different content sequences (see Table 3.2). For example, subject-matter experts, who naturally relate to content-centric designs, typically gravitate to one of three sequences—simple to complex, chronological, or hierarchical. These sequences are based on theoretical analyses of the content.

### TABLE 3.2   Sequencing Models

| | |
|---|---|
| Content-centric | Simple to complex |
| | Chronological |
| | Hierarchical |
| Learner-centric | Known to unknown |
| | Misconceptions to latest techniques |
| | Goal decomposition |

Content sequences that appeal to experts may and quite likely will be confusing and overwhelming to learners. Even worse, they will be boring. Learners can't appreciate clever or efficient organization of unfamiliar and meaningless information. They can't appreciate the advantage of knowing terms for things they cannot yet recognize, value, or use. Nor can learners appreciate classification systems for meaningless items.

Learners are much more interested in knowing the value of what they are learning and how it will lead to meaningful abilities. Learners are interested in surprising facts, paradoxes, and effort-saving insights. In short, they are interested in how the content relates to them, rather than how the content can be systematically or logically structured. It's therefore important to use the relationship between each content segment and the learner as a guide to sequencing.

## A Simple Approach

One way to do this is to help learners determine what they need to do in order to reach their performance goals. With guidance, "goal decomposition" exercises lead learners to identify the subtasks necessary to learn. Of course, this information could simply be presented to learners, but having them analyze the components of target abilities builds an individually meaningful learning map.

Learner-centered sequences:

- Determine the learner's initial competencies and then build on them.

- Chunk content into a map of meaningful, performance-related events.

- Advance in steps meaningful to the learner, but not so gradually as to present no challenge or sense of reasonable progress.

- Allow learners to attempt almost any task at their request, including those that are probably too difficult; the results identify undeveloped abilities that learners can pursue.

- Allow learner-controlled review at almost any time.

## Structuring Events

In building learner-centric e-learning systems, we want the learner to be an active participant—to be busy alternating among:

- Actively thinking about learning and thinking about the content
- Testing conclusions by working problems that will either confirm or refute learner hypotheses
- Practicing to strengthen skills and speed performance

We want learners at one moment to be thinking *inductively* to generalize their successes in specific, carefully chosen activities and to draw valid conclusions. At another moment, we want learners to be thinking *deductively* to determine from general concepts some specific principles—perhaps principles never actually presented or demonstrated to them. And finally, at other moments, we want learners to be rehearsing behavior patterns based on their learning.

For example, when learning mathematics, learners generally memorize specific math facts and procedures that, with familiarity, they begin to generalize so they can perform successfully on new problems (induction). At the same time, we want learners to grasp in some way the theoretical nature of mathematics—what it means to add two numbers—which will provide a way for them to develop math skills based on principles rather than arbitrary facts (deduction). And whatever behaviors the learner gains, mathematics will become memorable only by reinforcing skills and application of principles through practice. The challenge is to balance these three things appropriately for each learning situation.

Optimal content definitions for e-learning need to yield defined, purposeful learning activities. It is essential to define interesting events that conjure up insights, hold attention, and inspire behavior change. While theoretical organization, such as codification and clustering, may be compatible with this priority—and therefore advisable—the value of such approaches to structuring is secondary to creating engaging learning activities. Theoretical content organization does not justify mind-numbing learning experiences. (See Part 2, especially Chapter 5, for some easy and very effective means of structuring desirable learning events.)

## Three Pitfalls

There are three prevalent pitfalls with respect to content selection and structuring that one must be vigilant to avoid. Consider the following:

- Giving insufficient attention to the learner's perspective
- Teaching people things they already know—you will only irritate them by trying

- Teaching people things they can't understand—you will only irritate them by trying

Let's look at each of these precursors to boring learning events individually.

## Giving Insufficient Attention to the Learner's Perspective

It's very hard to focus design equally on both content and learner experiences, although both are critically important. One of these perspectives will tend to lead—to dominate your thoughts and focus. Choose wisely!

If you work primarily for content thoroughness and clarity, you will end up with a very different product than if you center your focus on what the learner will be thinking, doing, and feeling. It's important to let questions such as the following guide your thinking:

- What is the learner wondering?
- What challenges would increase the learner's curiosity and increase his or her interest in participation?
- What common misconceptions does the learner probably hold?
- What does the learner probably know already?
- What do learners in the field aspire to?
- What in the desired performance looks easy, but is difficult?
- What in the desired performance looks difficult, but is easy?
- In what contexts does the learner enjoy learning?

Note that in answering these questions, applicable content is essential and can often be identified rather easily. Content will be identified in contexts that should enhance its appeal to learners.

Almost by definition, information that learners find boring is either information that's meaningless to them or information they don't see how to use. You can be assured that it will not be boring if you put new information and skills in a context that clearly reveals how they will help learners. Be sure to present the information and skills in a way that relates to what learners already know, and you will help to make it meaningful for them. Learners fairly want to know what's in it for them.

## Teaching People Things They Already Know—You Will Only Irritate Them by Trying

One of the precious powers of e-learning is its ability to *individualize* instruction—that is, its ability to fit the sequence of events and even the nature of the events themselves to the needs and readiness of each individual learner. The instructor-led classroom environment doesn't have good capabilities for individualization. Teachers typically assume the role of presenting information to their students and leading activities. Unless all their students are identical in readiness and ability to learn, instructors have the challenge right from the start of simultaneously trying to reach those learners who have little background and need to cover basics thoroughly, and trying to pacify students who are already familiar with the basics and ready to move on. Even if they succeed in pacifying students who are essentially treading water, valuable time is lost in waiting for something beneficial to happen.

Most of us don't enjoy putting our time under someone else's control. If we're not getting value for our time investment, we can easily move from disappointment to irritation and beyond. In short, the positive attitude of interest and readiness to learn can be lost in minutes if learning events appear to be of no value, either for learning or entertainment. Without an appropriate frame of mind, no learning occurs. Remember, you can't learn someone. People must do the learning themselves. Try not to disable their abilities by boring learners to death.

## Teaching People Things They Can't Understand—You Will Only Irritate Them by Trying

The process of learning is a process of building. It's a process of building associations between stimuli and responses. Most important, it's a process that potentially results in a sustained change in behavior.

Although intellectual behaviors appear to be quite different from simple physical skills, similar underlying processes are at work in both instances. Theories suggest a process of learning which moves from perception to short-term memory to long-term memory (Figure 3.17; see Atkins and Schiffrin 1971).

Practice or rehearsal is necessary to move through the process, with increased practice leading to more permanent learning and behavioral change.

To begin the process, learners become aware of a relationship. If I said, "Say 1 when you see A," you wouldn't have much trouble. You have already learned to recognize the letter A. You know the number 1. Because both A and 1 are the first elements in symbol sequences known to

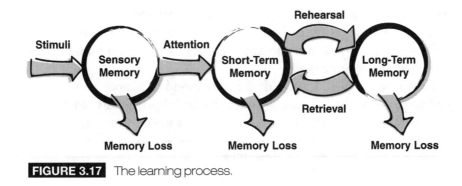

**FIGURE 3.17** The learning process.

you, the relationship is easy to build. A couple of quick rehearsals in your mind, and you're ready to perform.

In many senses, the assignment to respond with "1" to the letter "A" is *understandable* to you. But what if I asked you to respond to a complex Chinese symbol that appears quite similar to other Chinese symbols for which I wanted different responses? Unless you've learned Chinese, you might have quite a lot of trouble deciding what response to give or even whether you had ever seen a particular symbol before.

Consider another case:

| Symbol | Response |
|--------|----------|
| A | 3 |
| B | 1 |
| C | 4 |
| D | 2 |

You would have the advantage of being able to recognize all the symbols and you would:

- Formulate a simple mental rule that all replies are numbers and all matching symbols are letters.
- See that numbers are matched to only one unique letter.
- Know that only the numbers 1 through 4 are being used.
- Know that only the first four letters of the alphabet are being used.

Although you would have to be mentally active to prepare yourself, there are many important structures you can observe about this task and many things you already know that would help you understand and perform it, even if the overall purpose of the task isn't clear (which would add more understanding and make the task even simpler to learn and perform). The framework you can apply comes to your aid and makes this task a relatively simple one.

Okay, now suppose I wanted you to respond in a more complex way—by adding one to the base assignments (as listed previously) each time a letter was repeated. Sample correct responses would now be:

| Symbol | Response | |
|--------|----------|---|
| D | 2 | |
| C | 4 | |
| A | 3 | |
| D | 3 | Because 2 + 1 = 3 |
| C | 5 | Because 4 + 1 = 5 |
| C | 6 | Because 5 + 1 = 6 |

Further, suppose I did not explain this relationship at first, but would just correct you each time you gave a wrong response. You would be very confused. It would require many corrections before you could figure out what was going on. You would have a hard time learning, because the content simply would not make sense. In the process of trying to learn how to respond correctly, you might become quite upset. Your frustration might increase your attentiveness or it might make learning nearly impossible for you. If you just threw up your hands and thought the whole experience was poorly designed, you might just detach yourself and not even try. After a bit, you'd become thoroughly bored and look for ways to escape.

Although it seems ridiculous to imagine any learning situation in which learners wouldn't be assisted with aids for understanding, they exist widely because of the focus on the organization and expression of content from the expert's point of view. A learner's perspective varies greatly from that of the expert, the business owner, the manager, or the trainer. Designers must account for variances in learner readiness and ability to understand, or they must face the very real risk that learners will have needless difficulty in learning and may actually become unable to learn because of their rising levels of frustration. Ironically, when designers let content drive design and use up their resources on meticulous presentation of the content, they neglect the very aspects of training that most facilitate content comprehension.

Try to avoid the preceding pitfalls. These three are common entrapments capable of snaring even experienced, vigilant designers.

When I entered college, I had the intention of majoring in math. I had done well in math at our small Iowa high school, enjoyed it, and expected to meet the challenges relatively easily.

My first class, a calculus class, was a traumatic experience, however. The professor launched into long presentations during which he primarily thought out loud and addressed the whiteboard while continuously writing mathematical expressions that were completely foreign to me. He did not like being interrupted. He cautioned us that he might lose his train of thought and thus omit something we needed to know!

Talk about focus on content presentation!

# Navigation

We can't see all the content of an instructional application on the screen at one time (not that we would probably want to, anyway). Imagine taking all the pages of a book and covering a wall with them. After scanning over many pages and probably lingering over a few that appear to have the more interesting material, you'd realize that to get better value from the experience, you should pick a starting point and read at least a block of the material in the intended sequence. At the same time, however, you would appreciate having had the opportunity to appraise the total amount of material included, learn the book's organizational structure, assess how many interesting elements there appear to be, and make some strategic decisions about how you might peruse it.

Books are much simpler in structure than e-learning applications. It's easy to get an overview of them. Even before you've opened the cover, you have a sense of how many pages they have. You know if it's a small, medium, or large book. Books usually have a simple linear sequence running from beginning to end. Yet to size them up, we find it very helpful to have titled chapters and sections, a table of contents, numbered pages, and a good index.

e-Learning applications are not so quickly assessed. You can't even determine easily if they're small, medium, or large. You can't flip through them in a second to determine if they're well illustrated, highly interactive, or truly individualized. In fact, you probably can't determine very much at all about an e-learning application, except perhaps its style and general appeal, until you've invested a fair amount of time in it.

## Learner Needs Addressed by Navigation

Navigation structures in e-learning serve many purposes, some identical to their counterparts in other media, some unique to the nature and capabilities of computer-supported delivery. Navigation is not just a bothersome necessity of less concern than the learning events. Some applications actually derive a great deal of their instructional power directly from the strength of their navigation.

Navigation in e-learning applications can provide many valuable services, including:

- The ability to preview and personally assess:

    What can be learned

    How valuable it will be

    How much time it will take

    How difficult it will be

- Once into the application, the ability to determine:

    How much you have accomplished

    How much remains to be learned

- Overall, the ability to:

    Back up and review

    Back up and try different answers or options

Electronic performance support systems (EPSSs) are a good example of applications that focus heavily on navigation. EPSSs provide real-time information, prompting, and data processing tools to guide performers. In contrast to e-learning applications which help users perform based on internalized information and practiced skills, EPSS logic provides the expertise needed to guide users as they work. Users may remain dependent on the system for support, but such dependence may not be detrimental or even undesired in many situations, such as those where data entry is part of the transaction anyway and where procedures change frequently or where oversights and errors might have grievous consequences.

See Chapter 7 for an example of an EPSS application.

Skip ahead, preview, and return

Bookmark and return to points of interest or concern

Call up services such as glossaries or examples

Restart and resume where you left off

## Navigation Can Help or Hinder Learning

It's really frustrating to be uninformed and not know what to expect. Unless initial impressions are extremely positive, perhaps elevated by a fascinating opening (which I strongly recommend) or by reputation or trusted endorsement, people naturally become suspicious that lack of information means bad news. Expectations of a delightfully beneficial experience are replaced by doubt, if not dread. Not a good start.

Expectations set initial attitudes. Attitudes, in turn, assist or hinder the effectiveness of e-learning. With all the challenges facing us in the attempt to get people to do what we want them to do, a positive attitude is definitely something to foster. In many ways, all our efforts to shape behavior are much like processes of sales. We need to get people to want what we have to sell before we can expect them to buy. Constant focus and restatement of benefits is important. Navigation provides one of the ways people can pick up and examine our products and distinguish their benefits. It's the packaging that can cause our product to go home with the learner or be put back on the shelf for later consideration.

As you can see, navigation in e-learning is far more than just getting from point A to point B. Navigation facilities provide a major component of the learning experience. Good capabilities not only enhance the power of presentation and interactive components, but also provide learning experiences directly by allowing learners to compare and research.

See Chapter 6 for more detail on navigation design.

# Instructional Interactivity

The purpose of instructional interactivity is to wrestle our intellectual laziness to the ground—to reawaken our interest in learning, strengthen our ability to learn, and provide an optimal environment in which to learn.

Instructional interactivity is *not* the same as:

- Navigation
- Presentation
- Buttons
- Scrolling
- Browsing
- Information retrieval
- Paging
- Animation
- Morphing
- Video

These features are used, of course, in creating instructional interactivity, but they can and frequently are used for other purposes and in ways that do not result in the kinds of interactivity necessary to achieve success. Their presence does not signify instructional interactivity, nor the lack thereof, even though they are often promoted as evidence of interactivity.

Instructional interactivity creates not only external, observable events, such as clicking the mouse button or dragging an icon, but also (and more important) internal events, such as recall, classification, analysis, and decision making (i.e., thinking).

## A Functional Definition

It is easier to note the results of interactivity than to define it directly, because the presence of typical interactivity components does not guarantee that true instructional interactivity is present. The essential concept of interactivity has to do with how the components are used. A functional definition that has value is this:

> **instructional interactivity**   Interaction that actively stimulates the learner's mind to do those things that improve ability and readiness to perform effectively.

## Beneficial Activities

In order to assist learners to build skills, we have to help them become active participants. We cannot do the learning for them; they must do it themselves. Further, choosing the most beneficial activity is not something learners always do well. Instructional design, therefore, involves both designing activities that result in learning and designing structures that attract learners to them.

To strengthen new skills so they can continue to grow and be useful, it's important to exercise them—to apply them, to compare and contrast them with other procedures, to generate examples and counterexamples, to rehearse, and so on. Just as a physical trainer uses *activity* to keep exercisers moving, working at appropriate levels, and using reasonable but strength-building weights, inter*activity* is all about helping learners actively work at beneficial tasks. It's powerful stuff when used appropriately.

The challenge is to use optimal learning events at the right times to achieve the best return on the learner's time and our investment.

## Using It Wisely

Failures are often blamed on inadequate funding, while successes are often credited to singular talent. Exceptional talent can overcome many obstacles (and a lack of funds can be a very uncompromising obstacle), but there are ways to produce very effective interactivity with average abilities and a limited budget, especially if one is careful to use interactivity where its unique capabilities have the greatest benefit.

## Unique Characteristics of Interactivity

While multimedia is often used simply for fancy window dressing, interactivity is a technology which can take unique advantage of multimedia and create something far more valuable for our purposes than inactive books. Because books are learning tools with which everyone is familiar, let's think one more time about books in contrast to the unique properties of interactivity.

Books are much simpler in structure than e-learning applications. They are not generally interactive at all, but as a reader, you can become active with the content in many ways. You can look away and see if you can restate for yourself what you have just read. You can recall instances in which the information you've read would have been helpful, would have applied, or might not have been possible. You can think about why you're not doing what is suggested and what the consequences of changing what you're doing might be. You can recall problems that have occurred and determine if the book is providing solutions.

Further, you can make flash cards. You can outline the content. You can quiz fellow learners. You can try role-playing. You can draw cognitive maps (sometimes called *mind maps*). You can invent mnemonics or stories that help you recall the components of sets or the order of steps.

There are many activities you can invent and undertake that will help you learn material presented in noninteractive ways. They take time, energy, creativity, and commitment. It also takes skill to do this effectively and efficiently. Not all of us are as good at it, and we certainly do not always do the best we can—nor do many of us do much of anything at all when we have to take the full initiative ourselves. Books and many other resources simply leave the activity up to learners. Sure, they might include some self-test questions or propose some helpful activities. But it's very difficult, if at all possible, for books to simulate an active learning partner and mentor as computers can.

When questions are posed in a book, you can check the answer if it's provided anywhere without having to commit yourself to an answer. When you see the correct answer, you're likely to give yourself the benefit of the doubt and think, "Oh, sure. I knew that." The question is, if you had been taking a test, would you really have been able to answer? Quite possibly not. If learners are left to judge their own competencies without the help of an objective measure, they are quite likely to err.

The importance of objectively assessing learner abilities was addressed long ago by Sidney Pressey (1926; 1927) and further examined by B. F. Skinner (1987). In his pioneering work, Pressey began with devices that presented questions to students and hid the correct answers under a cover. Students could decide the correct answer and then check their work—or check first, then answer.

The results were disappointing. The rehearsal, thought Pressey, should have led to better performance. Later, he decided that students cheated themselves by not performing the mental exercises he intended. His next teaching machine was very simple, but required the exercise he prescribed: Students had to poke an answer sheet with a pin before checking their answers.

The results were dramatically different. And better.

With today's computer technology, one of the things we can do well and must do if we are to best help learners, is to get them to commit to answers before we reveal to them the consequences of their thinking.

Consider working a crossword puzzle. If answers are provided, you can easily think to yourself that you really knew the correct answer, even when you discover the provided answer is different from your first thought. Funny how much harder those puzzles are when the correct answers aren't there just to "confirm" your thoughts.

Interactions with the computer can force learners to commit to an answer or to perform a task before receiving feedback. Learners may be reticent to attempt a task, but it's in their best interest to review what they already know and to apply their current skills to see how close they can come to the desired behavior. This helps us, as the instructors behind the electronic curtain, to continuously determine the learner's current ability levels and select the next activity accordingly. Just as important, however, learners see what they can and can't do for themselves. It sometimes takes a little adjustment for some learners, but with well-designed interactivity, learners quickly come to see the advantages of being able to make mistakes and learn from them in privacy.

Good instruction:

- Causes learners to think
- Helps learners synthesize new information and integrate their knowledge
- Helps learners rehearse skills and prepare for performance
- Promotes awareness of competencies, readiness, and needs
- Contributes to self-confidence.

Good e-learning accomplishes all this and can also help learners:

- Learn privately from mistakes without public humiliation
- Experiment to see the effects of poor decisions or poor performance
- Explore in response to individual levels of interest
- Test their knowledge whenever they might like a progress check

## Making Good Interactivity Happen

Chapter 7 takes up interactivity in detail. It looks at the anatomy of good interactions, identifies their components, and looks to see how they integrate to achieve the important learning events of which they are capable. Examples are provided so you can personally experience the power of interactivity.

Next up, however, Chapter 4 turns to the overall process of designing and developing applications sporting the full magic of well-designed e-learning methods. Traditional processes attempting to deal with the complexities of learning application design and development have been tedious, often resulting in considerable friction among players, such as between subject-matter experts and instructional designers. Unfortunately, all the strife and long hours of work rarely achieve the kind of powerful and fun learning experiences we're talking about here. Happily, I have a new, better process to share with you. It overcomes many of the traditional problems while fully embracing the need to be learner-centric.

# Summary

Good design is essential for success but uncommon in e-learning. Perhaps this is because teaching is confused with presentation of information or perhaps because so much attention is given to technology that little remains for dealing with instructional concerns. Whatever the reason, good design can't be achieved without careful attention to learner motivation, user interface, content structure and sequencing, navigation, and interactivity.

Motivation is often not directly considered or addressed at all in designs. User interfaces often distract and frustrate learners. Content is often structured for completeness or logical sequencing without regard to making the learner's excursion through it meaningful, compelling, or even interesting. Navigation is often confused with interactivity and yet fails to provide user support that makes e-learning comfortable and convenient. Finally, the precious powers of interactivity are often not enlisted to either challenge learners or demonstrate their advancing proficiencies. Clearly, there are missed opportunities.

Part 2 takes up these design issues in detail, but for now, we have identified the issues. The next chapter deals with the process of identifying needs and creating solutions. The proposed process breaks with traditional methods in some important ways. It does so in recognition of the added complexity of striving not only for accuracy and clarity, but also for highly motivating, meaningful, and memorable events.

# GETTING THERE THROUGH SUCCESSIVE APPROXIMATION

- "With adequate funding we will have the cure for cancer 6 months from Thursday."

- "In my administration, taxes will drop 50 percent while lifelong full-coverage health benefits will be extended to all citizens."

- "We will deliver a strongly motivating, high-impact e-learning application as soon as you need it within whatever budget you happen to have set aside."

Some challenges are truly tough challenges. Although it might get a program launched, setting expectations unrealistically high doesn't help solve the real challenges at hand.

Designing effective e-learning applications is one of those truly tough challenges if you don't have the benefit of an effective process. This chapter talks about the design process and how to involve stakeholders so that expectations can be an ally rather than an additional burden.

## A Multifaceted Challenge

Developing learning experiences that change behavior is a tough, multifaceted challenge, no matter how few constraints are in place and how generous the funding. Just as in designing modern buildings, setting up a new business operation, or manufacturing an aircraft, in e-learning design there are multifarious complexities requiring a tremendous breadth of knowledge and skill. It's easy for newcomers to be unaware of this until they see their dreams fade in projects that struggle for completion and fail to achieve the needed results.

# Constraints

As if the inherent challenges of good training weren't enough, constraints always exist. Typical constraints include one or more of the following:

- Too little budget for the magnitude of behavioral changes needed
- Conflicting opinions of what outcome behaviors are important
- Unrealistically high expectations of solving deeply rooted organizational problems through training
- Preconceptions about what constitutes good instruction or good interactivity
- Short deadlines
- Inadequate content resources and sporadic availability of subject-matter experts
- Unavailability of typical learners when needed
- Convictions about applicability of specific media
- Undocumented variances in delivery platforms
- Restrictions on distribution or installation of workstation software

Further, regardless of how forward thinking and flexible an organization may be, typical challenges are always exacerbated by additional constraints en route, whether they are foreseeable through experienced analysis or are quite unexpected "pop-ups."

Who expects to find that the critical subject-matter expert has changed midstream into a person with very different views? Who expects the procedures being taught to be changed just as simulation software is receiving its final touches? Who expects information systems policies to change, no longer allowing access to essential databases for training purposes?

No one succeeds in e-learning design and development who hates a challenge. Complexity abounds from the primary task of structuring effective learning tasks and from the constantly changing tool sets and technologies. Challenges emanate from within the content, the learners, the client, the learning environment and culture, the technology, and so on. Each project is unique, and if one fully engages the challenge, construction of an effective solution cannot be simple and routine.

# Dealing with Design Challenges

The question is how to approach the challenges in a manner that ensures success, or at least an acceptable probability of success. Many approaches have been tried.

## EVERYTHING OLD IS NEW AGAIN

You might be surprised to know how much was happening with computer-assisted instruction (CAI) in the late 1960s and early 1970s. The Ohio State University (OSU), for example, had multiple efforts going on, involving many academic departments. I worked in the general university's computer-assisted instruction department as a graduate student and later as a full-time employee and director. Because of the support given to researching CAI at OSU, it was a great place to be. In 1973, after consulting with Control Data Corporation (CDC) for some time, I was asked to take a bigger role in CDC's efforts to improve learning opportunities through computer technology. PLATO (Programmed Logic for Automated Teaching Operations) began in 1963 at the University of Illinois with support from CDC and the National Science Foundation. The technology had amazing capabilities for its time, including vector graphics, touch panels, and rapid response time. By 1973 it seemed that CDC was looking for someone to help turn PLATO the research project into PLATO the commercial product and service offering. By 1973, CDC held marketing rights to PLATO.

### A Mess—Just Like Today

As hard as it was for me to imagine, activity at CDC was even more enticing than that at OSU/IBM. It was also very different; in fact, it was very much like today's e-learning activity: lots of very busy people, working hard to create training; high energy, enthusiasm, optimism, and pride; abundant hardware; funding with reasonable, but minimal, constraints; very little bureaucracy; and instructional approaches based on everything from very strong opinion to admitted guesswork. Little effort was based on acknowledged, if sometimes weakly substantiated, principles of instructional design and user interface.

Almost everyone had their own domain and was left alone. The energy of this work environment was invigorating, and everyone felt like an instant expert, so proud of their work. The development effort focused not so much on learning theory but on computing and communications technology, with the intent to deliver, on a large scale, interactive capabilities believed by most to be distant future possibilities at best. Many of those in the thick of development clearly didn't know what they were doing. If challenged on any design issue, the easy and ready rebuff was to declare the field totally new. Entirely new notions of instruction and learning environments were needed. The educated knew they didn't have all the needed answers and had to admit the field was, indeed, very much in its infancy. Anybody's idea deserved a chance. Play time! The guesswork and imprecise instructional design was somewhat frustrating to the few individuals who had relevant backgrounds. It really wasn't clear which principles of instruction were applicable in this new arena, but surely not all ideas had equal promise. At the very least, a systematic approach might have provided answers that haphazard design and development could not. Many fundamental errors were being made on a large scale because so many projects were in development.

## Can We Learn from the Past?

I convey this history here in my déjà vu anxiety. The world of e-learning today looks much like that of the early days of PLATO, where so much energy, excitement, and money resulted in a glut of poor instructional software. Don't get me wrong—PLATO efforts also resulted in some of the best learning applications yet. PLATO offered learning management systems (LMSs), e-mail, and instant messaging systems in the 1970s that are still unequaled. Even the mistakes are to be appreciated, because many alternative directions were explored. It is probably the most definitive effort in support of technology in learning on record. It demonstrated both the good that is possible and the waste that can be generated by inexperienced, unguided hands.

I convey this history with a plea—a plea that responsible individuals will insist on knowing what has already been learned, before capriciously and wastefully darting into application development as if there were no hazards and no vital expertise. In other words: There is a body of helpful knowledge to build on, and we won't ruin the fun inherent in developing today's e-learning by taking advantage of it as we go forward.

## EVERYTHING OLD IS NEW AGAIN, INCLUDING COST ESTIMATING

One problem I faced almost instantly at CDC was that budgets were set before learning outcomes were well defined and the gap between them and entry skills was assessed. Budgets were based on typical classroom training time and desires for certain percentages of content to be presented via specific media (e.g., video or interactive software).

When I objected to the budgets, the response was, "Okay, so you don't like the distribution of media. Fine. Give us better percentages, and then we can calculate the cost." When I responded that I couldn't know what the percentages should be until I better understood the learning tasks at hand, people rolled their eyes and moved on down the hall to other meeting rooms, where they carried on budget battles without critical information or the critic.

They battled over what were the most appropriate percentages of video versus text versus independent workbook time versus lecture versus computer interaction, and so on. They needed a cost before the project started, which was understandable, but it was like pricing a relocation before you know what is to be moved where or pricing a custom-built house before you know how many rooms are needed.

If management didn't like the cost answer, the project might not be undertaken at all. Fine, I thought. If you can't afford an effective solution, why squander what resources you have on an ineffective one? Some things aren't affordable, no matter how much you may want them. The practice, however, was to adjust the budget until it was acceptable, then go build something. Too expensive? Less video. If video hadn't been included in the first place, something else would have been chopped out.

## EVERYTHING CHANGES EXCEPT "POP-UP" CHANGES

Do unexpected changes pop up when you least expect them? Was your budget miraculously supposed to take them into account somehow? Been there? Done that? What a mess—ludicrous and immensely frustrating. It's where I lived.

I tried to fit in and do what I could. We worked together to define objectives, both outcome and enabling objectives; we carefully defined expected entry skills and built tests to assure initial learner readiness; we devised exercises that determined whether mastery had been achieved and, if not, what specific weaknesses required remediation; and so on. Good stuff. We performed all the basic tasks of analysis, test development, criterion specification, content scoping and sequencing, and documentation in readiness for design and development of instruction. Fine so far.

When we began the design of interactive activities, there would be much brainstorming and reiteration of content points. We would storyboard the designs, get approvals, and get our programmers busy. With pride, we would then present the new lessons to our clients. Always, some things were accepted enthusiastically, some halfheartedly, and some were rejected. More brainstorming followed, leading to revised designs and reprogramming, all to be repeated again and again.

Fairly often, large content changes occurred: "Add these modules and drop those." When a topic was deemed too difficult to handle through the chosen medium, we were told to switch media: "Produce a video instead." Diagrams taken from previous course material didn't now seem as effective as expected: "Let's show this in a different way." New drawings were made.

Perhaps the testing was too difficult and criteria were set too high. "Rewrite the tests so more students can pass them." "Adjust all related training components to match the less idealistic outcomes we're now going with. And, by the way, keep this within the project budget. We've got to stick within it."

Some questions have to be answered before e-learning development costs can be estimated. Answering questions does carry a cost, but it is far cheaper than wasting a whole project budget through invalid assumptions. It would be wonderful if there were formulas, percentages, or some other metrics to estimate costs, but it just doesn't work that way. Sadly, many people involved in developing e-learning are trapped in this myth. The good news is that there is a way to answer these questions (more on that later).

## Of Camels, Horses, and Committees

You know the old joke that a camel is a horse designed by committee? No doubt the horse committee was given an excellent design document, perfectly detailing the specifications and description of the horse. But that's what happens with committees, due to bureaucratic and political problems, compromises, and efforts to maintain harmony—the result is never better than a camel. While there may be big functional differences between a committee and a team, some of the same "camel" difficulties often arise with e-learning teams.

> Some years ago, Dr. Bruce Sherwood, a luminary in the respected PLATO team at the University of Illinois, made a fascinating presentation on the topic of teaming in the design and development of instructional applications. At that point, just as now, nearly everyone assumed that teams of specialists were needed to produce reasonable volumes of reasonable quality instructional software. Optimal team composition was something of a continuing debate, but a general consensus endorsed teams composed of a project manager, instructional designer, subject-matter expert, graphics artist, and programmer. Sometimes a single individual would carry multiple responsibilities, while in larger projects, certain tasks would be handled by teams within the team or even by departments that provided specialized on-demand services.

What do you think Professor Sherwood observed when he looked at the origins of exemplary e-learning applications?

> Sherwood found that the outstanding e-learning applications of the time, as rated by a panel of experts, were nearly all produced by teams of size 1—a single individual. Among the 10 best applications identified (it was hard to find 10 agreed to be outstanding), only 3 were produced by teams; the other 7 were created by individuals who worked long hours for months, if not years, to maximize the

effectiveness of the learning experiences they were creating. These people included the celebrated Sharon Dugdale and Stan Smith—extraordinarily insightful educators who have searched for more effective methods of teaching their respective disciplines throughout their careers and whose work remains exemplary of what can be accomplished—by an *individual*.

These findings, unfortunately, give us little solution to the problems of generating high-quality e-learning design in the quantities needed. It's possible that the top, most inventive solutions will be designed and developed by individual geniuses, but with the ever-widening array of technology and tools to be harnessed, it seems less and less likely. We need an effective alternative.

## Persistence versus Genius

What else has been tried to address the challenges of good e-learning development? Persistence seems like a possible substitute for rare genius. There's nothing wrong with persistence as a path to excellence, except that it can take a long time—a very long time, if talent, knowledge, and skills aren't very strong. The opportunities to err are pervasive. Unguided dedication can waste a lot of resources and frustrate everyone involved.

It's a lot of work when you know what you're doing, and even more when you don't. Many are so passionate about their e-learning projects that they make the necessary sacrifices to work until they are satisfied— or, more often, until they can't do any more. Results are most often disappointing, but sometimes are astounding and inspiring. They sometimes add to the proof that it's possible to use learning technology in meaningful ways. Passion is good, possibly even a prerequisite for producing excellent e-learning designs, but clearly passion and persistence alone aren't guarantees of success. Through such means, the actual costs in terms of work hours is prohibitive anyway. We need a better way.

## Genius versus Persistence

Genius, often born of insatiable curiosity, incites and demands *dedication*—serious dedication, requiring innumerable sacrifices over an extended period. We may think genius makes notable accomplishments easy, but geniuses often struggle for a lifetime to achieve that deed we

Fairly early in my career, I encountered a college professor who had worked nearly two years on a computer-assisted learning project. He had painstakingly prepared content, crafted test questions, and validated his mastery criteria. He had overcome countless technical problems, programming challenges, and funding issues. Finally, he was able to introduce students to the learning experiences he had sacrificed so much to create. Unfortunately, the results were not the glowing outcomes and flowing admiration he had anticipated. Students didn't understand their options, clicked the wrong things, and asked innumerable questions.

In something very close to rage, with a red face and wringing of his hands, he recounted for me how ungrateful modern-day students can be. How could they tell him it was boring, confusing, and ineffective after he had put so much work into it! There it was, on the computer! Interactive! Individualized! It deserved student admiration, but it didn't get it.

He debated between punishing students for their impertinence and giving up ever trying to do something special for his students again. I suspect he pursued both courses of action rather than attempting to create well-designed, compelling learning experiences his students would appreciate. Effort doesn't guarantee success.

applaud and mistakenly attribute more to rare ability than to prolonged effort. Genius is composed of talent (or predisposition toward talent), capability, focus, and being in the right place at the right time.

Sometimes genius is mostly persistence. If you work at something hard enough and long enough, your chances of success increase greatly—you improve your chances of doing the right thing at the right time and being rewarded for it. There's nothing wrong with applying genius as a means to excellence, except that there isn't enough of it handy.

I've had and continue to have opportunities to work with some incredibly talented people—people who have extraordinary insight and a range of talents that permit them to do what their unique vision challenges them to do. Unfortunately, there aren't enough of these geniuses ready to lead the design and development of all needed e-learning applications.

By the way, the task of excellent e-learning development has frequently been a challenge even for the gifted. They also have to work hard and explore many ideas to create great learning experiences. They too must persuade clients that there's a better, more interactive way. They meet with technology entanglements and organizational confusions just as do the rest of us.

There are many easier ways to fame and fortune than building valuable learning experiences. Exceptionally gifted designers who remain in the field of teaching and technology-based learning are too few, very busy, and often exhausted.

## Is There a Viable Solution to e-Learning Development?

If teams have problems producing effective solutions, if geniuses are too few, and if both persistence and genius are too slow, where does that leave us? Are regular folk doomed to produce the typical e-learning that doesn't work, that everybody hates, and that costs a fortune? Is the task of inventing effective interactive learning experiences so difficult that success will be the exception? Given that there are so few genius-level designers, is it just being pragmatic to consider e-learning an unrealistic solution for most performance problems and learning needs?

e-Learning might well be discounted as a potential mainstream tool if the answer to all these questions proves to be yes. Under such conditions, corporations shouldn't even consider e-learning as a solution to performance problems, or as a means for achieving business goals.

Some companies have clearly had great disappointments in e-learning, although they are often loath to publicize it. Undaunted, many expect that later efforts will lead to a positive return on investment (ROI), even if their initial efforts have not been successful. They just keep going, hoping somehow things will get better. "It's a learning curve issue," say some. "We just have to get the hang of it. One can't expect extraordinary successes in the first round."

e-Learning investments are growing to unprecedented, even colossal levels. Optimism remains strong. Organizations either are unaware of how ineffective their e-learning design is or they have the same confidence I have that there is a way good e-learning design can happen within realistic bounds. Some organizations, however, are anxiously looking for easier paths and quick fixes.

We have arrived at a critical question. What can we turn to for reliable and cost-effective production of timely, first-rate e-learning applications? Is there a viable solution?

*Yes.*

# An Issue of Process

Again, the lessons of early e-learning development offer some hope, and that hope lies in an effective process.

In 1979, William C. Norris, chairman and CEO of Control Data Corporation, sent down through his organization a challenge that landed at my feet. It was the challenge to find a way that "mere mortals could shape the interactive powers of computing into beneficial learning experiences *within reasonable time and effort constraints.*"

So here it was, within the prestigious and exhilarating realm of PLATO, where thousands of courseware development projects were undertaken, that I received the daunting but privileged challenge summed up in three words: "Make it easier." Well, actually, it was these three words: "Make it cheaper." (We are still hearing these words today.)

I, of course, wanted the three words to be "Make it better," because already I was seeing a plethora of boring applications beginning to swamp the exemplary applications. Manufacturing-style methods were being set up and used to roll out instructional courses in volume. Frightening. (And we are still seeing this today.)

With the backing of very significant resources, I was truly blessed with being at the right place at the right time. It was easy to see the make-it-cheaper challenge as an opportunity to lower costs so that people could afford to *make it better.* Our point of departure was from the then current methodology—an approach known as *instructional systems design* (ISD).

## What Should Have Worked, But Didn't: The ISD Tradition

Instructional systems design (ISD) is sometimes referred to as the *ADDIE method* for its five phases of analysis, design, development, implementation, and evaluation. (Actually having its roots in engineering design approaches, some may recognize the similarity of ISD to the information system development life cycle. One can only hope that this methodology works better in that context!)

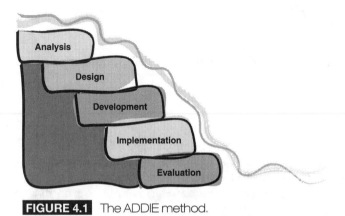

**FIGURE 4.1** The ADDIE method.

ISD is classified as a *waterfall methodology*, so called because there is no backing up through its five sequential phases or steps (Figure 4.1). Each phase elaborates on the output of the previous phase, without going back upstream to reconsider decisions.

Checks are made within each phase to be sure it has been completed thoroughly and accurately. If errors are found, work must not move on to the next phase, because it would be based on faulty information and would amplify errors and waste precious resources.

In many ways, this approach seems quite rational. It has been articulated to great depth by many organizations. But the results have been far from satisfactory. A few of the problems we experienced with it in the development of thousands of hours of instructional software included:

- *Considerable rework and overruns* because subject-matter experts couldn't see the instructional application in any meaningful way until after implementation (i.e. programming) had been completed. Then, errors and omissions were found and had to be corrected, with additional costs and schedule delays.

- *Contention among team members* because each would be visualizing something different as the process moved along, only to discover this fact when it was too late to make any changes without blame.

- *Boring applications* arising from a number of factors. One was that we couldn't explore alternative designs, because that requires execution of all five ADDIE steps to some degree *without* finalization of any. Another was that we focused on content and documentation rather than on learners and their experiences. Finally, we lacked helpful learner involvement (because learners had no prototypes to evaluate, and they couldn't react meaningfully to a sea of highly structured documentation that made no sense to them).

## A Fatally Flawed Process

By attempting to be fully complete and totally accurate in the output of each phase, the ISD or ADDIE waterfall method assumes that perfection, or near perfection, is possible. It requires a high degree of perfection as a safeguard against building on false premises promoted in previous phases. Many attempts to refine the process have tried to tighten it up through clearer definitions, more detailed documentation, more sign-offs, and the like. They have tried to make sure analyses were deep and accurate, content was clarified in full, and screen designs were sketched out in detail almost to the pixel: no errors of omission, no vagary—and no success.

Efforts to complete each phase with precise, unequivocal analyses, specifications, or programming, in our case at CDC and perhaps typically in similar projects elsewhere, increased the administrative burden, increased the focus on documentation, and, even worse, decreased the likelihood of creative, engaging learning activities. Costs increased and throughput decreased. Applying the process became the job, mediocre learning experiences the output.

## Iterations Make Geniuses

Fortunately, there is a viable alternative to ISD. Imagine a process that:

- Helps teams work together more effectively and with enthusiasm
- Is more natural and involves more players in meaningful participation from beginning to end
- Focuses on learning experiences rather than on documentation
- Produces better products
- Is based on iterations rather than phenomenal performance
- Can be a lot of fun

There is such a process. It's called *successive approximation*. Successive approximation is a term I borrowed from psychology. In operant conditioning, it means that the gap between the current behavior and the desired behavior gets smaller as you give rewards for behaviors that are getting closer to the desired behavior. Its primary power in the world of e-learning comes from making repeated small steps rather than perfectly executed giant steps, which very few can do successfully.

In exploratory work with PLATO, "successive approximation" seemed to describe a software development process we devised for the design and development of complex applications that involved significant learner-interface invention. It actually incorporates most ISD notions and all ADDIE activities, but they are applied repetitively at the micro level rather than linearly at the macro level. Most important, successive approximation rejects the waterfall approach. It is instead an *iterative* approach. It not only allows, but prescribes, backing up. That is, it prescribes *redoing* evaluation, design, and development work as insight and vision build (Figure 4.2).

Some ISD or ADDIE defenders suggest that these differences are minor, but I feel that successive approximation is nearly an antithesis of those terribly burdened processes. Let's look at successive approximation in closer detail.

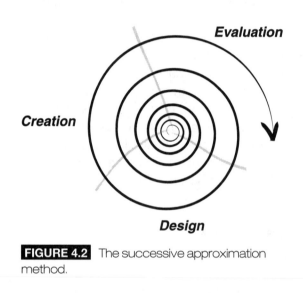

**FIGURE 4.2** The successive approximation method.

# The Gospel of Successive Approximation

There is an approach, a set of values, a way of thinking that is truly the essence and strength of successive approximation. Three primary tenets are enough to set you on your way to seeing the light. Once you get into it, all the critical nuances become natural and self-evident, rather than things to be memorized and applied dogmatically. Here is what the successive approximation flock believes:

- No e-learning application is perfect.
- Functional prototypes are better than storyboards and design specs.
- Quick and dirty is beautiful.

## No e-Learning Application Is Perfect

First and foremost is the recognition that no software application—or any product, for that matter—is perfect or ever will be. All applications can be improved, and as we make each attempt to improve them, we work to move successively closer to, or approximate, the theoretical ideal. We must be content to know that perfection is not achievable. Thankfully, it's not a prerequisite to success. We will never get to perfection, but a desirable process will ensure that each step we take will get us significantly closer.

Quite pragmatically, with successive approximation we are looking for the most *cost-effective* means we can find to enable learners to do what we want them to do. We want to spend neither more nor less than is necessary to achieve our goal. Both overspending and underspending are expensive mistakes. Without conducting some research and gathering critical information beforehand, there's no way of knowing what is the right amount to spend on a project, although everyone wishes there were. So it's important that the process be sensitive to the costs and diligent in determining appropriate investments at the earliest possible moment.

## Functional Prototypes Are Better than Storyboards and Design Specs

Next is the observation that storyboards and design specifications are unacceptably weak in comparison to functional prototypes. A *storyboard* is a hard-copy mock-up of the series of screens a learner will see in the completed e-learning piece, including feedback for each choice shown on the screen (Figure 4.3). These detailed screen images are presented in the order in which the learner is likely to encounter them, in the vain hope of avoiding errors and omissions in the finished e-learning application. Similarly, *design specifications* (or *specs* for short) include written descriptions and rough drawings of the interface, navigation, instructional objectives,

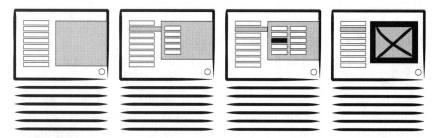

**FIGURE 4.3**  Storyboards typically include screen layout sketches and detailed written descriptions of how interactions should work.

content text, and so on. Again, the hope is that subject-matter experts and others on the design team will be able to fully grasp the nature of the envisioned interactions and successfully appraise the impact they will have on learners, and somehow will be able to spot errors and omissions in the design specs and so prevent them from becoming part of the final e-learning application.

By using functional prototypes, successive approximation sidesteps the risks inherent in storyboards and design specs, and reaps many advantages from using the actual delivery medium as a sounding board.

A true story: A large legal publisher formed a multimedia department to provide, among other things, training for its printing press operators. At first, a very linear design process was used. An instructional designer would follow ADDIE to the T and hand over fully scripted storyboards and design documents to the production people (media people and programmers).

As experience would predict, the applications had to be redesigned, because once the developers received the design documents and started producing the application, nobody liked what they saw. Everyone realized that very few people would get anything out of the training.

The organization learned from experience and changed its design process. Rather than creating design documents in a vacuum, the whole team (including end users) met for the project kickoff. Prototypes were built before filling in all the content. Once the appropriate design was determined, iterative development cycles took place.

The outcome? The production time was reduced by one-third to one-half, depending on the project.

## Storyboards and Design Specs

Storyboards have been valued tools to help clients, subject-matter experts, instructors, managers, programmers, and others understand and approve proposed designs. The logic is clear enough. Look at the sketches of screen designs, read the annotations of what is to happen, look at the interactions proposed and the contingent feedback messages students are to receive, and determine whether the event is likely to achieve the defined learning outcomes.

Storyboards are far better than nothing and much better than design specs that attempt to describe interactions verbally. Unfortunately, no matter how detailed storyboards may be, experience indicates that they fall short in their ability to convey designs adequately to all the concerned individuals. They are inferior as props for testing design effectiveness with learners. The sad truth is that storyboards almost invariably lead to problematic surprises when their contents have been programmed and their prescribed interactivity can be witnessed and tested.

I know that significant numbers of my much-appreciated readers are very much attached, both intellectually and emotionally, to storyboards. They find storyboards so valuable they wouldn't know any way of proceeding without them. Some, if not many, will feel that their storyboards have been the keys to many successes. Just between you and me, I'm actually thinking that these successes probably weren't such great successes anyway and weren't, in any case, all they might easily have been. How much more might have been achieved had a more effective process been used? What opportunities were lost by not being able to present and discuss aspects of the actual interactions to be *experienced?*

True instructional interactivity (see Chapter 7) cannot be storyboarded or effectively communicated through design specs. Yes, this may seem a radical, even rash, assertion. But consider the nature of a storyboard, and the nature of true instructional interactivity, and try to reach any other conclusion. Storyboards, by their nature, are static documents. Just displaying a static document changes its nature. What looks good on paper rarely looks good on the screen and vice versa. Even bigger differences become apparent between interactions described in documents and operational interactions created through a developer's interpretation of the documents. Even with sketches and detailed descriptions, the original vision will mutate in the most unexpected ways. Further, the original vision often doesn't seem so good when illuminated on the screen, even if no permutations have occurred.

## Prototypes

Functional prototypes have an enormous advantage over storyboards. With functional prototypes, everyone can get a sense of the interactive nature of the application, its timing, the conditional nature of feedback, and its dependency on learner input. With functional prototypes, everyone's attention turns to the most critical aspect of the design, the interactivity, as opposed to simply reviewing content presentation and talking about whether all content points have been presented. Design specs aren't even in the running. Unlike using storyboards or design specs, users of prototypes may have to personally decide on responses to make and actually make them in order to see how the software will respond.

I can hear the objection: Developing prototypes takes too long! My answer is that, for a skilled prototype developer, a useful prototype can usually be turned out in about two hours.

## THE BIRTH OF A PROTOTYPING TOOL

My leave from OSU was about over and I was preparing to return. I didn't think I could bring about the changes I felt were needed at CDC, but the company made a preemptive move. It allowed me to hire a team of the best people I could find. Through searching and many interviews, I found some great graduate students with relevant degrees in education who were just coming into the labor market or had been employed for a bit in leading research centers. They were fast thinkers, fun and inspiring to work with. We also hired some talented programmers from the outside who saw themselves on a mission of greatness (rather than on one of effort reduction and risk avoidance—the in-house crowd I had been given originally). They were up for experimentation to see how many original ideas we could put in motion. Things happened.

We didn't really want to enforce final approvals and prohibit changes in order to make projects easier to manage. We knew that the best ideas didn't—in fact, *couldn't*—surface until we all had something to see, touch, and feel. But the constant requests for changes blew our budget and schedules time and again. Without a flexible tool that allowed meaningful changes in both display and interactive logic to be implemented in seconds, it was necessary to have finalized specifications for programmers.

Specifications of any significance couldn't change without disrupting the programming effort, if not actually requiring significant reprogramming to core structures. Repeated changes to developing code made it difficult to maintain clean software structures and eventually caused programming nightmares, errors, and inflexibility. Changes were expensive and needed to be avoided.

One member of this new CDC team, Bill Bonetti, took on an effort to make it much easier for us to mock up display screens. Rather than drawing storyboard designs that often seemed much different when on the screen than when reviewed (and approved) on paper, we could draw our designs on the screen quickly. Instead of programming coordinates for display elements (imagine having to enter commands like "draw x=30, y=122 to x=18, y=430" just to draw a single line segment on the screen), you could literally touch the screen to position text or to draw lines, circles, and boxes. You could fine-tune objects through easy keyboard commands. You could move them, delete them, or duplicate them without having all objects on the screen erase and slowly replot with each change. It was fast and easy. Anyone could do it. We discovered that, even with only a few primitive capabilities, the ability to explore alternatives on the computer in the learners' delivery environment provided indispensable value.

It's hard to appreciate today how radical this capability was in the 1970s. It truly changed everything. It changed how we thought, how we did things, and eventually what we did. It created possibilities far beyond those we anticipated. It was helpful to be able to mock up screen displays for our clients far more quickly than before. We could make many design changes inexpensively and be responsive to shifting winds of thought. Clients could see designs in the presentation medium rather than on paper, and this alone reduced the number of design-program-redesign-reprogram cycles. But beyond anything we had considered, we discovered that our clients could take our proposed designs and rework them on their own as many times as they wanted, until they hit on something they found acceptable.

Building on the success of the screen editor, Bill went further and added a simple branching structure so authors could even build some basic interactivity. In some cases, this "unprogrammed" interactivity was powerful enough to make mock-ups that were deliverable as completed applications! If not that, they were easily powerful enough to test with learners in order to confirm whether designs were likely to work well for them. If the prototyping tool didn't produce the final application, it certainly helped everyone to evolve the design and to communicate the final blueprint in great specificity to the programmers.

Teams can produce excellent products if members have effective ways to communicate with each other. They need to see—*literally* see—the same design rather than imagine different designs and assume a common vision that really doesn't exist. If projects could be built by only a single person, it would usually take far too long. Teamwork is necessary, but it must be effective. Teams need a way to share a common vision, lest they all start on individual journeys leading to very different places. Without help from each other, no one arrives anywhere desirable.

## Ability to Evaluate

Think of the difference between watching *Who Wants to Be a Millionaire* and actually being in the hot seat. With nothing at risk, we casually judge the challenge to be much easier than it actually is. Imagine if, in storyboard fashion, *Millionaire's* correct answers were immediately posted for us on the screen as each question appeared, just as we'd see in storyboards. We'd easily think, "Oh, I know that. What an easy question!" But we wouldn't actually be facing the dreaded question: "Is that your final answer?" In the hot seat, we might actually have quite a struggle determining the answer. Obviously, many contestants do. Quite possibly, our learners would have much more trouble than we would anticipate from prototypes—you just can't tell very easily without the real tests that prototypes allow.

Comprehension of displayed text is inferior to comprehension of printed text. We also know that many designs that are approved in a storyboard presentation are soundly and immediately rejected when they are first seen on the screen, and they are even more likely to be rejected when they become interactive. Prototypes simply provide an invaluable means of evaluating designs. Otherwise, with the storyboards approved and the programming completed, changes are disruptive at best. More likely, they cause budget overruns and the work environment becomes contentious.

## Two-Hour Prototyping

We built Authorware specifically to address prototyping needs. Authorware is an icon-based authoring system for developing media-rich e-learning applications, marketed by Macromedia, Inc. To provide the most value, prototypes must be generated very quickly—we're talking minutes to hours here, not weeks—so they can be reviewed as early as possible and discarded without reservation. Prototypes must have interactive functionality so that the key characteristics of the events can be evaluated. Many teams today use Authorware primarily for this purpose even if the final product will be developed using tools more specifically optimized for Internet delivery, but any tool that allows very rapid proto-typing and very rapid changes to prototypes can serve well.

## Quick and Dirty Is Beautiful

Finally, quick iterations allow exploration of multiple design ideas. Successive approximation advocates believe attempts to perfect a design before any software is built are futile and wasteful. Alternative designs need to be developed with just enough functionality, content, and media development for everyone to understand and evaluate the proposed approaches.

I hasten to point out that there are problems with this approach if there are unindoctrinated heathens among the believers. Skeptics may lose confidence when asked to look at screens with primitive stick figures, unlabeled buttons, no media, incomplete sentences, and dysfunctional buttons. Although these are the characteristics of valuable rapidly produced prototypes, some may be unable to see through the roughness to the inner beauty. Indeed, this is a radical departure. I plead with you, however, to keep the faith. Converts are numerous, even among previously devout antagonists. To my knowledge, none of my clients would ever return to other processes; they have all become evangelists.

Converting disbelievers, however, can take time and patience. ("Most of our so-called reasoning consists in finding arguments for going on as we already do." —*James Robinson*.) It is often worthwhile, therefore, to produce a few polished screens to show what can be expected later in the process. Also, communicating your production standards for the project in advance will help curb the tendency to nitpick designs that are ready only for high-level evaluation.

### Brainstorming

The first version of a new application will typically be furthest from perfection, the furthest from what we really want, no matter how much effort is applied. To optimize chances of identifying the best plan possible, alternative approaches need to be explored. In this brainstorming mode, divergent ideas aren't judged before they've been developed a bit.

Brainstorming sounds like fun and can be. But the process isn't always obvious to everyone, and it can be difficult to keep on track. Check Table 4.1 for some approaches my teams have found effective.

## TABLE 4.1    Brainstorming Techniques

| Technique | Description |
|---|---|
| Using word reduction | Take the whole problem and reduce it to two sentences. Then one sentence. Then five words. Then one word. The idea is to really get at the *conceptual heart* of the process. As people go around the room and share their one word, you may find that everyone focuses on a different word! This ridiculous exercise reveals the direction for interactivity and also the potential conflicts. |
| Acting it out | Role-play the situation: the problem, how it's working now, how it's not working. |
| Playing the opposite game | What's the opposite of what's desired? For example, the opposite of what's needed is to slam the phone down on a customer after screaming "Don't call back!" This backhanded example reveals a goal: End conversations with the customer eager to call back. This approach can be a very goofy, funny brainstorming approach, but don't lead with this one first— there has to be some group trust before you start handling the client's content with humor. |
| Oversimplifying | Have the subject-matter experts explain the problem as they might to a class of 8-year-old kids. This forces them to use easy words, explain jargon, and reduce the problem to its most basic elements. It sheds unnecessary complications. |
| Drawing it | Draw the problem statement instead of using words. |
| Finding analogies | "Our problem is like the problem furniture salespeople have when a customer doesn't want to buy a bed that day. . . ." "Our problem is like when you go to the dentist and you haven't flossed and you feel guilty. . . ." Find creative ways of expressing the problem other than directly—this will suggest paths for interactivity and reduce the problem to basic elements. |
| Setting a 10-minute limit | Pretend that your users only have 10 minutes to experience all of the training. What would you expose them to? What would you have them learn? This activity can help users prioritize what's important in the interactivity or the problem analysis. |

## Alternatives at No Extra Cost

The total cost of a set of smaller creative design efforts (that is, prototypes) is easily affordable, because you don't spend much on any given
one. A quick review of alternatives incurs far less risk than single-pass or
phased approaches that bet everything on one proposal. Further, with the

iterative approach, course correction is performed routinely and early enough to prevent full development of ultimately unacceptable (and therefore extremely costly) designs.

With a prototyping approach, expenses are kept to a minimum while the search for the best solution is being conducted. Each prototyping effort means minimal analysis, leading to minimal design work, which leads to minimal development (prototyping) for evaluation. Note that this is just the opposite of ISD, which works for perfection at each point and intends to perform each process only once. Instead, following a small amount of effort, ideas are available for evaluation by everyone—including *students*, who can verify what makes sense and what doesn't, what is interesting and what isn't, what's funny and what isn't, what's meaningful and what's confusing, and so on. No more money needs to be spent on anything that seems unlikely to work if there are more promising alternatives to explore.

Please put your savings in the offering tray as we pass it around!

## Unsuccessful Designs Provide Insight

Early evaluation is input that either confirms or refutes the correctness of the analysis or design. In either case, additional analysis will lead to new design ideas that can be programmed and evaluated. Again, it's critical that early prototyping be regarded as disposable. In fact, it's healthy for organizations to work with the expectation of discarding early prototypes and a commitment to do so. There's no pressure for this early work to be done with foresight for maintenance, standards compliance, or anything else that would detract from the challenge of identifying the most effective learning event possible.

Again, prototyping requires the availability of flexible tools and the experience to use them, because it is often valuable to perform prototype development *live*—in front of the brainstorming team. Choose a tool that allows you to build your prototypes very quickly, concentrate on the learner experience instead of implementation details, and make modifications almost as quickly as ideas arise. Each correction will be a step forward.

## It's Catching On

Successive approximation is catching on in many organizations largely because alternative processes are not producing the quality of software and instruction expected and required. Even organizations that create general computer software are turning to similar approaches. (See the work of the Dynamic Systems Development Method Consortium at http://na.dsdm.org/.) Costs for development of even rather primitive interactive software remain high even with our best approaches. It is therefore important that projects return value, because they otherwise risk substantial losses.

Successive approximation requires neither the intellect of Albert Einstein nor the imagination of Walt Disney. Yet, by putting teams in the best possible position to be inventive—to see and explore opportunities while they still have resources to pursue them—successive approximation can reliably produce outstanding, creative learning experiences that are meaningful and memorable.

## It's Not Catching On

The successive approximation approach is a radical departure from the development processes entrenched in many organizations. I don't think this is unfortunate in itself. What's unfortunate is the inability to change.

## Change Requires Leadership

I have worked with many organizations that have rigid software development processes, defined in detail—painful, unending detail. These processes not only are blessed by top management, but also are rigorously enforced. Unfortunately, the underlying methodology is typically a waterfall method, and corporate standards are implemented to enforce completion of each phase, irreversible sign-offs, and systematic rejection of good ideas that come later than desired. Although I've invariably found that individuals within these organizations ingeniously find ways to employ some of the processes of successive approximation, they frequently have to do it surreptitiously.

The successive approximation approach also conflicts with many widespread notions of project management, so managers not fully versed in its principles may be uncomfortable and edgy, if not actively resistant. They may try to impose constraints that seem both logical and harmless but handicap the process enough to call its effectiveness into question.

It's an interesting situation—those who have had success with successive approximation cannot comprehend how any organization would stick to older methods, and those who are working to perfect traditional methods are unable to see the innumerable practical advantages of successive approximation. It appears that you have to get wet in order to swim, but some just aren't willing to put even a toe in the water.

They need a shove! Go ahead and push!

 **Advisory**

# Savvy—A Successful Program of Successive Approximation

Unfortunately, just understanding and appreciating the three key principles of successive approximation doesn't lead an organization easily to fluent application. To see how the principles can translate into some critical details, let's look at my own organization's application of successive approximations as a case study.

*Savvy* is the name Allen Interactions has given to an articulated application of successive approximation. *Savvy*, by the way, is not an acronym—because, frankly, we couldn't come up with anything that wasn't hokey, especially with *two* Vs in the middle of the name.

Because of its continuing success from almost every point of view, we hold dearly to the postulates of successive approximation and apply them in a program that involves:

- A Savvy Start
- Recent learners as designers
- Typical learner testing
- Breadth-over-depth sequencing of design and development efforts
- Team consistency and ownership
- Production with models

Let's explore them individually:

## A Savvy Start

Savvy begins with attempts to collect some essential information that is critical to making a succession of good decisions. The information doesn't have to be totally correct or complete. It's just a place to start.

Just as it's too expensive and ultimately impossible to make a perfect product, it's too expensive and ultimately impossible to get perfect information at the outset of a project (see Rossett 1999 for practical tips)—or any other time, for that matter. Waiting for attempts to extract this information from discussion, analysis, synthesis, report generation, report review, comment, modification, and approval is also expensive.

### Ready, Fire, Aim

Radically, and in perhaps an audacious manner, Savvy begins with the Savvy Start, and the Savvy Start begins with a short discussion and some on-the-spot rapid prototyping. Design, development, and evaluation of off-the-cuff prototypes stimulate information discovery. While this may seem akin to a trial-and-error process, many strongly held tenets, including such cornerstones as what should be taught to whom when, which values are appropriate, and how technology can be used to improve performance may actually be seen in a new light. Staunchly held preconceptions are quite often modified, if not totally discarded, in the process.

One Savvy Start began with 11 people in the room and a lot of resistance. We kicked out people who didn't need to be there, cut off their attempts to have long-winded discussions, and started making prototypes. By the end of the two-day experience, a 20-plus-year instructional designer said to the Savvy Start team: "You changed my life."

We assumed for the better.

### Unchangeable Things Change

Experience warns us about taking initially stated requirements to be absolute. No matter how strongly they may be supported at first, assuming that requirements can't be changed is precarious and probably unnecessarily restrictive. Things do change. In fact, learning is all about change. As people learn more about training and e-learning in particular, their preconceptions and premature plans can and often do change.

In corporate training arenas where custom courseware is developed under contract with external vendors, it's hard for contractors to know quickly what the real anchors are, what is actually negotiating posture versus a truly immutable constraint, and where hidden flexibility lies or can be created. If you're trying to help clients (whether internal or external) achieve significant success rather than simply trying to please them by delivering good-looking courseware, you will be focused on creating events that get people to change their behavior. Simultaneously, you will probably have to change your clients' minds about a lot of things, including what are and aren't effective uses of technology.

The earlier you can learn the lay of the land, the more credibility you will have to shape the training into what's really needed. But you need to get a foothold in order to investigate.

### Who's on First?

Prototypes help get discussions focused on solutions, not on who is in control, whose opinion counts the most, who knows the content best, who has the most teaching experience, or who can make the best-sounding arguments for certain design decisions. Prototypes stimulate brainstorming and creative problem solving. Prototypes get projects started and help clients determine what really is and isn't important to them. Prototypes help align clients' values for success rather than for maintenance of the status quo.

The excerpts from the Allen Interactions Savvy documentation presented in Figure 4.4 suggest the importance of client education. The process is paradoxically both similar to many things we do in life and surprisingly unexpected and foreign as a commercial process for creative product development. This document is provided to Allen Interactions' clients to set expectations and convey a clear picture of what happens just before and during a Savvy Start.

## Recent Learners as Designers

There is a fascinating paradox about expertise. The more expert we become, the more difficulty we have explaining how we think and how we do what we do, especially to those with very little knowledge of the particular field. Experts often experience difficulty and frustration as they try to help or teach novices.

Consider this: Who knows the most about driving, a person who has been driving safely for 20 years or a 16-year-old? The 20-year veteran, right?

# ALLEN INTERACTIONS SAVVY START

The training goal is to "Get People to Do the Right Thing at the Right Time." Backgrounding and the Savvy Start are efforts to determine, as cost-effectively as possible, who are the people, what is the right thing they should do, when should they do it, and how might we make this happen.

Before Savvy Start sessions begin, it's valuable to gather whatever pertinent information is readily available relating to the problem definition, content domain, audience, technical options, schedule, budget, available resources, and so on. A small investment from stakeholders to articulate their thoughts can be helpful, but investing too much effort or attempting finality too soon is detrimental.

In order to keep the process simple, clear, open, and objective, it's not imperative that information go through formal approval processes at this point. However, we encourage stakeholders to share their thoughts. If there are multiple points of view and perhaps differing goals among stakeholders, it's important for this information to surface as early as possible. Multiple goals can be addressed simultaneously if they aren't by nature conflicting and mutually exclusive. If differences resolve in the process of collecting information, that's great. If differences aren't even realized until the Savvy Start sessions begin, that's ok too.

Our Backgrounding and Savvy Start activities are described below:

## Backgrounding

Problem Statement

When any project is beginning, it's very tempting to jump directly to solutions—a process we actually promote more than refute; however, in order to keep the project focused and to know whether we have succeeded in the end, it's vital to look carefully at the problem, need, or performance gap that inspired the project in the beginning.

We know that the Savvy Start will help define the problem, perhaps even reframe it in some surprising ways as we progress, but some initial time spent getting a consensus definition amongst the stakeholders of the core problem is invaluable.

| | |
|---|---|
| Target Audience | One size does not fit all. Training appropriate for senior level executives, for example, requires characteristics different from training for entry-level computer operators. A function of Backgrounding and the Savvy Start is to define the target audience, their demographics, their experience, and what motivates them to learn and to perform. |
| | Because it's difficult to predict what anyone, including even ourselves, will actually find appealing and engaging, prototypes will help test our thoughts and expectations early. We will avoid expensive development based on poor assumptions, and we will continue to validate designs through subsequent, iterative evaluations. |
| Project Objectives | Once we have confidence in the problem statement and have defined the characteristics of the target audience, we will work with the client stakeholders to define specific project objectives. |
| | Clear, well-defined project objectives are necessary to guide the project, set values, define and select alternatives, keep the scope on track, and give us a way to evaluate progress. |
| Technical Issues | We define the basic technical issues involved with the project. Will delivery be via Web, intranet, or CD-ROM? What platform will our audience have (display capabilities, processor speed, network connection, speakers/headphones, etc.)? What browser plug-ins can we use? Can we use audio or video? Can we put data on the hard drive? What performance data can we store and in what format? Will a commercial, proprietary, or custom learning management system (LMS) be used? |

| | |
|---|---|
| User Interviews | Even at this early point, it's valuable to talk with end users to discover what their issues and concerns are, help us understand their needs, define training constraints and opportunities, and ensure that we can get learners involved throughout the process. Interviews typically include one-on-one discussions with managers of the people to be trained because manager expectations and views can differ significantly from all other stakeholders. Sometimes, support training for managers must be considered so that trained behaviors will be understood, supported, and encouraged. |

## Savvy Start

| | |
|---|---|
| Attendees | Who attends a Savvy Start? |
| | Participants at a Savvy Start include a producer and a developer from Allen Interactions. The producer provides project management and often instructional design leadership. The developer is there to provide technical support and create prototypes. Client participants usually include the project manager, representative stakeholders, and subject-matter experts (SMEs). |
| | It's usually best to keep the group small. Four or five people (1–2 from Allen, 2–3 from the client) will be able to reach consensus and keep moving to make the best use of Savvy Start time. |
| Prototyping | Prototyping is the heart of the Savvy Start and much of the continuing design process. We create rough functional prototypes to test interaction possibilities and determine their usefulness. |
| | To begin prototyping, everyone (Allen consultant(s), stakeholders, and subject-matter experts) brainstorms to select content for one or more experimental interactions. Our consultants will help in content |

selection to ensure maximum gain from the activity.

Some of the criteria to be considered include choosing content that is:

- Considered challenging to teach or most often misunderstood
- Critical to learn in order to perform targeted tasks
- Helpful in evaluating alternative instructional paradigms and use of media

Brainstorming produces rough ideas for sample interactions. Often several ideas are identified at almost the same time. At this point, client participants leave the room, and the Allen Interactions producer and developer spend 60–90 minutes to develop an interactive, functional prototype based on ideas discussed. Client participants then return to interact with and evaluate the prototypes. Immediately, essential information, values, opinions, and creative thoughts surface and initiate brainstorming for the next prototype.

| | |
|---|---|
| User Testing | It's always enlightening, if not vital to the efficient discovery of optimal solutions, to put prototypes in front of typical learners as soon as possible. All design ideas are just hypothetical until their effectiveness with learners is evaluated. Learners are truly the customer to be served, and, without their feedback, the risk of doing poorly is unnecessarily high. |
| Outline Project | In the final afternoon of the Savvy Start, typically after 3–5 prototypes have been created, all participants have a much deeper understanding of the big picture, including client values and goals and promising approaches to achieving performance success. At this point, we discuss how the remainder of the project will be completed. It will typically include the use of iterative |

prototyping to address other types of objectives yet to be identified and classified.

| | |
|---|---|
| Objectives × Treatments Matrix | A critical parameter for estimating project cost and duration is the Objectives × Treatments Matrix. As soon as possible, it is important to prototype a treatment for each type of objective (behavior) to be learned and estimate of how many objectives will be covered. |
| | When similar types of targeted behaviors are identified, we consider building or using models from our library that allow substitution of content without reprogramming. Project effort is largely a total of the number of unique interactions and models to be designed and built. Not all interaction paradigms and models need to be prototyped to get a good idea of the total project resources required, but the more that is known about them and the number of objectives needed to achieve required outcome behaviors, the more precise budget, schedule, and resources plans can be. A final discussion will be held to gather as much information as possible for estimating the matrix parameters. |
| Determine Project Parameters | We also discuss the other significant project parameters that need to be defined (project roles, dates, technical specifications, etc.) in order to write the preliminary project plan. |
| Savvy Start Deliverables | After the Savvy Start, Allen Interactions will deliver the following items: |

- Packaged and (if requested) source versions of the prototypes
- A preliminary project plan
- A budget estimate for course development based on stated assumptions

As appropriate, we may also send:

- Revised versions of the prototypes based on client feedback
- A summary of the end-user interviews
- An analysis plan
- A detailed schedule for the project

**FIGURE 4.4** Excerpt from Allen Interactions Savvy documentation. *(Copyright © 2002 Allen Interactions Inc., Minneapolis, MN, www.alleninteractions.com.)*

Who can best help you prepare for a driver's license exam? Probably someone who recently took the test, such as a 16-year-old. Not the more expert driver!

The mental gymnastics of experts are quite incomprehensible to novice learners. It appears experts come to their conclusions mystically. The rationale eludes learners. With mounting anxiety, feelings of inadequacy, and doubts about ever succeeding, novices working with experts begin to turn their focus on their emotions and their lack of progress. In the process, their learning abilities wane, and their expert instructors become even more frustrated.

## Experts Know Too Much

Experts become able to think in patterns and probabilities. They look for telltale signs that rule out specific possibilities or suggest other signs to investigate. While their rationale could conceivably be mapped out for novice learners, the skills needed to identify and evaluate each sign would have to be developed. Further, these skills would have to be refined and perhaps reshaped and combined with others to be effective for specific contexts. Although much of this would be fascinating for experts, almost none of it would be meaningful to the beginning learner. Attempts to fashion training based on a model of expert behavior are unlikely to succeed.

What does all this mean for the design of effective learning events and for successive approximations?

- Although their input can be invaluable, seasoned experts are not likely to be good designers of instruction on topics and behaviors in their field of expertise.

- The most advanced experts may have difficulty providing the services of subject-matter experts.

## Recent Learners Know More

We have to be careful about relying on subject-matter experts to articulate content to be learned, the most appropriate sequence of events, or the needed learning events themselves. While their review of content accuracy is obviously important to make sure learners aren't misled, there is a frequently overlooked source of valuable expertise: recent learners. The paradox continues.

Perhaps surprisingly, recently successful learners can provide an important balance and valuable insights. While the behavior of experts may indeed define the target outcome, experts often have trouble remembering not knowing what they now know so well and do without thinking.

Recent learners, however, can often remember:

- Not knowing what they have recently come to know
- What facts, concepts, procedures, or skills where challenging at first
- Why those facts, concepts, procedures, or skills were challenging
- What happened that got them past the challenge
- What brought on that coveted "A-ha!" experience

In an iterative process that seeks to verify frequently that assumptions are correct, that designs are working, and that there are no better ideas to build upon, recent learners are invaluable contributors. Guessing what will work for learners is an unnecessary risk. You can't speak for learners as well as they can speak for themselves, and waiting until the software is fully programmed is waiting too long. Once recent learners get in on the vision they can:

- Review even the earliest prototypes and access the likely value to learners.
- Propose learning events.
- Propose resources helpful in learning, such as libraries of examples, exercises, glossaries, and demonstrations.

- Help determine whether blended media solutions might be vital and which topics might be taught through each medium, including instructor-led activities.

- Review learner-interface designs for intelligibility.

Finally, although recent learners can be expected to make valuable contributions to the project from start to finish, it can be valuable both to continue working with the same individuals and to bring in others who will be seeing the project for the first time after some iterative work has been accomplished. Fresh eyes will make another layer of contribution, perhaps by seeing opportunities or problems that no one who has been on the team from the beginning is noticing.

Of course, the practicality and cost of working with an expanded review team must be considered. A small number of recent learners might be enough. Perhaps only three will be sufficient, particularly if you can find articulate, insightful, introspective, and interested individuals. Consider also the cost of *not* providing a learning event that really works for learners and reliably engenders the behaviors you need.

Don't miss the value recent learners can provide without seriously considering the advantages.

## Typical Learner Testing

Again we turn not to the usual sources of expertise, but to a nevertheless invaluable one: typical learners. Just as it is risky to think you know what a teenager would want to wear, it's really dangerous to make assumptions about what will appeal, engage, and be meaningful to learners without testing. Experience certainly helps increase the probability that proposed designs will work, but the confluence of factors determining the effectiveness of learning events is complex. Just as with television commercials and retail products, many good ideas don't turn out so well in practice, even when conceived by experts.

Thankfully, e-learning development tools allow easy and rapid modification of learning events. There won't be recalls, trashed products, or even filled wastebaskets, but mistakes can certainly be expensive if they aren't caught soon. The iterative process of successive approximation seeks to catch mistakes as soon as possible, well before the first version of the product is distributed. Thus, typical learner testing is a critical component of the process.

The timing of learner testing in the successive approximation approach is what differentiates it from other processes. Typical learners are brought in after each cycle of design. They are even brought in to look at prototypes resulting from the Savvy Start or prototypes that will be used to help schedule and budget the project. While everyone knows the prototypes will undergo major revision, perhaps several times, the reaction of typical learners can have a profound impact on the project. Learners may report that too much effort is being put into facts that are quite obvious and easy to understand. They may report the opposite. They may find that your enthusiastically endorsed ideas are quite boring, or that your simple game is way too complicated.

Surprises in the reactions of typical learners should be expected. It is difficult to put yourself into someone else's mind-set, but easy to be convinced that you have done so. The reality of the situation will surface, bluntly and frustratingly at times, if typical learners are truly comfortable expressing their opinions. While it may be deflating and hard to accept their input, it is invaluable to get it early and often. And, of course, it is necessary to accept it and work with it to garner the process advantages.

It takes *discipline*.

Just as with the participation of recent learners, participation of typical learners requires effort, cost, and coordination. For example, arranging for a steady stream of typical learners who haven't yet seen the evolving application can be difficult. Providing computers at the times and places needed, arranging for responsibilities to be covered while people are away from their workstations, providing orientation, and gathering feedback in useful forms is a lot of work. Perhaps none of these is as difficult to come by, however, as the discipline required just to make it happen. It's so easy to assume you're on the right track and that there's little guidance a typical learner can provide.

Designers readily fall into the trap of designing for themselves, assuming much more similarity of their needs, likes and dislikes, abilities, readiness, comfort with technology, and so on than actually exists with targeted learners. They conclude that there's little to be gained by stopping for discussion and feedback. It's a comforting and desirable conclusion, because there's always a push to keep the project moving. It seems that evaluation takes time away from development; although, in the long run, it should reduce total development if it catches design errors early enough.

No one likes to show their work in progress. We especially don't like to hear about deficiencies we know are there, as if we didn't recognize them and intend to address them. We don't like to expose mistakes. So, our natural tendency, if not our immutable rule, is to hide our work from view until it is finished and polished. But the longer a project goes on without verifying its course, the more costly it will be to make changes should they be required.

It cannot be said strongly enough: You must involve learners early and frequently. It's really quite irresponsible to do otherwise. It has to fit within the constraints of the overall project, as do all activities, but frequent learner testing is an essential component of successive approximation.

## Breadth-over-Depth Sequencing of Design and Development Efforts

The successive approximation approach has a built-in risk. Although many instructional designers are instantly attracted to the process, managers quickly see a red flag. The concern is that because it is an iterative process, projects will never be completed but will continue in perpetual revision as new ideas inevitably surface. Managers are concerned that attempts to refine the first components will consume all the project time and that insufficient resources will remain to complete the work. In the jargon of successive approximation, this would be a *depth-over-breadth* approach. And it's a gospel sin.

The managers' fears might be valid if successive approximation were not a *breadth-over-depth* or *breadth-before-depth* approach. The process depends on proposing design solutions for *all* performance needs as quickly as possible and implementing functional prototypes to verify the soundness and affordability of each approach. Like layers of a cake, each iteration covers the entire surface, then builds on the previous layer until a satisfactory depth is achieved.

Let's see why it's so important.

### Everything Is Related

Although there may be facts, concepts, procedures, and skills which seem very much unrelated, design work in all corners of an e-learning application affects work in the other corners. Like making a bed, you can't complete the process by perfecting each corner one at a time. You first loosely position sheets and blankets, then revisit each corner to tuck and tighten. If you need to adjust one corner, it will be easier to do so if the other corners haven't been completed. If they have been completed, there will be some unmaking and remaking—an effort that wouldn't have been necessary had you waited to check all four corners before perfecting them.

The analogy speaks strongly to notions of breadth over depth: Get through all the content before finalizing designs. Learner-interface notions, context development, testing and scoring structures, feedback and progress protocols, and many other design decisions may have to be adjusted several times until all of the content has been accommodated. You must not dig deeply into one area, assuming that all others have similar needs. If you perfect one "corner," the odds are high that you will have to undo a lot of work.

## Setting the Budget

We've already asserted that no application will reach perfection. In a way, that's good news for the budgeting process. It doesn't make good business sense to set an unreachable goal, because failure would be certain. Because perfection can't be reached, it's not the goal. Pragmatically, the goal is to spend exactly the right amount, no more or less than is necessary to achieve the desired outcome behaviors efficiently.

The successive approximation approach is capable of two very important outcomes:

- Successive approximation can produce the best learning application possible within the constraints of a preestablished schedule and budget.

- Successive approximation can help determine an optimal budget through iterative improvement and evaluation.

Within constraints, as many alternatives as possible are considered. Because of the breadth-over-depth rule, however, instruction for all targeted behaviors will be developed before refinement is applied to any of them. Minimal treatment of all content is therefore ensured.

When budgets are inadequate to meet needs, and sometimes they are, opportunities for later improvement are identified in the normal iterative process. Everything is set and ready for further refinement should funding become available.

Iteratively comparing the impact of each successive revision yields data relevant to the appropriateness of further spending. Through early revisions, gains are likely to be very high, but as the quality of the application continues to improve, successive gains will begin to decrease. Taking specific value factors into consideration—such as the cost of errors, the opportunities for expanded business, improved productivity, and so on— one can then make relatively objective decisions about whether additional cycles would yield an acceptable return on the investment.

In the meantime, and most important, the best possible application, within allocated resources and constraints, will be available for use.

## Three Is the Magic Number

A plan to revisit all areas of design three times proves quite effective in practice. Sometimes only one revision is necessary, especially when a previously validated model is being used.

Figure 4.5 shows a practical application of successive approximations with three prototyping iterations. Three iterations of the design, creation, and evaluation process are applied. The first prototyping is done during the Savvy Start and is based on initial analysis information that is always modified and extended during Savvy Start sessions.

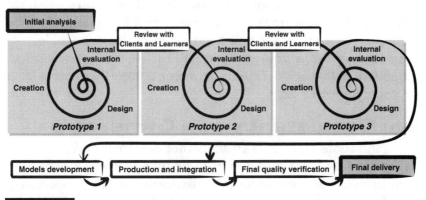

**FIGURE 4.5** A three-iteration application of successive approximation.

When the initial prototypes have been completed, they are tested with typical learners. This provides input for the second prototype and iterations of the design, creation, and evaluation process.

Sometimes the second prototype is sufficient, but it is important to reserve time and budget for a third prototyping effort, just in case. Better to come in under budget than over. Experience indicates that it is seldom necessary to go beyond three prototypes to finalize a design.

## Creeping Elegance

It's hard not to want to perfect media, interactions, and even text as they are initially developed. It is important, actually, to develop the look and feel enough that stakeholders can get a very clear picture of what is being proposed. It's also valuable to develop style sheets (you know, those irritating documents you have to refer to that specify what branding colors to use, what fonts are allowed, what margins are necessary, and so on) and to fully render some interactions so that everyone is clear about the extent of refinement that is eventually intended for all interactions.

Refinement should be confined to representative components of the final product, rather than applied to all prototypes. In fact, some later prototypes may be even more primitive than the first ones, because everyone will already understand how media and interface standards will be applied.

Temptingly, after the development of standards, it will be as easy to fully apply some of them as to wait for late iterations. There's no sense in doing things twice if standards can be applied with only about the same time and effort as placeholders. One must guard carefully, however, against creeping elegance. Unnecessarily refined prototypes work contrary to the effectiveness of successive approximation. Regardless of how much more satisfying it is to present refined prototypes, rewards should go to those who achieve consensus on the first iteration as quickly as possible.

Remember, *breadth over depth*. Cover all the content at modest levels of refinement, then go back over all the content iteratively to make successive layers of improvements.

## Team Consistency and Ownership

Many organizations work to keep all members of their design and development staffs busy. It makes sense that idle time is an expense to be avoided. In fact, most organizations departmentalize their specialists, with designers, programmers, artists, and so on each in their respective departments. As projects call for various tasks to be done, available people are assigned from each department. Department managers are responsible for providing services as needed while minimizing excess staff.

In my experience, this is perhaps the worst conceivable organizational structure. (I've tried it, of course.)

One has to admit that there's logic and simplicity to it. Unfortunately, it doesn't seem to work. Why not?

### Total Immersion

Crafting a multimedia experience to change behavior requires merging the talents of many individuals. As I've already asserted, documents describing interactive multimedia fall far short as tools for defining and communicating design vision. You have to feel the clay in your hands to know what's happening. To contribute, you have to be there, thinking, contributing, listening, working. You have to understand the business and performance problem being addressed as if it were your own problem to solve.

An effective team is not just individuals who show up from time to time, provide an illustration, and bow out. It's a team whose members stay with a project from beginning to end, think about solutions during lunch, and daydream about the most effective project solutions.

The level of individual involvement may change from time to time, especially in production activities, and not everyone assists in all tasks, of course. But beginning no later than with the initial prototypes, it's important that all team members be participants.

Artists and programmers can make important contributions to instructional design, just as designers and managers can make important observations on media design. As the team works together, knowing that each of the players will be there at the finish line, everyone looks to take advantage of what is being done in the successive cycles to make the application better, stronger, and more effective in later iterations. Issues aren't dismissed because the concerned individual probably won't be back tomorrow. Committee design anomalies don't occur, because each individual will be there to see if the specified outcome behaviors result. No one succeeds if the application fails; everyone succeeds if it does.

### Studios

Allen Interactions' greatest success has come from organizing into studios. A *studio* is a full complement of professionals capable of designing and developing all aspects of a powerful multimedia learning application. Clients work with the same team, the same individuals, from beginning to end. They meet and get to know every individual. They communicate directly about any and all issues and ideas.

The studio structure is not only a comforting and flexible structure for clients, it's the only one I've found to consistently produce the kind of learning solutions everyone wants.

## Production with Models

It is important to leverage technologies wherever helpful and to find every way possible to develop powerful learning experiences at the lowest cost. One very effective way to do this is to search for and identify similar learning tasks among the types of behaviors people must learn. Whether teaching dental assistants, airplane mechanics, telesales operators, or office managers, there are likely to be some similar tasks or repeating tasks with only content variations, not structural differences.

Sometimes the similar tasks are found to reoccur within one e-learning application. Other times, similar tasks are found in each of several different applications. Once an instructional approach has been designed and the delivery software is developed, it likely can be used repeatedly with specific content substitutions.

Models can vary in size from small structures, such as utilities for students to make notes in a personal notebook as they pursue their e-learning, to complex structures that are nearly complete training applications. Several applications used as examples in this book are actually models of varying size and complexity.

The corrective feedback model is a logic model shown in two applications: Who Wants to Be a Miller? and Just Ducky (see Figures 7.25 to 7.29). The user interface, graphics, and content vary tremendously from application to application, but the elegant and effective logic of this application is the same in each.

The task model is a structure that's particularly effective in teaching procedural tasks, such as the use of a software application. Shown in the *Breeze Thru Windows 95* application (Figures 7.22 to 7.23), this model has been used many times with a variety of content, such as teaching the use of custom and commercial software systems, medical devices, and restaurant seating and food-order-processing systems.

A problem-solving investigation model (Figures 7.30 to 7.38) was developed by DaimlerChrysler Quality Institute to require learners to practice applying statistical quality-control methods in an environment that simulates the complexities of large, real-life manufacturing processes. Rather than being given all the information needed as might be done in an academic approach, learners must think who might have needed information, find what is known, interpret data, and determine what information is relevant to solve problems that have actually occurred but have proved difficult to solve. Once the structure was built, it was only a matter of substituting new content to build additional cases for learners to study.

When there are enough uses of an approach, it pays to develop formalized templates or models that are structured specifically for easy content substitution. (See Table 4.2.) Sometimes, it's even worth going further to provide options for quick customization of how a model will work.

## When to Consider Models

Some projects are highly design-intensive. Almost every interaction is uniquely tailored to specific activities and outcome behaviors. As a result, models are not likely to be very helpful. Generalizing code so that content can be substituted is sometimes a costly and trivial effort, and it shouldn't be undertaken just in case the structure might be used again when the prospects for reuse haven't been identified. On the other hand, there are

**TABLE 4.2   Advantages and Disadvantages of Programmed Models**

| Advantages | Disadvantages |
| --- | --- |
| Speed development. | Force design compromises. |
| Reduce costs. | Generate content-insensitive interactions. |
| Centralize software bugs and repairs. | May be incompatible with the design context or may force adoption of a vanilla context. |
| Provide interface consistency. | Lead to monotonous repetition. |
| Reduce risk of programming errors. | May not be adaptable as needs change or more appropriate interactivity is identified. |

times when a logical structure can be used very widely. Not only is it then appropriate to generalize the code, but it is also important to document its use very carefully and sometimes even provide a number of options to help tailor the structure to a wider variety of applications.

## Spotting Opportunities for Models

In the first pass of interaction design, one objective is to be certain that a prototype is developed for every type of learning activity. Although we reviewed in detail why it's important to avoid refining these prototypes too early, there is yet another reason to delay refinement. Quite often, an approach used in one area of the application will be appropriate in another, but with only a slight twist. Sometimes in reviewing the original intended use, the twist will be valuable there as well. Sometimes not.

Because minimal effort was put into the early prototypes, ideas and structures remain temporary and fluid as instructional designs are considered for all of the content (breadth over depth). It is appropriate to reconsider individually developed designs that appear to be similar to each other to see if they might be evolved into a single, more generally useful structure. This will tap the advantages of models, and, unless inappropriate comprises are made to force compatibility, it will also avoid most of the disadvantages of models. More interesting, it may be possible now to build a more powerful, sophisticated set of interactions because of their broad utility.

 Advisory

Models can save development time and dollars. In the hands of an instructional design expert, they are powerful tools. But there are serious risks for inexperienced designers, who often find models especially attractive. Overuse of models leads to monotonous repetition and boring interactions. Nuances of the subject matter and needed interactions are often neglected or compromised while trimming content to fit properly into templates. If you're seriously undertaking an effort to improve performance, it's important and more cost-effective to do it right. There are enough challenges to meet without additionally trying to fit the solution into misshapen, predefined boxes.

# Summary

The challenges of designing and implementing excellent e-learning applications are many and varied. Team approaches are necessary, even though some of the best work has been done by dedicated individuals working over long periods of time. Most projects cannot wait for the extended development time needed by individuals. Unfortunately, traditional team approaches have had their unique disadvantages as well, resulting in mediocre products, delayed implementation, and organizational tension.

Successive approximation is a pragmatic approach that has overcome many of the problems experienced with team design and development. It is an iterative process that begins with rapid prototyping and evolves the most promising designs into the best application possible within given constraints. Frequent review of emerging applications takes the lead, rather than single-pass development working from design documents. Above all else, the process *must* be iterative to be cost-effective.

A successful example of successive approximation called *Savvy* involves six key principles and activities:

- A Savvy Start
- Recent learners as designers
- Typical learner testing
- Breadth-over-depth sequencing of design and development efforts
- Team consistency and ownership
- Production with models

# PART 2

# DESIGN

The second part of this book turns to specific design principles that lead to positive learning experiences. Although the perspective imparted in Part 1 may be paramount to full success, I'm also convinced that the design principles described here will improve any e-learning design effort.

Who should read Part 2? Everyone interested in using e-learning to achieve success—to get people to do the right thing at the right time. This includes executives, business strategists, consultants, buyers, and others responsible for the success of organizations.

It may seem strange that principles seemingly of interest only to instructional designers are presented here for review by managers, buyers, and others. But, I do strongly recommend that both designers and managers read the design principles explored in Part 2, as it is important for all decision makers to be able to discriminate between weak approaches and powerful ones. Everyone needs to work together to adhere to essential values and principles. It is easy to go wrong, and there are so many false roads to success.

# Background

Part 1 looked at the reasons why e-learning is so often a waste of time and money and how organizations are sometimes oblivious to both waste and lost opportunities. It also looked at what it takes to succeed with e-learning and how extraordinary the return can be when e-learning design is done well. The methods and principles that lead to highly effective e-learning seem simple and obvious when reviewed and enumerated, and yet, when you look at most e-learning applications, you find boring and ineffective presentations sprinkled with simplistic, uninteresting interactions.

The effectiveness of individuals and the power of organizations depend on their ability to perform, adapt, and change in response to shifting conditions. Learning is essential in many cases. If people find their training programs to be agonizing experiences, they will resist them and fail to complete them when allowed to quit early. Those unable to get themselves excused are likely to start the training with a negative attitude, and they'll have a boring, unproductive experience. Desired performance changes will not come easily.

Just as problematic are courses of instruction that are pleasant and entertaining, but fail in their mission to effect learning. Learners enjoy the break from the daily routine, but return to the job no more able to perform than before the training.

# No Reason for Poor e-Learning

Regardless of the reason for the ineffectiveness of an e-learning application, poor e-learning fails to build competitive organizational and individual strengths. There is no reason to waste the valuable and costly time of employees through ineffective training. And because there are decades of experience in the design of effective interactive instruction methods, there's no longer any justification for building ineffective e-learning applications.

Because so much poor e-learning has been developed and high-impact e-learning applications have been so rare, many have concluded that there must be a strong cost correlation: Weak e-learning is cheap; good e-learning is expensive. They further conclude that while weak e-learning design can be done quickly, good e-learning design takes forever.

These hasty and truly misleading conclusions are dangerous for several reasons:

- They overlook advancements made by leading design and development organizations over the last few decades; these advancements point the way to much less expensive and far faster development of high-impact e-learning applications.

- They ignore the real costs of lost business opportunities and poor performance.

- They channel resources into alternative solutions that can have even less probability of making a lasting impact.

We don't need to run from the challenge, but we do need to change our approach to it. Change in behavior doesn't come easily, either for our employees or ourselves. Unfortunately, developing powerful, engaging learning events requires change. To succeed, we have to approach the problem differently, think differently, reorder values and priorities, and, in many circumstances, do things that are contrary to both intuition and common wisdom. We may, indeed, have to do things that seem contrary to popular conclusions drawn from formal education on instructional design.

# Buyer Beware

The type of e-learning design that is an effective tool to meet business challenges and opportunities is not similar to the e-learning designs typically seen today. Effective e-learning builds learner interest rather than depletes it. It actually transfers skills and knowledge rather than just describes them. It enhances learner self-esteem and confidence. It builds competitive performance and contributes meaningfully to both individuals and the bottom line. Unfortunately for the uninformed buyer, it's easy to be deluded into thinking that superficially appealing applications of instructional technology are actually effective or representative of what can be achieved. In fact, many impotent instructional designs look professional and can be defended on many grounds. When organizations stop using them because of unrealized expectations, decision makers are disappointed and baffled at best. At worst, they conclude that e-learning isn't up to the task.

There is a costly difference between e-learning that works and e-learning that merely looks like it would work but doesn't. While the measured effectiveness of a completed application is the ultimate test of a design and development process, trial and error is an expensive process to use. Discovering that a completed application doesn't deliver reveals a costly mistake. No one wants to uncover this news. Measurement is itself costly and often considered either an unaffordable luxury or simply unnecessary. So it isn't until an organization discovers it can set aside a training program without much ill effect that the weakness is finally realized. And then it appears as a cost-saving move to eliminate the program!

Give me a break!

# You Don't Have to Count on Luck

Much is known about what works and what doesn't. Mistakes can be avoided. It is possible to be quite certain an application is going to be effective and yield a high return. Unfortunately, this is not widespread knowledge and does not guide enough design and development efforts. Informed leaders need to know what can be achieved and what to look for; they must become informed and demanding buyers. We can and must approach e-learning projects armed with the knowledge of what can truly be achieved within given constraints. We must insist on value so great that it is apparent even without measurement.

These, then, are the purposes of Part 2:

- To arm leaders with the knowledge they need to ensure success in each e-learning investment
- To guide designers in the application of values-based authoring that ensures success.

# LEARNER MOTIVATION

I am sometimes asked why I've stayed in the field of technology-based instruction for so many years. I can tell you that once you experience some successes and see what is possible, the allure of repeating those successes is very strong. Let me tell you a story of an early success with the PLATO system:

A custodian at an eastern public school was at his wit's end. After repeatedly lecturing teachers and staff about turning the building lights off when they left in the evening, lights were still being found ablaze many mornings when the building was being unlocked for the day. No one would admit leaving lights on. To the contrary, everyone assured the custodian that lights were switched off as the last person left.

In desperation, a security guard was posted. Sure enough, the lights went off as the last employee left, but sometime later in the evening the guard heard a noise outside. While he was outside checking, lights came on inside the school building!

The guard quietly reentered the building to see what was happening. To his great surprise, he found a room full of kids hard at work studying math with their PLATO computers. The noise he had heard was the kids getting into the ventilation ductwork so they could crawl through to the classroom. Once in, of course, it was very dark. The kids turned on the lights!

How often do kids break into school to study? How many situations do you know of in which school children voluntarily assemble to buckle down to schoolwork?

I have had many experiences in which I have personally seen technology-based instruction make a dramatic difference in the lives of learners. Each one of them has given me a craving for more. Each one of them has shown me how much untapped potential lies in e-learning. One area that definitely deserves more attention is the ability of e-learning to motivate learners.

Although outstanding teachers do their best to motivate learners on the first day of class and continually thereafter, many e-learning designers don't even consider the issue of learner motivation, let alone take action to raise it. They tend to focus instead on the meticulous presentation of information or *content*. Perhaps they believe the techniques teachers use to motivate learners are beyond the capabilities of e-learning. Instead of looking for alternative ways to use the strengths of e-learning technology to address motivation, they simply drop the challenge.

# The e-Learning Equation

Learning is an action taken by and occurring within the learner. Instructors cannot learn their learners, and neither can e-learning technology with all its graphics, animations, effects, audio, interactivity, and so on. Learners must be active participants and, in the end, do the learning.

The learners' motivation determines, in large part, the level of their participation in the learning activity and their ability to learn. Motivation is an essential element of learning success.

With apologies to Albert Einstein, let me advance a conceptual model through a simple equation:

$$e = m^2c$$

where  $e$ = edification (or e-learning outcomes)
$m$ = motivation
$c$ = content presentation

The equation suggests that if there is no motivation ($m = 0$), there are no learning outcomes ($e = 0$), regardless of how perfectly structured and presented the content may be. Of course, if the content is also inaccurate or faulty ($c = 0$), the learning outcomes will also be null. However, the equation suggests that emphasizing motivation in the course can have an exponentially greater impact than simply being comprehensive in content presentation.

No matter what the speculative value of $c$ (content presentation) might be, when $m = 0$, $e = 0$. If you think about it, you know this is quite possible. Surely you've attended a class that went into a topic you didn't see as valuable or applicable to you. You started thinking about something else and later jerked to attention, realizing you had no idea of what had been said.

## Motivation and Perception

Our selective perception allows us to filter out uninteresting, unimportant stimuli. It's very important that we have the capability of ignoring unimportant stimuli; otherwise, we would be shifting our attention constantly. Without selective perception, we wouldn't be able to attend properly to important events.

There are countless stimuli vying for our attention; however, most of these are unimportant and need to be ignored. As we sit in a lecture, for example, we can study the finish of the ceiling, note the kinds of shoes people are wearing, and check to see if our fingernails are trimmed evenly and to the desired length. The more we attend to unimportant things, the more difficult it becomes to effectively attend to those things that might actually be quite important to us.

Our motivations influence our perceptions and the process of focusing our attention. We attend to things of importance, whether they paint exciting opportunities in our minds or present dangers. When we see the possibility of winning a valued prize by correctly and quickly answering a question, for example, we focus and ready our whole body to respond. At that moment, we become completely oblivious to many other stimuli so that we can focus exclusively on the question. Conversely, if we expect little gratification from winning or have almost no possibility of winning, we might remain fully relaxed, not trying to generate an answer, or not even listening to the question. We might, instead, begin watching the behaviors of those really trying to win. If people watching provides little entertainment, that ceiling may take on a new fascination. There's a good likelihood we'll never even hear the question or the correct answer, because we'll be listening to our internal thoughts instead.

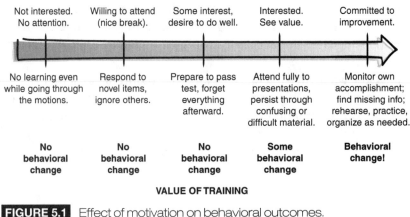

**MOTIVATION LEVEL**

| Not interested. No attention. | Willing to attend (nice break). | Some interest, desire to do well. | Interested. See value. | Committed to improvement. |

| No learning even while going through the motions. | Respond to novel items, ignore others. | Prepare to pass test, forget everything afterward. | Attend fully to presentations, persist through confusing or difficult material. | Monitor own accomplishment; find missing info; rehearse, practice, organize as needed. |

| **No behavioral change** | **No behavioral change** | **No behavioral change** | **Some behavioral change** | **Behavioral change!** |

**VALUE OF TRAINING**

**FIGURE 5.1** Effect of motivation on behavioral outcomes.

## Motivation and Persistence

As the gateway to learning, motivation first helps us attend to learning events. It then determines what actions we take in response to them. Viewed from the perspective of whether we achieve the behavioral changes targeted, success correlates with motivation as shown in Figure 5.1.

When we're motivated to learn, we find needed information even if it's not so easily accessed. We make the most of available resources. We stay on track with even a disorganized or inarticulate lecturer. We ask questions, plead for examples, or even suggest activities and topics for discussion. If the lecturer proves to be a steady, untiring adversary, we turn to other learners, the library, or even other instructors for the help we need. We might switch to another class if that's an option, but somehow, if our motivation is high enough, we learn what we want to learn. And to the extent possible under our control, we refuse to waste time in unproductive activities.

## Instructional Design Priorities

As we've seen, motivation controls our perception—what we see, hear, and experience. Motivation also fuels our persistence to achieve selected goals. Strong motivation, therefore, becomes critical for sustained learning.

**Premise:** Motivation is critical for learning. If motivation to learn is low, very little learning will occur. If motivation to learn is high, learning will occur even if instructional materials are poor.

There may be exceptions to this statement, as there are to most rules; however, many situations that appear to be exceptions are not. We learn things, for example, from simple observation. We learn from traumatic events, from surprises, and from shocking happenings. Are these exceptions? We find concurrent motivations at work even in these cases. Our motivations to belong, be safe, avoid unemployment, or win can all translate readily into motivation to learn. They cause what appears to be involuntary learning, but is, nonetheless, motivated learning.

Learning motivation is nearly always energized by other motivations, whether negative (such as avoidance of embarrassment, danger, or financial losses) or positive (such as competence, self-esteem, recognition, or financial gain).

---

**Conclusion:** It is as important, if not more important, to bolster learner motivation as it is to present content effectively.

---

# e-Learning Design Can Heighten as Well as Stifle Motivation

In a circular fashion, e-learning can help build the motivation needed for success. Heightened motivation strengthens the effectiveness of the e-learning and therefore promotes learning. This self-energizing system is to be fostered.

An opposing, deadly cycle is the alternative. Poor e-learning saps any motivation learners have. As learners suspect their e-learning work is of little value, they attend less and participate less, thus reducing the possibility that it will be of value. With evidence that e-learning isn't working for them, learner interest and motivation continue to drop. This self-defeating system is, of course, to be avoided.

## e-Learning Dropouts

Many e-learning designs tacitly assume, expect, require, and depend on high learner motivation, as evidenced by the good measure of persistence it takes just to endure them. If learner motivation wanes before the completion of instruction, learners drop out mentally, if not physically. Know what? This is exactly what is reported: 70 percent of learners drop out of their e-learning applications without completing them (Islam 2002).

Optimists claim (or hope) that high e-learning dropout rates simply reflect the attrition of learners who have gotten all they needed. Learners quit, it is reasoned, because their needs have been satisfied and they feel ready to meet their performance expectations. This may be their excuse, but I doubt that learners feel their initial e-learning experiences were so successful that they need not complete the training.

MOVIEGOER: This movie is so good, let's leave—quick, before it ends.
READER: This book is so good, I don't think I'll read any more of it.
E-LEARNER: This e-learning application is so good, I think I'll quit.

Does this logic sound right to you? e-Learners more likely drop out because they can't take the boredom and frustration than because the instruction has served their needs so well. The time, effort, and patience required are greater than the perceived benefit.

## Even Excellent Instruction Must Be Sold to the Learner

To create successful e-learning—or any successful learning program, for that matter—we need to make sure that value really is there. But perhaps just as important, we also need to make sure learners see and appreciate that value in concrete terms. Each learner must buy into the value of the learning—not just in general, but for specific, meaningful benefits. In other words, we need to *sell* learners on the *truthful* proposition that participation will provide benefits worth the time and effort. Doing so will stimulate vital motivation and give the program a chance to succeed.

I'm not talking about marketing spin meant to mask a miserable experience (although if the experience is going to be miserable, it's more important than ever to sell it successfully to the learner). Nor do I suggest cajoling learners or propositioning them: "If you struggle through this, you'll be much the better for it."

Adult learners are sensitive to manipulation. If they feel they are being manipulated, they are likely to react defensively. They may be motivated to prove the instruction was unnecessary or ineffective. Rather, everyone has much to gain if the learner sees the personal advantages of learning. Again, the value must truly exist *and* learners must be able to envision and appraise the win firsthand.

All of this is done to ensure that the $m$ in $e = m^2c$ reaches the highest value possible.

## It Isn't Bad News That Motivation Is Essential

Knowing the importance of learner motivation gives us an explanation of many e-learning failures and points the way to success. This is good news.

Actually, even better news lies in knowing that motivation levels change from situation to situation and from moment to moment. In other words, motivation levels are context-sensitive and can be influenced. We don't have to be satisfied with the levels of motivation learners carry into a learning event. If a learner's motivation is low, we can do things that are likely to raise it.

$$e = m^2c$$

You may have noted that, in contrast to Einstein's equation ($e = mc^2$), I have squared the motivation factor. This is done to emphasize not only that motivation is essential, as would be indicated simply by $e = mc$, but that the learning outcome is more likely to be affected by motivational factors than it is by the content presentation. Again, if motivation is high, learners will make the most of whatever content information is available. If motivation is low, refining presentation text and graphics may help to improve learning somewhat, but not to the same level as heightening motivation.

It's also critical that these two elements compliment each other. Content can be structured and presented in ways that are sensitive to the issue of motivation. That is, just as confusing and incomprehensible content presentation can extinguish motivation (i.e., $c$ can be 0), selection of the right content at the right time can stimulate motivation.

Further, interactivity allows learners to act on their motivations. Seeing their efforts advance themselves toward their goals reinforces motivation. We might, therefore, extend our equation to include the value of interactivity:

$$e = m^2ci$$

where $i$ = interactivity

The equation is not to be taken in any literal, computational sense, of course. We have no practical units of measurement applicable to content presentation nor standardized measures of motivation; however, the factors that determine learning shown here are functional and easily observed. The equation serves as a reminder not to omit attention to each factor.

### Motivation to Learn versus Motivation to Learn via e-Learning

Motivation has focus. It has a goal. We can have a varying set of multiple motivations with their individual goals simultaneously, and they are competitive with each other at all times. In certain contexts, one motive will sometimes have sufficient strength to dominate our attention. At these moments, stimuli unrelated to the dominant motivation won't even reach our consciousness.

Realizing the context sensitivity of motivations, we can also understand that e-learning events have the power to both increase and decrease learner motivation. Like every other aspect of human behavior, learner motivation is complex, but a simple view of motivation is sufficient to reveal powerful design principles for interactive instruction.

The simple view is this:

- If we want to learn, we will find a way.
- If we don't want to learn, we won't.
- If we want to learn but the e-learning application isn't working for us, we will turn to something else.

When we want the cost savings, quality control, easy access, and other advantages of e-learning, the question becomes, "How do we get learners to *want* to learn via e-learning?"

The answer: Seven Magic Keys.

# Seven Magic Keys to Motivating e-Learning

Yes, I have seven (rim shot please) "magic keys" to making e-learning experiences compelling and engaging.

It's never as easy as following a recipe in e-learning. I can't emphasize enough that there is a lot to know about instructional design, and that although good e-learning design may look simple to create, it isn't. A great idea will often look obvious, and an effective implementation of it may look easy when complete, but uncovering the simple, "obvious" ideas can be a very challenging task.

**TABLE 5.1  Ways to Enhance Learning Motivation—
the Magic Keys**

| Key | Comments |
|---|---|
| 1. Build on *anticipated outcomes.* | Help learners see how their involvement in the e-learning will produce outcomes they care about. |
| 2. Put the learner at *risk.* | If learners have something to lose, they pay attention. |
| 3. Select the right *content* for each learner. | If it's meaningless or learners already know it, it's not going to be an enjoyable learning experience. |
| 4. Use an appealing *context* | Novelty, suspense, fascinating graphics, humor, sound, music, animation—all draw learners in when done well. |
| 5. Have the learner perform *multistep tasks.* | Having people attempt real (or "authentic") tasks is much more interesting than having them repeat or mimic one step at a time. |
| 6. Provide *intrinsic feedback.* | Seeing the positive consequences of good performance is better feedback than being told, "Yes, that was good." |
| 7. Delay *judgment.* | If learners have to wait for confirmation, they will typically reevaluate for themselves while the tension mounts—essentially reviewing and rehearsing! |

It is therefore important to set out in promising directions right from the start. The magic in these keys is that they are such reliable and widely applicable techniques. Their presence or absence correlates well with the likely effectiveness of an e-learning application—at least to the extent that it provides motivating and engaging experiences. Thankfully, these features are not often more difficult to implement than many less effective interactions. These are realistic, practical approaches to highly effective e-learning. Let's begin with Table 5.1, which lists seven ways to enhance motivation—the Seven Magic Keys—and then discuss them in more detail with examples.

# Using the Magic Keys

You don't have to use every Magic Key in every application. You would be challenged to do it even if you were so inclined. On the other hand, the risk of failure rises dramatically if you employ none of them.

Although it's rather bold to say so, I do contend that if you fully employ just one of these motivation stimulants, your learning application is likely to be far more effective than the average e-learning application. Everything else you'd do would become more powerful because the learner would be a more active, interested participant.

# Magic Key 1: Build on Anticipated Outcomes

We have motives from the time we are born. As we mature, learned motives expand on our instinctive motives. All our learned motives can probably be traced to our instinctive motivations in some way, but the helpful observation here is that all persons have an array of motivations that can be employed to make e-learning successful (Figure 5.2). A simple and effective technique to build interest in an e-learning application is to relate its benefits to learner desires for comfort, power, self-esteem, and other prevalent motivations.

## Instructional Objectives

Much has been made of targeted outcome statements or *instructional objectives*, perhaps beginning with Robert Mager's insightful and pragmatic how-to books on instructional design, such as *Preparing Instructional Objectives* (Mager 1997c), *Measuring Instructional Results* (Mager 1997b), and *Goal Analysis* (Mager 1997a; Atlanta, GA: Center for Effective Performance). Instructional designers are taught to prepare objectives early in

**FIGURE 5.2** Prevalent motivations.

the design process and to list learning objectives at the beginning of each module of instruction. Few classically educated instructional designers would consider omitting the opening list of objectives.

Mager provides three primary reasons why objectives are important:

> Objectives . . . are useful in providing a sound basis (1) for the selection or designing of instructional content and procedures, (2) for evaluating or assessing the success of the instruction, and (3) for organizing the learners' own efforts and activities for the accomplishment of the important instructional intents. (Mager 1997c, p. 6)

There's no doubt about the first two uses. If you don't know what abilities you are helping your learners build, how can you know if you're having them do the right things? As I've emphasized before, success depends on people doing the right thing at the right time. If no declaration of the right thing is available, you can neither develop effective training nor measure the effectiveness of it—except, perhaps, by sheer luck. Objectives are a studied and effective way of declaring what the "right thing" is. As Mager says, "if you know where you are going, you have a better chance of getting there" (Mager 1997c, p. 6).

It's the third point that's of interest here—using objectives to help learners organize their learning efforts. Certainly objectives can help. When objectives are not present, learners must often guess what is important. In academic or certification contexts, learners without objectives must guess what will be included in the all-important final examination. After they have taken the final exam, learners know how they might have better organized their learning efforts. But, of course, it's too late by then.

For objectives to provide benefits to learners, learners have to read, understand, and think about them. Unfortunately, learners rarely spend the time to read objectives, much less use them as learning tools. Rather, they discover that the objectives page is, happily, a page that can be skipped over quickly. Learners think, "I'm supposed to do my best to learn whatever is here, so I might as well spend *all* my time learning it rather than reading about learning it."

## Lists of Objectives Are Not Motivating!

Many designers hope objectives will not only help learners organize their study, but also motivate them to want to learn the included content. Will they? Not if learners don't read them. How readable are they? It depends, of course, on how they are written.

Accomplished writers know that objectives should have three parts:

- A description of behavior that demonstrates learning
- The criterion for determining acceptable performance
- The conditions in which the performance must be given

Writers have learned the importance of using the right vocabulary; see Table 5.2 to get the gist of it.

Measurable behavioral objectives are, indeed, critical components to guide the design of effective training applications. Designers need such objectives, and none of these components should be missing from their design plans. But the question here is about their use as motivators.

You can hardly yawn fast enough when you read a block of statements containing such "proper" objectives as:

Given a typical business letter, you will be able to identify at least 80% of the common errors by underlining inappropriate elements or placing an "X" where essential components are missing.

Motivating? I don't think so. Objectives are certainly important, but listing such statements as this in bullet points at the start of a program is boring and ineffective. There are better ways to motivate learners.

**TABLE 5.2 Behavioral Objectives— Acceptable Verbs**

| Not Measurable | Measurable |
| --- | --- |
| To know | To recall |
| To understand | To apply |
| To appreciate | To choose |
| To think | To solve |

## How about Better-Written Objectives?

You can certainly write objectives in more interesting ways and in ways more relevant to the learner. Frankly, when deciding just how much energy and involvement to commit, learners want to know what's in it for them (i.e., how it relates to their personal network of motivations). Effective objectives answer the question and give motivation a little boost; see Table 5.3.

**TABLE 5.3  More Motivating Objective Statements**

| Instead of Saying . . . | You Could Say . . . |
|---|---|
| After you have completed this chapter, given a list of possible e-learning components, you will be able to list the essential components of high-impact e-learning. | In a very short time, say about two hours, you will learn to spot the flaws in typical designs that make e-learning deathly boring and you will know some ways to fix them. Ready? |

Remember that the more fully we can sell the learner on the advantages of learning the material at hand, the more effective the material will be. But if you've come to agree on this point, you might wonder whether textual listings of objectives are really the best way to sell anyone on learning. Good thought. We can do better!

Break the Rules

## Don't List Objectives

If learners aren't going to read objectives, even valuable and well-written objectives, listing them at the beginning of each module of instruction isn't a very effective thing to do.

In e-learning, we have techniques for drawing attention to vital information. We use interactivity, graphics, animation—in short, all the powers of interactive multimedia—to help learners focus on beneficial content. Why, then, shouldn't we use these same powers to portray the objectives and sell the learning opportunity to the learner?

Instead of just listing the objectives, provide meaningful and memorable experiences.

## Example 1:  Put the Learner to Work

Perhaps the clearest statement of possible outcomes comes from setting the learner to work on a stated task. If learners take a try and fail, at least they'll know exactly what they are going to be able to do when they complete the learning.

In this example of an award-winning application to teach users the ins and outs of Microsoft Windows (Figures 5.3 to 5.8), individual objectives are quite clear in the presentation of the task itself. Learners are immediately put to work to see if they can select a printer. Many learning aids are available, including a complete demonstration, a demonstration of the next step, hints, and sometimes an amusing video that puts the overall utility of knowing how to perform the task in context. Learners, engaged in their task, are motivated to seek and apply help as needed.

**Demo
on CD**

**FIGURE 5.3**  A meaningful task challenge takes the place of a traditional objective statement.

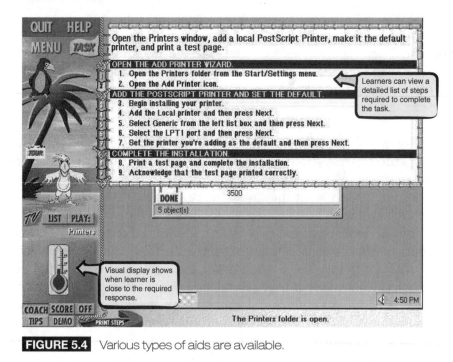

**FIGURE 5.4**  Various types of aids are available.

*Figures 5.3 to 5.8 from* Breeze Thru Windows 95 Basics. *Courtesy of Allen Interactions Inc.*

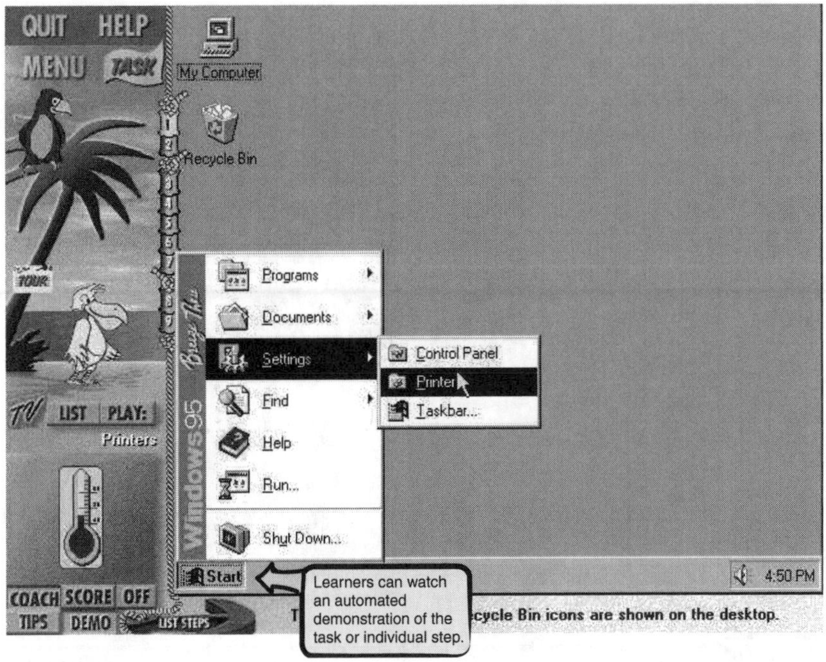

**FIGURE 5.5** Learners can request a demonstration.

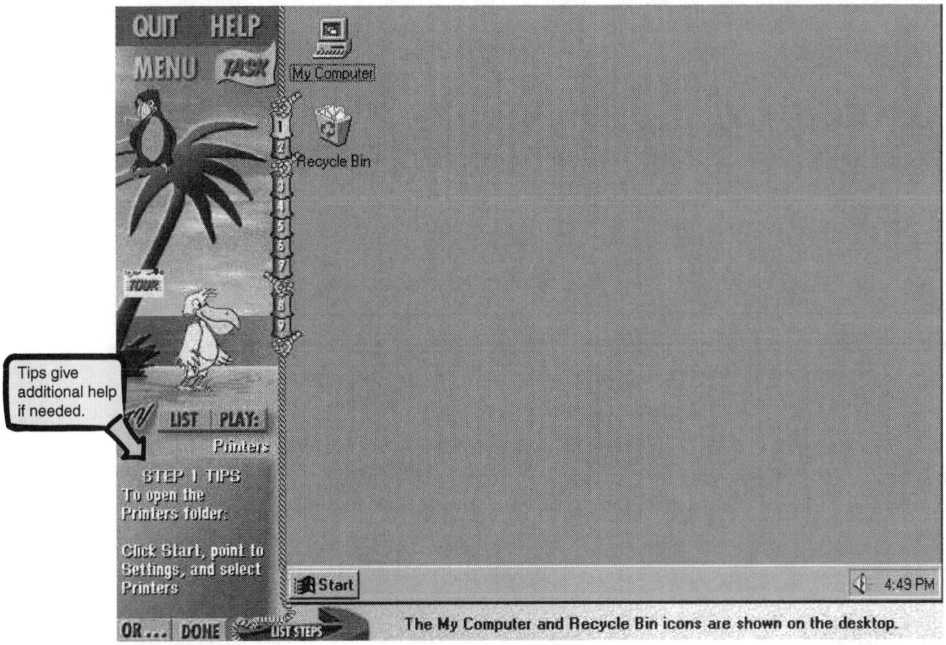

**FIGURE 5.6** Tips are available to suggest alternate ways of completing the task.

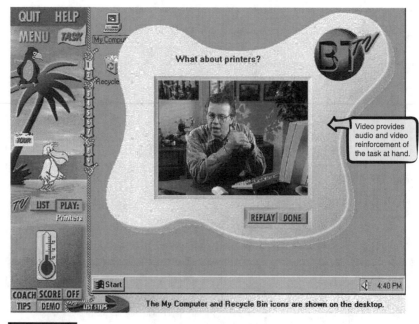

**FIGURE 5.7** Videos add humor and perspective.

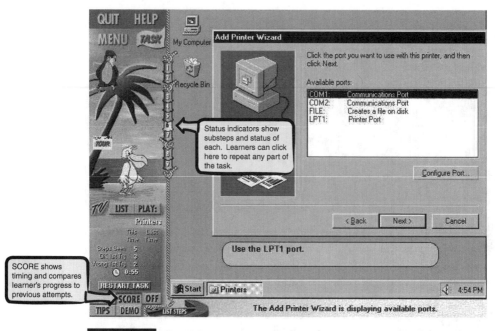

**FIGURE 5.8** Scoring and progress indicators encourage learners to practice for perfection.

You might be concerned that some failures, especially early on, will frustrate or demoralize learners. This is an appropriate concern. Interactive features must be provided to help all learners work effectively with risk. Please see Magic Key 2 for a discussion of risk management.

## Example 2:  Drama

Motivation is not an exclusively cognitive process. Motivations involve our emotions and our physiological drives, as well. Good speakers, writers, and filmmakers are able to spirit us on to take action, to reevaluate currently held positions, and to stir emotions that stick with us and guide our future decisions.

Imagine this scenario. Airline mechanics are to be trained in the process of changing tires on an aircraft in its current position at a gate. You can easily imagine the typical first page of the training materials to read something like this:

> At the completion of this course, you will be able to:
>
> • Determine safety concerns and proper methods of addressing each.
> • Confirm and cross-check location of tire(s) to replace.
> • Obtain appropriate replacement tire.
> • Select appropriate chock or antiroll mechanisms and secure according to approved procedures for each.

Now imagine this approach. You press a key to begin your training. Your computer screen slowly fades to full black.

> Lightning sounds crash and your screen flickers bright white a few times. You see a few bolts of lightning between the tall panes of commercial windows just barely visible. Through the window, you now see an airplane at the gate. The rain is splashing off the fuselage. A gust of wind makes a familiar sound.
>
> The scene cuts to two men in yellow rain slickers shouting at each other to be heard over the background noise of the storm and airport traffic.
>
> "You'll have to change that tire in record speed. The pilot insists there's a problem, and that's all it takes to mandate the change. There's going to be a break in the storm and there are thirty-some flights hoping to get out before we'll probably have to close down again."
>
> "No problem, Bob. We're on it."

Return to the windows, where we now can see people at the gate—a young man in business attire is pacing worriedly past an elderly woman seated near the windows.

"Don't worry, young man. They won't take off if the storm presents a serious danger. Even in a storm and with all the possible risks of air travel, I still think it's the safest way for me to get around."

"Oh, thanks, ma'am. But you see, my wife is in labor with our first child. I missed an earlier flight by ten minutes, and now this is the last one out tonight. I'm so worried this flight will be delayed for hours—or worse, even cancelled due to weather. I'm not sure what my options are, but I need to get home tonight."

Back outside, Bob runs up to three mechanics as they run toward him in the rain.

"All done, Bob. A little final paperwork inside where it's dry, and she's set to fly."

"Your team must have set a record. Even under pleasant circumstances, I don't know any other employees who could have done such a good job so fast. The departure of this aircraft won't be delayed one minute because of that tire change. A lot of people will benefit from your work tonight."

"This is going into the company's newsletter!"

I hope you can see how this dramatic context can much more effectively communicate the learning objectives *and* motivate learners to pursue them. Who wouldn't want to be a hero in this circumstance? Who wouldn't begin thinking, "I'll bet I could learn to do that . . . maybe even do it better." And then, "I wonder what it takes. Hope I get a chance to find out in this learning program."

## Example 3:  Game Quiz

Many interactive courses start with an opening assessment. It's a sound instructional principle. In order to select appropriate experiences for our learners, we need to know which skills our learners already have and which they don't.

The problem is that taking a test isn't an eagerly sought out experience. Many learners, in fact, become terribly fearful just at the thought. They would go to great lengths to avoid being tested, and, if not able to escape the test, may perform far below their actual abilities simply because of fright.

So, while there are good reasons to begin training activities with an assessment, there are also very good reasons not to. The challenge is how to:

- Motivate learners.
- Create a positive attitude about engaging with the e-learning application.
- Determine learner skill levels.
- Communicate what can be learned in the course.
- Set expectations in a convincing manner.

Sometimes it is not so much what you do as how you do it. One of the advantages of technology-based instruction is that learning experiences can be very private. Some of the fear of testing comes from apprehension about what others will think of a poor public performance.

There's much emotional carryover into e-learning from other experiences, even when concerns about embarrassment truly are not applicable. These concerns cannot be simply ignored, appropriate or not. Experience does show that nearly everyone can become accustomed to, and even appreciate, private testing when the results are kept private and are used to make learning experiences more fitting and enjoyable.

Not all quizzes are alike. While many are threatening, it's possible to make them fun. By creating as much distance as possible between the feared, graded academic test and a game in which not knowing an answer is fully acceptable and knowing one is a happy surprise to everyone, it's possible to meet all the challenges previously mentioned. Learners get into it and are energized. They see that there will be humor about mistakes and opportunities to address weaknesses (that's what the training is all about). They see whether they are beginners, intermediate performers, or even too advanced for the course. They see what content is covered and see some of the things that are important. And finally, if the testing is done very well (perhaps even involving some simulations), they see what kinds of tasks they will be able to perform once the training has been completed.

In this example, Fallon Worldwide (an advertising agency) wanted to assess each employee's level of Internet knowledge to best provide appropriate training. The idea of a formal test was unlikely to be an attractive

**Demo
on CD**

**FIGURE 5.9** Opening sequence sets expectations for challenge and fun.

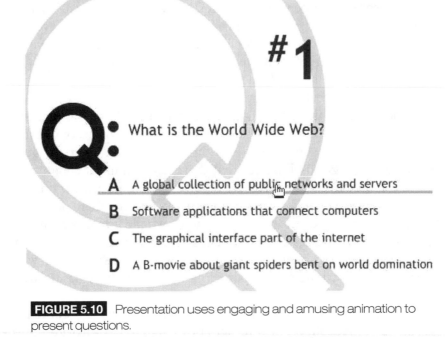

**FIGURE 5.10** Presentation uses engaging and amusing animation to present questions.

*Figures 5.9 to 5.11 from* Internet Readiness Quiz. *Courtesy of Fallon Worldwide.*

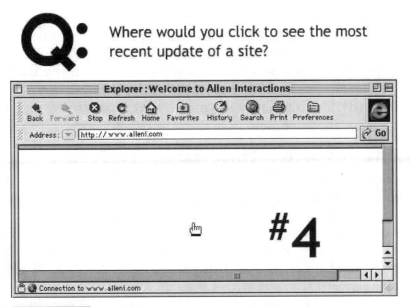

**Q:** Where would you click to see the most recent update of a site?

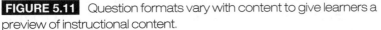

**FIGURE 5.11** Question formats vary with content to give learners a preview of instructional content.

proposition and would unnecessarily prejudice learners against the effort. This engaging quiz plays more like a game than an assessment tool. It moves quickly, is entertaining in its visual and audio effects, previews and highlights important information about the Internet, and still manages to gather all the desired information (Figures 5.9 to 5.11). You'll need to check this one out on the CD to get full impact.

## Magic Key 2: Put the Learner at Risk

When do our senses become most acute? When are we most alive and ready to respond? It's when we are at risk, when we sense danger (even pretended danger) and must make decisions to avert it. It's when we see an opportunity to win and the possibility of losing.

Games energize us primarily by putting us at risk and rewarding us for success. Although it's easy to point to the rewards of winning as the allure, it is also the energizing capabilities of games that make them so attractive. Risk makes games fun to play. It feels good to be active, win or lose.

Proper application of risk seems to provide optimal learning conditions. I used to think, in fact, that putting learners at some level of risk was the only effective motivator worth considering in e-learning and the most frequently omitted essential element. While I have identified other essential elements—the other Magic Keys—I continue to believe that risk is the most effective in the most situations. There are positives and negatives, however; see Table 5.4.

## Problems with Risk as a Motivator

Consider instructor-led training for a moment. In the classroom, putting the learner at risk can be as simple as the instructor posing a question to an individual learner. The risk to the learner goes far beyond failing to answer correctly. Public performance can affect social status, social image, and self-confidence for better or worse. Even if we're in a class in which we know none of our classmates, being asked a question typically causes a rush of adrenaline because of what's at stake.

Competition is a risk-based device used by many classroom instructors to motivate learners. In some of my early work with PLATO, I managed an employee who considered one of PLATO's greatest strengths to be its underlying communication capabilities, which were able to pit multiple users against each other in various forms of competitive combat. Although these capabilities were often used just for gaming, he was intrigued with the idea of using them to motivate learners.

Competitive e-learning environments can certainly be created, but, unfortunately, pitting learners against each other often constructs a win/lose environment. It may be true that even the losers are gaining strengths, and they may be effectively motivated to do their best as long

**TABLE 5.4   Risk as a Motivator**

| The Positives | The Negatives |
|---|---|
| Energizes learners, avoids boredom | May frighten learners, causing anxiety that inhibits learning and performance |
| Focuses learners on primary points and on performance | May rush learners to perform and not allow enough time to build a thorough understanding |
| Builds confidence in meeting challenges through rehearsed success | May damage confidence and self-image through a succession of failures |

as they aren't overly intimidated by the situation or their competitors. But it's difficult to prevent the nonwinners from seeing themselves as losers.

## Private versus Social Learning Environments

There are advantages to being in the company of others when we learn. We are motivated to keep up. We learn from watching the mistakes and successes of others. Communication with others helps round out our understanding. Successful public performance gives us confidence.

On the other hand, the risk of public humiliation is, for many, a fearful risk. While a successful public performance can easily meet our two essential criteria of being a meaningful and memorable learning event, the event may be memorable because of the fear associated with it. And although traumatic experiences may be memorable, the emotional penalty is too high. For many individuals, practice in a private environment avoids all risk of a humiliation and can bring significant learning rewards.

Interestingly, research finds that people respond to their computers as if they were people (Reeves and Nass 1999). We try to win the favor of our computers and respond to compliments extended to us by computer software. Quite surprisingly, solo learning activities undertaken with the computer have more characteristics of social learning environments than one would expect. Talented instructional designers build personality into their instructional software so as to maximize the positive social aspect of the learning environment.

Asynchronous electronic communications such as e-mail and synchronous learning events such as are now possible with various implementations of remote learning can build a sense of being together. Where resources are available to assist learning through such technologies, a stronger social learning environment can be offered, although here, just as with other forms of e-learning, design of learning events, not the mere use of technology, determines the success achieved.

For many organizations, though, one of the greatest advantages of e-learning comes from its constant availability. When there's a lull in their work, employees can be building skills rather than being simply unproductive while waiting for either more work assignments or scheduled classes to roll around. Unless you can count on the availability of appropriate colearners, it is probably best to design independent learning opportunities.

# Don't Baby Your Learners

Some organizations are very concerned about frustrating learners, generating complaints, or simply losing learners because they were too strongly challenged. They are so concerned, in fact, that they make sure that learners seldom make mistakes. Learners can cruise through the training, getting frequent rewards for little accomplishment.

The organization expects to get outstanding ratings from learners on surveys, and may get them regardless of whether any significant learning occurred. But even greater ratings may be achieved by actually helping learners improve their skills. More important, both individual and organizational success might be achieved.

Break the rules and put learners at some measure of risk. Then provide structures that avoid the potential perils of doing so. Here are some suggestions:

## Avoiding Risk Negatives

The positives of risk are extremely valuable, but they don't always outweigh the negatives. Fortunately, the negatives can be avoided in almost every instance, so that we're left only with the truly precious positive benefits. Effective techniques include:

- *Allowing learners to ask for the correct answer.* If learners see they aren't forced into a risk and can back out at any time, learners often warm up to taking chances, especially when they see the advantages of doing so.

- *Allowing learners to set the level of challenge.* Low challenge levels become uninteresting with repetition. Given the option, learners will usually choose successively greater challenges.

- *Complimenting learners on their attempts.* Some encouragement, even when learner attempts are unsuccessful, does a lot to keep learners trying. It is important for learners to know that a few failures here and there are helpful and respected.

- *Providing easier challenges after failures.* A few successes help ready learners to take a run at greater challenges.

- *Providing multiple levels of assistance.* Instead of all or nothing, learners can ask for and receive help ranging from general hints to high-fidelity demonstrations.

Using these techniques, it is possible to offer highly motivating e-learning experiences with almost none of the typical side effects that accompany learning risk in other environments.

## Example:  Stacked Challenges

Why do kids (and adults) play such video games as the classic Super Mario Bros. for hours on end? Shortly after home versions of the game became available, our son and all the children on our block knew *every* opportunity hidden throughout hundreds of screens under a multiplicity of changing variables. They stayed up too late and would have missed meals, if allowed to, in order to find every kickable brick in walls of thousands of bricks (Figure 5.12). They learned lightning-fast responses to jump and duck at exactly the right times in hundreds of situations. And for what? Toys? Money? Vacations? Prizes? Nope.

We play these games as skillfully as possible to be able to continue playing, to see how far we can get, to avoid dying and having to start over, to feel good about ourselves, and to enjoy the energy of a riskful, but not harmful, situation.

In the process of starting over (and over, and over), we practice all the skills from the basics through the recently acquired skills, overlearning them in the process and becoming ever more proficient. We take satisfaction in confirming our abilities as our adrenaline rises in anticipation of reencountering the challenges that doomed us last time.

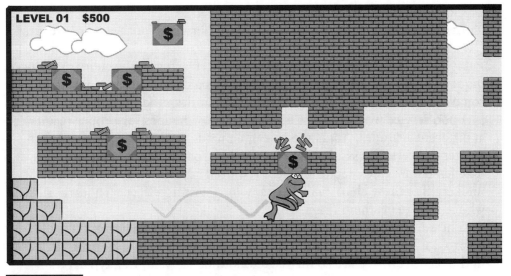

**FIGURE 5.12**  Computer games successfully teach hundreds of facts and procedures.

Imagine, in contrast, the typical schoolteacher setting out to teach students to identify which bricks hide award points. There would be charts of the many thousands of bricks in walls of various configurations. You can just imagine the homework assignments requiring students to memorize locations by counting over and down so many bricks and circling the correct ones. In class, students would grade each others' papers.

Students would be so bored that behavior problems would soon erupt. The teacher would remind students that someday in the future, they would be glad they could identify the bricks to kick. Great success would come to those learners who worked diligently. After several years of pushing students through these exercises, the teacher might turn to e-learning for help. With a happy thought of transferring the teaching tedium to the computer, the teacher would create an online version of the same boring instructional activities.

To me, this sounds similar to a lot of corporate training. While we might not see our trainees pulling each others' hair, making crude noises, and writing on desks, we can be sure they will be thinking about things other than the training content when learning tasks are so uninteresting.

Just teaching one task within the complex behaviors of the venerable Super Mario Bros. player would be a daunting challenge for many educators, yet millions of people have become adroit at these tasks with *no instruction*—at least with no *typical* instruction. Why aren't the obviously effective instructional techniques applied to e-learning, with all its interactive multimedia capabilities?

Good question. Why not, indeed!

In a project done for the National Food Service Management Institute (NFSMI), *Cooking with Flair: Preparing Yeast Breads, Quick Breads, Cakes, Pasta, Rice & Grains*, there were two goals: to teach specific culinary techniques and to teach concepts to give learners a deeper understanding of some of the more complicated aspects of quantity food preparation.

Food service workers must be able to adjust recipes for proper results at different altitudes. Adjustments can be made to the leavening, tougheners, tenderizers, liquids, baking temperature, pan greasing, and storage. The lesson provides details of these required adjustments, but it is unlikely that these charts will have any long-lasting effect on a learner who simply reads them (Figure 5.13).

The adjustment tasks are not complex, difficult to understand, or difficult to do: Increase leavening, reduce liquids, and so on. The problem lies in the fact that there are so many factors to be learned. In a typical training design, there would be concern about how you could keep people

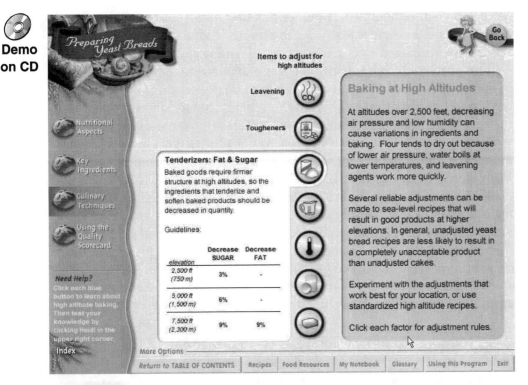

**Demo on CD**

**FIGURE 5.13** Explanation of high-altitude baking adjustments provides a lot to remember.

awake and focused on the task while you tried to train them on all these pieces of information.

But think about how many specific pieces of information children eagerly learn in the Super Mario Bros. games. If they can learn all of that information, then we should similarly be able to teach this information. What techniques can we borrow from the Nintendo game to make an e-learning experience successful?

## Repetition and Goals

Repetition is a primary way of getting information stored in our brains (see Figure 3.17). Most theorists believe we first perceive new information, transfer it to short-term memory, and then, through repetition, eventually integrate new information with existing information already

*Figures 5.13 to 5.19 from* Cooking with Flair: Preparing Yeast Breads, Quick Breads, Cakes, Pasta, Rice & Grains. *Courtesy of National Food Service Management Institute, University of Mississippi.*

held in long-term memory. Whether this description of the internal process is exactly correct really doesn't matter. What is clearly observable is that repetition facilitates learning, recall, and performance.

The problem is that repetition is generally boring. So, we need a way to make repetition palatable. This is where goals come in. By establishing goals we draw attention away from the repetition itself and can focus on the results that repetition achieves. If learners fail over and over again, they will generally want to stop. However, if they fail in a more advanced place each time, they're motivated to keep working toward perfection. Visible progress keeps learners trying.

These motivators were incorporated fully into the Heidi altitude baking exercise in *Cooking with Flair*. NFSMI used the visual context of a mountain that the learner's character (in this case Heidi rather than Mario) has to climb. She wants to visit her grandfather, who lives at the top, and prepare some baked goods for him to enjoy (Figure 5.14).

Along the way, she stops to visit his neighbors, who live at different altitudes (Figure 5.15). Her task is to prepare gifts of baked goods as she

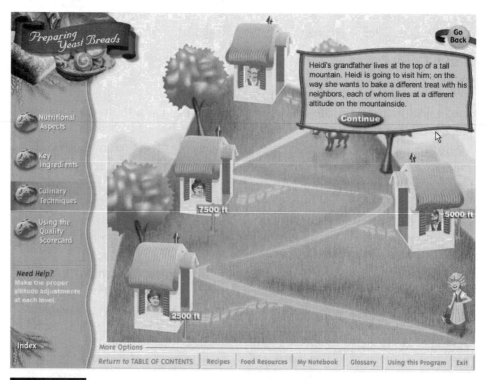

**FIGURE 5.14** Learners face the challenge of helping Heidi climb a mountain to reach her grandfather.

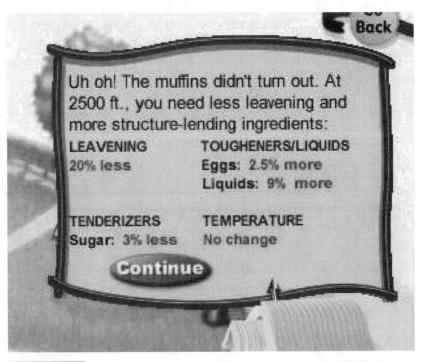

**FIGURE 5.15** Learners attempt to adjust recipes for each altitude.

travels along (Figure 5.16). The problem is that all her recipes expect preparation at sea level. If she doesn't adapt them properly, her baked gifts will be terrible (Figure 5.17), and the mountain's goat will knock Heidi down to the base of the mountain (Figure 5.18). She rolls down giggling—no injuries or violence here (Figure 5.19). The learner must start all over again.

Learners don't need to remember all the detail. Instead, they respond at the generalization level. "At this altitude, do I put in more or less

**FIGURE 5.16** When learners fail to adjust recipes properly, detailed information supports the learning opportunity.

**FIGURE 5.17**  When recipe adjustments fail, Heidi meets the goat.

flour?" Decisions the learner must make to adapt recipes for each altitude are simple check boxes, but the challenge is a considerable one, given all the possibilities. Feedback is both specific and dramatic.

Specific information is provided in response to the learner's choices.

Because learners must start over each time they fall, they get the most practice making adjustments at the 2,500-ft level. The extra practice at 2,500 ft is especially important because, on the job, more learners will have to make adjustments for this sea level than any other.

Intense learner involvement builds quickly in this exercise. Learners feel great satisfaction when they finally get Heidi all the way up the mountain to her grandfather (Figure 5.19).

Memory and interest continue to build as Heidi moves up the mountain and *closer to her goal.*

**FIGURE 5.18**  Heidi rolls down the hill to start all over again.

**FIGURE 5.19**  After succeeding with several altitude adjustments, learners put extra effort into their final challenges.

# Magic Key 3: Select the Right Content for Each Learner

What's boring? Presentations of information you already know, find irrelevant, or can't understand.

What's interesting?

- Learning how your knowledge can be put to new and valuable uses
- Understanding something that has always been puzzling (such as how those magicians switch places with tigers)
- Seeing new possibilities for success
- Discovering talents and capabilities you didn't know you had
- Doing something successfully that you've always failed at before

Moral? It's not enough for learners to *believe* there is value in prospective instruction (so that they have sufficient initial motivation to get involved). There must also be *real value* for them as learners. The content must fit with what they are ready to learn and capable of learning.

## Individualization

From some of the earliest work with computers in education, there has been an alluring vision: a vision that someday technology would make practical the adaptation of instruction to the different needs of individual learners. Some learners grasp concepts easily, whereas others need more time, more examples, more analogies, or more counterexamples. Some can concentrate for long periods of time; others need frequent breaks. Some learn quickly from verbal explanations, others from graphics, others from hands-on manipulation. The vision saw that, while instructors must generally provide information appropriate to the needs of the average learner, technology-delivered instruction could vary the pacing and selection of content as dictated by the needs of each learner.

Not only could appropriate content be selected for each learner's goals, interests, and abilities, instruction could also be adapted to learning styles, cultural backgrounds, and even personal lifestyles and interests. Perhaps no instructional path would ever be exactly the same for two learners. It would be possible for some learners to take cross-discipline paths, while others might pursue a single topic in great depth before turning to another. Some learners would need to keep diversions to a minimum while working on basic skills; others would benefit from putting basic skills into real-life contexts almost from the beginning. Areas of potential individualization seemed almost endless, but possible. And given enough learners across which to amortize the cost of development, the individualization could be quite practical.

Many classroom instructors do their best to address individual needs, but they know there are severe limits to what they can do specifically for individual learners, especially when there are high levels of variation among learners in a class. The pragmatic issues of determining each learner's needs, constructing an individual road map, and communicating the plan to the learner are insurmountable even without considering the mainstay of the typical instructor's day: presenting information. It's impossible to handle more than a small number of learners in a highly individualized program without the aid of technology.

With e-learning, we do have the technology necessary for truly exciting programs that can adapt effectively to the needs of individual learners.

Through technology, the delivery and support of a highly individualized process of instruction is quite practical, and there are actually many ways instruction can be fitted to individual needs.

Fortunately, it's not necessary to get esoteric in the approach. The simplest approaches contribute great advantages over nonindividualized approaches and probably have the greatest return on investment. It may require an expanded up-front investment, of course, as there's hardly anything cheaper than delivering one form of the curriculum in the same manner to many learners at the same time. But there are some practical tactics that result in far more individualized instruction than is often provided.

Let's look at some alternative paradigms to see how instruction can be individualized. Our emphasis here will be on just one parameter—content matching. Efforts to match learning style, psychological profiles, and other learner characteristics are technically possible. But where we haven't begun to match content to individual needs, we'll hardly be ready for the more refined subtleties of matching instructional characteristics to learners.

## Common Instruction

The most prevalent form of instruction makes no attempt to adapt content to learners. Learners show up. The presentations and activities commence. After a while, a test is given and grades are issued. Done. Next class, please.

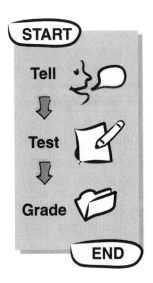

This form of instruction has been perpetrated on learners almost since the concept of organized group instruction originated. It's as simple and inexpensive as you can get, and it's credible today due not to its effectiveness but to its ubiquity.

It's unfortunate that so many use common instruction as a model for education and training. This tell-and-test paradigm is truly content-centric. With honorable intentions and dedication, designers frequently put great effort into the organization and presentation of the content and sometimes also into the preparation of test questions, but they do nothing to determine the readiness of learners or the viability of planned presentations for specific individuals. Although the application easily handles any number of learners and has almost no administrative or management problems, it doesn't motivate the learner.

The effectiveness of common instruction ranges widely, depending on many factors that are usually not considered, such as motivation of the learners, their expectations, their listening or reading skills, their study habits, and their content-specific entry skills. It is often thought that the testing event and grading provide sufficient motivation, so the issue of motivation is moot. Besides, motivation is really the learners' problem, right? If they don't learn, they'll have to pay the consequences—and hopefully will know better next time.

Wrong thinking, at least in the business world. It's the employer and the organization as a whole who will pay the consequences—consequences that are far greater than most organizations contemplate (as discussed in Chapter 1).

Individualization rating for common instruction:

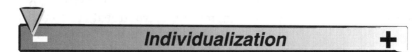

## Selective Instruction

A front end is added to common instruction in the creation of selective instruction. The front end is designed to improve effectiveness of the inevitable common instruction by narrowing the range of learners to be taught. Clever, huh? Change the target audience rather than offer better instruction.

Most American colleges and universities employ selective instruction at an institutional level; that is, they select and prepare to teach only those learners who meet minimum standards. Students are chosen through use of entry examinations, measures of intellectual abilities, academic accomplishments, and so on. The higher those standards can be, the better (well, the easier) the teaching task will be, anyway.

It makes sense that learners who have been highly successful in previous common instruction activities will be likely to again deal effectively with common instruction's unfortunate limitations. Organizations of higher learning will, therefore, find their instructional tasks simplified. They need to do little in the way of motivating learners and adapting instruction to individual needs. They can just find bright, capable, energetic learners, and then do whatever they want for instruction. The learners will find a way to make the best of it and learn.

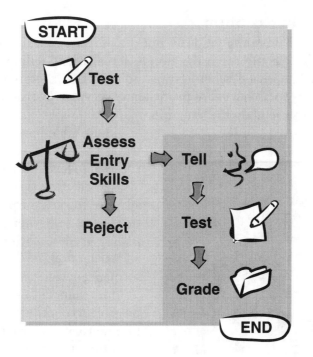

It dismays me that our most prestigious institutions boast of the entrance examination scores achieved by their entering learners. What they know, but aren't saying, is that they will have minimal instructional challenges, and their learners will continue to be outstanding performers. By turning away learners with lower scores, they will have far less challenging instructional tasks and will be able, if they wish, to devote more of their time to research and publishing. They actually could, if they wished (and I don't mean to suggest that they do), provide the weakest instructional experience and still anticipate impressive learning outcomes.

We do need organizations that can take our best learners and move them to ever higher levels of achievement. But perhaps the more significant instructional challenges lie in working with more typical learners who require greater instructional support for learning. Here, common instruction probably has been less effective than desired and should be supplanted by instruction that is based more on our knowledge of human learning than on tradition.

Individualization rating for selective instruction:

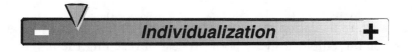

## Remedial Instruction

Recognizing that issuing grades is not the purpose of training, some have tried modifying common instruction to actually help failing learners. In this remedial approach, when testing indicates that a learner has not reached an acceptable level of proficiency, alternate instructional events are provided to remedy the situation.

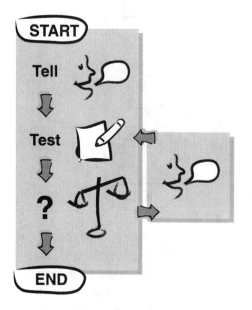

These added events, it is hoped, will bring failing learners to an acceptable level of performance.

Remediation is something of an advance toward purposeful instruction, because, rather than simply issuing grades, it attempts to help all learners achieve needed performance levels.

If learners fail on retesting, it is possible to continue the remediation, perhaps by providing alternate activities and support, until they achieve the required performance levels.

One has to ask, if the remediation is more likely to produce acceptable performance, why isn't it provided initially? The answer could be that it requires more instructor time or more expensive resources. If many learners can succeed without it, they can move on while special attention is given to the remedial learners.

The unfortunate thing about remedial instruction is that its individualization is based on failure. Until all the telling is done, instructors may not discover that some learners are not adequately prepared for the course, or don't have adequate language skills, or aren't sufficiently motivated. Although more appropriate learning events can be arranged after the testing reveals individual problems, precious time may have been wasted. The instructor and many learners (including those for whom the instruction is truly appropriate) may have been grievously frustrated, and remedial learners may be more confused and difficult to teach.

All in all, remediation represents better recognition of the true goals of instruction but employs a very poor process of reaching them.

Individualization Rating for remedial instruction:

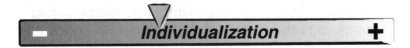

## Individualized Instruction

The same components of telling, testing, and deciding what to do next can be resequenced to achieve a remarkably different instructional process. As with so many instructional designs, a seemingly small difference can create a dramatically different experience with consequential differences.

A basic individualized system begins with assessment. The intent of the assessment is to determine the readiness of learners for learning with the instructional support available. Learners are not ready if, on one hand, they already possess the competencies that are the goal of the program, or, on the other hand, they do not meet the necessary entry requirements to understand and work with the instructional program. Unless assumptions can be made accurately, as is rarely the case despite a common willingness to make assumptions regarding learner competencies, it's very important to test for both entry readiness and prior mastery.

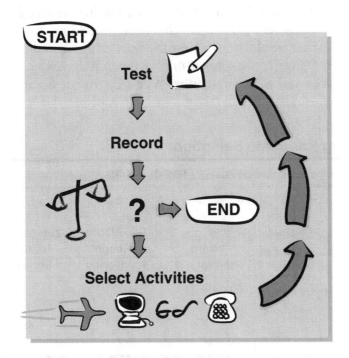

Record keeping is essential for individualized programs to work, because progress and needs are frequently reassessed to be sure the program is responding to the learner's evolving competencies. Specific results of each testing event must be kept, not just as an overall performance score, but as a measurement of progress and achievement for every instructional objective each learner is pursuing.

As progress is made and records are updated, the questions of readiness and needs are asserted. If there are (or remain) areas of weakness in which the training program can assist, learning activities are selected for the individual learner. Any conceivable type of learning activity that can be offered to the learner can be included, electronically delivered or not, including workbook exercises, group activities, field trips, computer-based training, videos, and so on.

The learning system is greatly empowered if alternate activities are available for each objective or set of objectives. Note that it is not necessary to have separate learning activities available for each objective, although it helps to have some that are limited to single objectives wherever possible. An arrangement suggested by Table 5.5 would be advantageous and perhaps typical. However, great variations are workable; it is often possible to set up an individualized learning program based on a variety of existing support materials.

Looking at the Table 5.5, you can see how an individualized learning system works. If a learner's assessment indicated needed instruction on all four objectives, what would you suggest the learner do? You'd probably select resources A and D, because we don't happen to have one resource that covers all four and because together A and D provide complete coverage of the four objectives.

**TABLE 5.5 Learning Resource Selection**

| | Learning Resources | | | | | |
|---|---|---|---|---|---|---|
| Objective Number | **A**<br>Basics Manual Text, Chapter 1 | **B**<br>Basics Manual Exercises, Chapter 1 | **C**<br>Intro Videotape | **D**<br>CD-ROM on Recent Discoveries | **E**<br>Tutorial on Problem Solving | **F**<br>Group Discussion on Science |
| 1 | X | | X | | | |
| 2 | X | X | | | | |
| 3 | | | X | X | X | |
| 4 | | | | X | | X |

Further, to their benefit, these two resources cover more than one objective each. When resources cover multiple objectives, it is more likely that they will discuss how various concepts relate to each other. Such discussions provide bridges and a supportive context for deeper understanding. Some supportive context, particularly important for a novice, is likely to be there in the selection of A and D in the preceding example, whereas it would be less likely in the combination of C, B, and F.

Just as with remedial instruction, if a prescribed course of study proves unsuccessful, it's better to have an alternative available than to simply send the learner back to repeat an unsuccessful experience. If the learner assigned to A and D were reassessed and still showed insufficient mastery of Objective 3, it would probably be more effective to assign Learning Resource E at this point than to suggest repetition of D.

The closed loop of individualized instruction systems returns learners to assessment following learning activities, where readiness and needs are again determined. Once the learner has mastered all the targeted objectives that the learning system supports, the accomplishment is documented, and the learner is ready to move on.

The framework of individualized instruction is very powerful, yet, happily, very simple in concept. Its implementation can be extraordinarily sophisticated, as is the case with some learning management systems (LMSs) or learning content management systems (LCMSs), whether custom-built or off the shelf. However, it can also be built rather simply within an instructional application and have great success.

Note that this structure does not require all learners to pursue exactly the same set or the same order of objectives. Very different programs of study are easily managed. Learners who require advanced work in some areas or reduced immersion in others are easily accommodated.

Individualization Rating for individualized instruction:

## Examples

As we have noted, there is a continuum of individualization. Some individualization is more valuable than none, even if the full possibilities of individualized instruction are beyond reach for a particular project. One of the most practical ways of achieving a valuable measure of individualization is to simply reverse the paradigm of tell and test in common instruction.

### Fixed Time, Variable Learning

With the almost-never-appropriate tell-and-test approach, exemplified by prevalent instructor-led practices, learners are initially told everything they need to know through classroom presentations, textbooks, videotapes, and other available means. Learners are then tested to see what they have learned (more likely, what they can recall). After the test, if time permits (since instructor-led programs almost always work within a preset, fixed time period, such as a week, quarter, or semester), more telling will be followed by more testing until the time is exhausted. The program appears well-planned if a final test closely follows the final content presentation and occurs just before the time period expires.

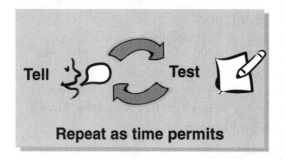

When e-learning follows this ancient plan, many of its archaic weaknesses are preserved.

### Fixed Content, Variable Learning

Instead of a predetermined time period, content coverage can be the controlling factor. The process of alternately telling and testing is repeated until all the content has been exhausted. The program then ends.

To emphasize the major weakness of this design (among its many flaws), the tell-and-test approach is often characterized as *fixed time, variable learning*—or, in the case of e-learning implementations, *fixed content, variable learning*. In other words, the approach does not ensure sufficient learning to meet any standards. It simply ensures that the time slot will be filled or that all the content will be presented.

### Fixed Learning, Variable Time and Content

To achieve success through enabling people to do the right thing at the right time, we are clearly most interested in helping all learners master skills. It is not our objective to simply cover all the content or fill the time period. To get everyone on the job and performing as desired as quickly as possible, we would most appropriately choose to let time vary, cover only needed content, and ensure that all learners had achieved competency.

Break the Rules

## Put the Test First

Many instructional designers embark on a path that results in tell-and-test applications. They may disguise the underlying approach rather effectively, perhaps by the clever use of technomedia, but the tell-and-test method nevertheless retains all the weaknesses of common instruction and none of the advantages of individualized instruction.

Let's compare the tell-and-test and test-and-tell methods (see Table 5.6). The advantages gained by simply putting the test first and allowing learners to ask for content assistance as they need it are amazing. As pre-

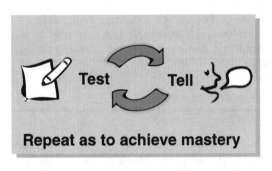

viously noted, just a slight alteration of an instructional approach often makes a dramatic difference. This is one of those cases. There is very little expense or effort difference between tell and test on the one hand and test and tell on the other, but the learning experiences are almost fundamentally different.

Getting novice designers to break the tendency to begin their applications with a lot of telling is not simple. Indeed, almost everyone seems to have the tendency to launch into content presentation as the natural, appropriate, and most essential thing to do. I have been frustrated over the years as my learners and employees, especially novices to instructional design, have found themselves drawn almost magnetically to this fundamental error. I have, however, discovered a practical remedy: After designers complete their first prototype, I simply ask them to switch it around in the next iteration. This makes content presentations available on demand and subject to learner needs.

Another example drawn from e-learning initiatives at NFSMI illustrates the power of the test-and-tell technique. A companion CD to the Breads and Grains module illustrated earlier, *Cooking with Flair: Preparing Fruits, Salads, and Vegetables*, teaches a range of facts and procedural information regarding the preparation of fruits and vegetables. The target

**TABLE 5.6   Selecting Content to Match Learner Needs**

| Tell and Test | Test and Tell |
| --- | --- |
| Because they have to wait for the test to reveal what is *really* important to learn (or it wouldn't be on the test), learners may have to guess at what is important during the extended tell time. They may discover too late that they have misunderstood as they stare at unexpected questions on the test that will determine their grades. | Learners are immediately confronted with challenges that the course will enable them to meet. Learners witness instantly what they need to be learning. |
| All learners receive the same content presentations. | Learners can skip over content they already know as evidenced by their initial performance. |
| Learners are passive, but they try to absorb the content slung at them, which they hope will prove to be empowering at some point. | Learners in well-designed test-and-tell environments become active learners; they are encouraged to ask for help when they cannot handle test items. The presentation material (which can be much the same as that used in tell and test) is presented in pieces relevant to specific skills. Learners see the need for it and put it to use. |
| It's boring. | Not likely to be boring. |

learners usually have some general but incomplete knowledge of the topics to be covered, but the gaps in their knowledge vary greatly. A typical strategy in such a context is to tell everybody everything, regardless of whether they need it. This is rarely helpful, as learners tend to stop paying attention when forced to read information that they already know. This is exactly the situation in which test and tell is most powerful.

We'll look at a content area called "Do the Dip," in which learners are to master information about how to keep freshly cut fruit from turning brown (Figure 5.20). The principle at hand is that fruits that tend to darken should be dipped in a dilute solution of citrus juice; some other fruits do not need to be treated in this way. The learner is to learn which common fruits this rule applies to. The setup here is very simple. Learners are given a very brief statement that sets the context. Then they are immediately tasked with the job of preparing a fruit tray. They can place the cut fruit directly on the serving tray, or they can first dip the fruit in a dilute solution of lemon juice.

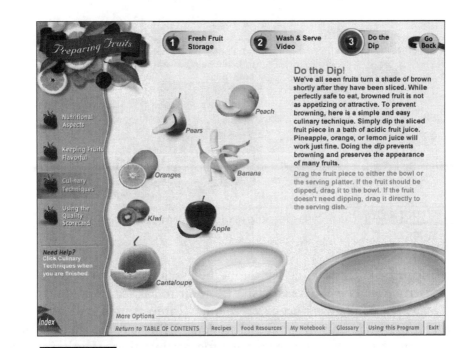

**FIGURE 5.20** Learner must decide whether it is appropriate to dip fruit in preparing fresh fruit tray.

If the user correctly dips a fruit, the information regarding that choice is confirmed with a message and a *Do the Dip!* flag on the fruit (Figure 5.21). Whether the learner already knew the concept or guessed correctly, the "tell" part of the instruction is contained in the feedback—presented after the learner's attention has been focused by the challenge.

How about when the learner is wrong? When a fruit is not dipped when it should be, the fruit turns brown and unappealing, while instructional text specific to the error is presented on the screen (Figure 5.22).

After the exercise is complete, the learner is left with a summary screen: a complete and attractive fruit platter and screen elements that further reinforce the lesson of which fruits require a citrus treatment (Figure 5.23).

This is a small and straightforward application of the test-and-tell principle. You should notice this magic key in action in more sophisticated ways in nearly every other example described in this book. It's

*Figures 5.20 to 5.23 from* Cooking with Flair: Preparing Fruits, Salads, and Vegetables. *Courtesy of National Food Service Management Institute, University of Mississippi.*

Do the Dip!

Apple

Yes, apple slices need to be dipped into a fruit bath before serving. Dipping the fruit will help prevent the apple from browning.

**FIGURE 5.21** Correct response is reinforced with *Do the Dip!* stamp on selected fruit.

engaging, efficient, and effective. Nonetheless, a common response from instructional designers is, "Isn't it unfair to ask learners to do a task for which you haven't prepared them?" (Interestingly, we rarely if ever hear this complaint from actual students!) But it really isn't unfair at all. Quite the reverse: The challenge focuses learning attention to the task at hand, allows learners with experience with the content to succeed quickly (saving time and frustration), provides learning content to the right people at the right time, and motivates all learners to engage in critical thinking about a task instead of simply being passive recipients of training. When the "tell" information is presented in the context of a learner action (i.e., right after a mistake), learners are in an optimal

Apple

Apples need to be dipped into a bath of acidic fruit juice before serving. This will help prevent browning. Try another apple slice. This time drag the apple slice to the bowl of juice.

**FIGURE 5.22** Incorrect response results in brown, unappealing fruit; user must repeat this fruit correctly.

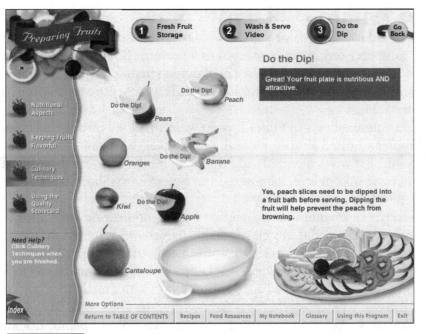

**FIGURE 5.23** Success results in completed tray and review of learned content through markers on fruit.

position to assimilate the new information meaningfully into their existing understanding of the topic.

## Magic Key 4: Use an Appealing Context

Learning contexts have many attributes. The delivery system is one very visible attribute, as is the graphic design or aesthetics of an e-learning application. More important than these, however, are the role the learner might be asked to play, the relevance and strength of the situational context, and the dramatic presentation of contextual content.

It's easy to confuse needed attributes of the learning context with other contextual issues. Unfortunately, such confusion can lead to much weaker applications than intended. However, strong learning context can amplify the unique learning capabilities of e-learning technologies. Let's first look at some mistakes that have continued since the early days of e-learning.

## The Typing Ball Syndrome

When I did my first major project with computer-based instruction, it was with computer terminals connected to a remote IBM 360 central computer. The terminals were IBM 3270s, which had no display screen but were more like typewriters, employing an IBM Selectric typewriter ball (Figure 5.24).

Continuous sheets of fanfold paper were threaded into the machine. A ball spun and tilted almost magically to align each character to be typed. With thin flat wires manipulating the ball's mechanism, the ball, like a mesmerized marionette, hammered the typewriter ribbon to produce crisp, perfectly aligned text.

Selectric typewriters were something of an engineering fascination. They so quickly produced a clean, sharp character in response to a tap on the keyboard, it was hard to see the movement. And yet, since a perfect character appeared on the paper, you knew the ball had spun to precisely the correct place and had tapped against the ribbon with exactly the right force.

If the Selectric typewriter was fascinating, the IBM 3270 Terminal was enthralling. Its Selectric ball typed by itself like a player piano! Looking very much like the Selectric typewriter with a floor stand, the terminal was able to receive output from a remote computer and could type faster than any human. The keys on the keyboard didn't move. The ball just did its dance while letters appeared on the paper.

The computer could type out information and learners could type their answers to be evaluated by the computer. The technology was fascinating. There was much talk about this being the future of education. Classroom delivery of instruction was clearly near the end of its life span, and, despite fears of lost teaching jobs, there was great excitement that

**FIGURE 5.24** IBM Selectric typewriter and ball.

private, personalized learning supported by amazingly intelligent computers would truly make learning fun and easy.

## Novelty versus Reality

There were some very positive signs that technology-led instruction would indeed be a reality in the near future. Learners eagerly signed up for courses taught with the use of computer terminals. Seats filled up rapidly, requiring dawdling learners to sign up for traditionally taught classes or wait another term to see if they would be lucky enough to get into one of the computer-assisted classes.

But some disturbing realities crept in, realities that countered initial perceptions and rosy predictions. For one thing, it took a lot longer for information to be typed out than to find it in a book. While you didn't get to watch them being typed, books were pretty fast at presenting information—and they were portable, too. They didn't make any noise, either—so they could be used in libraries and other quiet places that are conducive to study. They often included graphics and visual aids—things our Selectric typewriters couldn't provide. You could earmark a page and easily review. You could skim ahead to get some orientation and get a preview of what was to come.

Learners, the harsh but insightful critics that they often are, did the most unexpected thing. Instead of sitting at the terminals waiting for the typing ball to spit out text, they simply took their "borrowed" copies of printouts to a comfortable location and studied them. Sometimes they'd work together in pairs or groups: One learner would read the computer's questions, and another learner would answer. The first learner would look up and read the feedback for that particular answer, and together, they would have a pleasant, effective experience learning. They were executing, in effect, the programmed instructional logic. It was much better than sitting at a typing machine.

Why bring up this "ancient" history? We're not dealing with typing balls anymore. Isn't this irrelevant?

Not at all. Each time a new technology comes on the scene, we expect too much of it and require too little of ourselves to use it effectively. We are ready to think each new technology solves everything. For learning, the Internet has repeated the typing ball scenario—almost to the letter!

The typing ball was not essential to learning in any way. Learners quickly dispensed with it and created a more effective context in which they could freely discuss the content not only in a more *convenient* manner, but in a more *meaningful* manner, as well. In fact, the typing ball context was not really an *instructional* context at all; it was simply a new technology for instructional delivery. This seems like an obvious confusion to us today, but this mistake has been made time and again as new technologies have arrived to save the future of education. It is happening now, with the Internet.

## Novelty Is Short-Lived

Any attribute of the learning context can be made novel. The reaction to the novelty, almost by definition, will be one of instant interest and enthusiasm. Novelty draws attention and energizes exploration.

After the initial novelty-based interest, however, the next level of evaluation sets in. Newness doesn't last very long. Once we see something, experience it, and put it in its place among other familiar notions, it is no longer new. If a novelty doesn't introduce something of real value, it quickly sinks to neutral buoyancy.

In other words, novelty has a single, short life—too short to sustain much learning and involvement.

## Much e-Learning Depends on Novelty

A terrible mistake many have made in e-learning is assuming that because new technology is employed, it must provide better instruction. Because it comes in a new form and has such incredible attributes as worldwide access and 24/7 availability, it appears that its instructional effectiveness is better. Inexplicably, many even assume instructional development will be faster and easier: "We can put our PowerPoint slides on the Web. They'll be fantastic for training."

Wrong on all counts.

Actually, e-learning tends to expose instructional deficiencies and exacerbate their weaknesses.

Weak instructional design applied on a small scale, perhaps in just one class, doesn't do much damage. When parts of a book are poorly structured, for example, an instructor can likely overcome the problem through use of supplemental materials, class activities, or in-class presentations.

However, when a poor instructional design is broadcast to hundreds or thousands of learners, it can wreak havoc that is not as easily corrected. As

I've noted, organizations tend to look the other way and avoid questioning instructional effectiveness, even though the damage in lost opportunities, wasted time, severe mistakes, and accumulated minor mistakes can be astronomical.

Much early Web-delivered e-learning repeated the history of computer-assisted instruction (CAI). Actually, in many ways, contemporary e-learning has been more unguided than early CAI systems, which in many cases did conscientiously attempt to develop and apply instructional theory. Almost from their introduction, Web-delivered e-learning applications have bet on the novelty of computer presentation. e-Learning proponents often base their enthusiasm on the novelty of using computers for new purposes, rather than on a true appreciation of the potential computers offer.

## ANTICIPATED BENEFITS OF e-LEARNING

- Quick, easy, fun learning
- Quickly developed training programs
- Access to current information 24/7
- Learning on personal time rather than during work time
- Access to reference material as needed
- Unrestricted time to review, answer questions, and so on
- Personalized programs
- Lower training costs

The pioneering applications drew attention because they painted a picture of people happily learning whenever and wherever it might be convenient. Easy, fast, cheap. But novelty, with its fleeting contributions, left exposed many weakly designed applications and put the effectiveness of e-learning in question.

Questions about what it takes to be effective are slowly—surprisingly slowly—coming to the front. Technoblindness, fueled by euphoric views of potentialities, neglects the truth. Many have charged into e-learning investments, empowered by not much more than a fascination with its novelty and some fanciful dreams. They need to carefully consider the learning context.

## Context Elements to Consider

There are many types of context decisions to make. Remember that we are vitally concerned about motivational aspects of everything we do in e-learning. We should make context choices first to stimulate learning motivation and second to assist learners in transferring their newly learned knowledge and skills to real-world tasks.

As David Jonassen observes:

> The most effective learning contexts are those which are problem- or case-based and activity-oriented, that immerse the learner in the situation requiring him or her to acquire skills or knowledge in order to solve the problem or manipulate the situation. Most information that is taught in schools, however, is stripped of its contextual relevance and presented as truth or reality. Our youth are daily subjected to acquiring countless facts and rules that have no importance, relevance, or meaning to them because they are not related to anything the learners are interested in or need to know. [Jonassen 1991, p. 36]

Although many consider content presentation to be most important and others dwell on user interface, neither of these orientations is likely to produce optimal or even excellent learning opportunities if a well-conceived context isn't used to make the experience meaningful and memorable. Jonassen reiterates, "Instruction needs to be couched in a context that provides meaning for the learners, a context that activates relevant schemata, that engages learners in meaningful problem solving" (p. 36).

Table 5.7 presents some contextual ideas to heighten motivation and facilitate meaningful transfer of learned skills.

# Learning Sequences and Learning Contexts

Breaking complex tasks apart and teaching components separately can be an effective instructional practice. *Part-task* training is effective and efficient because it allows learners to focus on component behaviors and master them before having to deal with the interrelationships among sequences of behaviors to be performed.

## Risk of Part-Task Training

One has to be careful here, however. Breaking instruction into pieces for reduced complexity and easier learning can have exactly the opposite consequences: increased complexity and learner frustration.

How many piano learners, for example, have given up the instrument entirely because they could not sit for hours and practice finger exercises and arpeggios? Fingering skills are certainly important, but such drills are

## TABLE 5.7 Motivating Contexts

### To Stimulate Learning

| Suggestion | Comments |
|---|---|
| Require the learner to solve problems and do things. | It is more interesting to assemble or operate simulated equipment or software, diagnose system faults, or find an accounting error, for example, than to simply answer a bunch of questions. |
| Use a timer for learners to beat. | A simple mechanism such as a countdown timer stimulates learner attentiveness. |
| Use suspense. | You can set up consequences for errors that accumulate. The learner must not make too many errors or a tower will topple, a company will lose a contract, or a chemical solution will explode. |
| Set a maximum number of allowed errors. | If the learner makes one too many errors, he or she has to begin all over again, as in many video games. |
| Dramatically demonstrate the impact of poor performance. | Drama gets our emotions involved and makes experiences more real and personal. |
| Dramatically demonstrate the impact good performance can have. | A positive impact on the organization or on the learner personally is a goal of interest. A dramatic revelation of what is possible can be very motivating. |

### To Transfer Skills

| | |
|---|---|
| Provide feedback from a simulated supervisor or coworker. | Feedback might stress how the consequences of the good or poor performance effect them personally, their team, and the organization as a whole. |
| Ask learners how they think what they are learning applies to their actual jobs. | Address the question head-on. Encourage learners to develop their own examples of realistic ways to apply what they've learned. They might even work out a personal agenda or timeline for fully implementing their new skills. |
| Create an unreal world. | It is sometimes more effective to invent a completely new world for the examples and situations that learners will be working with. This may help learners avoid getting caught up in the details of their own specific processes and see opportunities for improvement more easily. |
| Use job tasks as the basis for lesson design, case studies and examples, or follow-up projects. | Designing job-based training maximizes the probability that learners will be able to retrieve their new knowledge and skills when they are back at work. In other words, let the practical tasks that learners need to perform drive the content and sequence of the training. |

**TABLE 5.7** *(Continued)*

## To Transfer Skills

| | |
|---|---|
| Use guided discovery or cognitive apprenticeship. | The learning is inherently contextual or situated in the job. |
| Incorporate case studies and examples that reflect best practices of proficient employees. | It helps to set standards of excellence against which learners can evaluate their own performance abilities. |
| Provide a variety of examples and problems based on documented events. | To ensure that learners will be able to apply their new skills appropriately in work situations, ensure that the problems and situations presented during training reflect the richness and diversity of what they will encounter in their everyday tasks. |
| Use a high-fidelity simulation while training procedural tasks. | It's worth the effort to make the simulation as much like the real thing as possible, because transfer is enhanced to the extent that actual tasks share common elements with rehearsal tasks. |
| Assign projects to be completed during or after the class. | Learners may not always see how what they have learned can be applied. Immediately applying new skills outside the training context can be very helpful. |
| Space out the review periods over time. | Rather than giving learners one shot at learning a new skill and massing all practice activities into one episode, spread out the intervals of practice over time to facilitate retention of new skills. |
| Give practice identifying the key features of new situations in which learners might apply their new skills appropriately. | If learners begin analyzing where and when new skills are applicable, they may begin setting expectations of where and when they will personally begin to apply them. |
| Provide skill-based training at a time when learners actually need it (just-in-time training). | The smaller the separation in time between the learning episode and the application of that learning, the greater the likelihood that the learner will transfer skills to that situation. |
| Embed the physical and psychological cues of the job into the instruction. | This helps to guarantee that learners will retrieve the relevant knowledge and skills when they sense those same cues back in the work environment. |

far from the music learners want to play. They want to learn music that is enjoyable to play. If the finger exercises don't demotivate them, the simplistic nursery school songs strung one after another are enough to devastate many potential musicians. Every music learner wants to play cool songs as soon as possible. The songs don't have to be overwhelmingly complex or difficult to play, they just need to represent an accomplishment that is meaningful to the learner.

## Maintaining Context

Critical elements of a meaningful context can easily be lost when instruction is broken into pieces. Context can be maintained if instruction begins with a clearly defined and learner-appreciated goal. Then subtasks can be defined and learned. Removing some context momentarily can be helpful, as long as enough context exists for the learning to be meaningful, or the relationship of the content to the ultimate goal is clear. The importance and relevance of the subtasks must be clear to the learner and often revisited. It is easy to assume that learners see this relationship, when, in fact, they may not. There are some easy techniques that help considerably, although they again fly in the face of traditional instructional design practice.

**Break the Rules**

## Don't Start at the Bottom of the Skills Hierarchy

A valued tool of instructional designers is the skills hierarchy. Desired skills are broken down into their constituent parts, then ordered in a prerequisite sequence or hierarchy. The target skill resides at the top, while the most basic, elementary skills sit at the bottom, with intermediary skills building the tree (Figure 5.25).

If the hierarchy is accurately constructed, tasks in the tree cannot be learned or performed before the skills below them have been learned. The hierarchy therefore prescribes a useful sequence for teaching. You start at the bottom, where all learners can be assumed able to learn the

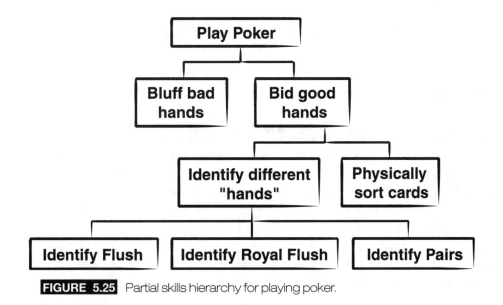

**FIGURE 5.25** Partial skills hierarchy for playing poker.

skills. Once these prerequisite skills have been mastered, you can move up a level.

Break the rules! Instead of beginning with the tedious task of explaining flush, royal flush, pairs, and so on to teach poker, deal the cards and play the game. Maybe you have all participants organize their cards and lay them face up. An experienced poker aficionado might announce who has the best hand and ask the learners to figure out why it's so strong. Of course, the *best* way to put the learners at risk is to give them a pile of chips and have them begin betting. Once students are in danger of losing chips (or gaining the whole multicolored pile), they ask good questions, learn winning combinations faster, and pay greater attention to explanations. There's no better way to learn about bluffing than to lose your chips to someone who wins the hand with two jacks!

## Boring!

QUESTION: Where do the *least* interesting tasks probably lie?
ANSWER: At the bottom of the hierarchy.

QUESTION: Where do the most interesting tasks probably lie?
ANSWER: Higher up the tree, probably near the top.

QUESTION: If you start at the bottom, is it clear to learners why they are learning these skills?
ANSWER: No, but we tell them these skills will be important. They'll see it later.

QUESTION: If you start at the bottom, are you starting with the most boring elements of the content with little contextual support?
ANSWER: Yes.

SUGGESTION: *Don't start at the bottom.*

## Keep Your Eye on the Target

If you want to be a lawyer, chemist, or romance novel writer, you probably have an expectation of what your life will be like in those occupations. It is this vision that motivates the necessary dedication of considerable time and effort to learn the many essential facts, concepts, and skills. Although we may well have misconceptions about what is involved in appealing professions, we often set out on major journeys with considerable optimism and enthusiasm, only to have that optimism and enthusiasm severely challenged by boring introductory courses. Many learners have told me that they gave up their interest in a profession because they couldn't imagine taking many more courses like the introductory course.

## A Great Learning Journey Starts . . . in the Middle!

Good e-learning designs do a lot to keep activities relevant and interesting. They don't work on the all-too-common instructor admonishment, "Trust me. Someday you'll be glad you know this." How do they do this? They start somewhere in the middle of the skills hierarchy, if not at the top, and let learners participate in leading the charge to fill in the missing pieces as necessary.

As you look at a skills hierarchy (and, by the way, you should construct one), scan up from the bottom in search of a point where a collection of prerequisites comes together in support of a skill or concept. Look at that skill or concept and see if it is a powerful or useful one. Points of convergence on a skills hierarchy often identify a capability that new learners can see as meaningful and desirable.

### Sometimes It Starts at the End

As presented in the discussion of Magic Key 3, a test-and-tell sequence is a useful strategy. I don't literally mean a test as a typical academic test, of course. You should build a context in which the learner has the opportunity and need to apply the skills resident at this selected point in the hierarchy.

The learner may or may not be able to perform well, but either outcome is helpful. If the learner does well, you might decide to jump up to the next point of convergence in the hierarchy and repeat the process. If the learner does not do well, you will be ready to respond to the learner's requests for help by supplying appropriate instructional experiences for all the prerequisite content. If the learner accurately identifies a need, you would respond to it, reinforcing the learner's perception of the need's relevance.

As you generate a contextual understanding, learners are learning much more than just a collection of skills. They are preparing personal perspectives, a set of values, and a cognitive map to guide performance and continuing learning.

In other words, context doesn't have to just sit in the background. It can be an important component of the interaction with learners to provide a structure for understanding, learning, and intelligent performance.

## Novelty Can Be a Valuable Tool

We earlier debunked novelty as an instructional context; however, it does have value. Novelty is powerful for only a short time, but it can be useful when applied thoughtfully and purposefully. Although it is not a substitute for effective learning interactions, novelty does have two important uses in effective e-learning:

- Novelty draws attention and energizes curiosity.
- Novelty can help make an experience memorable.

## Drawing Attention

As previously discussed, the most important thing designers must accomplish is motivating learners to learn. This is done by connecting with their needs and creating interest. And this means first getting their attention and helping them build positive expectations, curiosity, and a willingness to try (Figure 5.26).

Because novelty loses its value quickly, its use is well suited to attracting attention. It increases learner receptivity to messages that market the value of learning the content and skills at hand.

## Memorable Experiences

An unexpected quip, a fascinating morph, an amusing sound, or a simulated explosion could provide an element of appeal or surprise that learners will remember for some time. It's important, of course, that these elements be closely tied to important learning points. We don't want to end up with the effect of a clever TV commercial that viewers can remember in great detail, except for one minor point—the product or company being promoted.

As we know, to be effective, e-learning experiences must be *both* meaningful and memorable. A novel context can help tremendously to attract

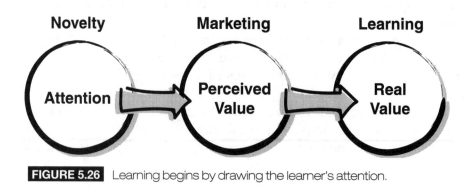

**FIGURE 5.26** Learning begins by drawing the learner's attention.

attention, but it can also hinder good interactive designs and disguise bad ones. It is potent stuff. It must be applied carefully, with clear purpose and intent, or it may easily destroy the learning opportunity by diverting attention from what is really important and of long-term value. One has to be careful in this arena to avoid self-delusion—mistaking ineffective novel experiences for effective novel experiences. Novelty is not the goal. It is a tool and means to better learning.

An example will help:

KTCA-TV and 3M Company, Inc., in association with ICONOS, Inc., created a series of outstanding CD-ROMs to accompany the public television program *Newton's Apple*. The intent was to provide highly interactive and educational experiences as companions to the television series. The "Why Does Glue Stick?" segment is a masterful example of how context—in this case novelty, sequencing, and skills transfer—can impact motivation.

The novelty in the challenge is apparent immediately (Figure 5.27). The learner needs to build a bridge to help an elephant cross a chasm. The tricky part is that the bridge must be built by gluing together such

**Demo on CD**

**FIGURE 5.27**   The learner can choose objects and glues to build a bridge.

*Figures 5.27 to 5.31 from* What's the Secret?, Vol. 2. Courtesy of KCTA-TV, St. Paul, MN.

diverse objects as a circular saw blade, a birdhouse, or an aquarium. Luckily, there are five adhesives available for use in solving this puzzle.

Again, the learner is thrown somewhat into the middle of the content. No boring discussions of glue characteristics here. While the context is unusual, it shines the spotlight fully on the content at hand: What are the characteristics of various adhesives that make them work with some surfaces but not with others? To build the bridge, the learner chooses an adhesive. If it is a successful combination, the elephant takes one step closer to its destination (Figure 5.28). If the adhesive does not hold, the learner gets a surprising but quite humorous result (Figure 5.29).

Now, critics might suggest that this is just unfair to the learner. How is the learner to know how to combine these unusual items into a bridge? Well, if this were all there was to the piece, the criticism might be justified. As it turns out, the background information necessary to make informed decisions is easily available to the learner. Clicking on the magnifying glass initiates an investigation mode, through which the learner can read about the adhesives and the surfaces, even to the detail of seeing electron-microscope images (Figure 5.30).

Learners can research adhesives and make informal decisions, or they can experiment with materials and adhesives to see what will work. Ulti-

**FIGURE 5.28** A successful combination.

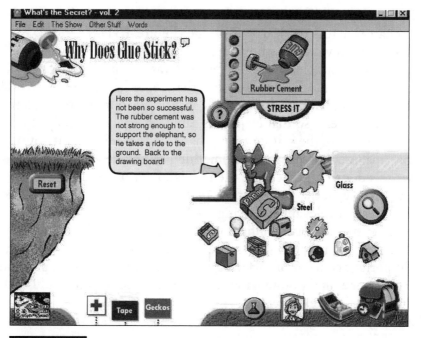

**FIGURE 5.29** An unsuccessful combination.

**FIGURE 5.30** The learner can choose the investigation mode for more detail.

mately, a successful effort is rewarded appropriately: A whole herd of elephants charges across the learner's bridge (Figure 5.31).

It should be obvious how novelty and learner sequencing work well to distinguish this example. But skills transfer was also included as one of the strong features of this design. How can that be? It hardly seems possible to imagine a less useful task than building a bridge out of a preposterous combination of items so that elephants can cross a gap. Actually, it's the preposterousness of the setting that enhances the transferability of this content. Imagine if the task were something more like gluing a metal number to a doorframe. Because the task is so reasonable, it is easy to focus too tightly on the details of the metal number and the doorframe, which are really irrelevant to the higher-level concept. Because it is non-sensical to even attempt to build a bridge from an aquarium and a saw blade, the learner naturally generalizes the learning to the underlying, more important concept of surface types. The learner is figuring out in general how one might bond paper to metal or glass to wood, and that is really the point of the exercise.

Carefully selecting the right context made all this possible. Brilliant.

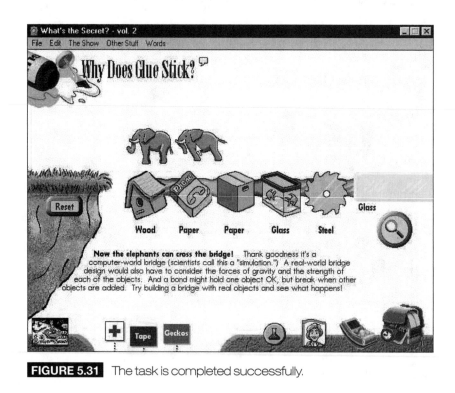

**FIGURE 5.31**  The task is completed successfully.

# Magic Key 5: Have the Learner Perform Multistep Tasks

Everyone likes doing things that are rewarding—things that have specific personal value. Most things of value require more than just recalling an answer, or even a bunch of answers; they require the performance of many small tasks, with multiple decisions to be made along the way. They frequently require execution of a multistepped plan that must be adapted to fit a specific situation.

In other words, life and job performance aren't very much like a school test. They are much more complex. They involve simultaneous or integrated performance of different types of behaviors, judgments, and often interpersonal skills. Judgments typically include setting priorities, sequencing steps (planning), deciding the degree of perfection necessary, and deciding how to use time and perhaps other resources most effectively. Contingencies often have to be considered in case things don't go as expected. New plans may be needed as more information becomes available.

## Have Learners Perform Authentic Tasks

Much has been made of standardized question forms, such as multiple choice, true/false, matching, and fill-in-the-blank structures. While they have their uses, they do not create engaging learning activities. Because they look at isolated points of knowledge, they frequently provide little of the critical performance context.

Learning tasks must be *authentic*—they must relate directly to the effective performance of tasks on the job. Authentic tasks are far more appealing than almost any rhetorical or academic task. They heighten our propensity to get involved. And that's what we are after: *involvement*, *engagement*, and *learning*—the kind of learning that leads to success.

## Example

The DaimlerChrysler *Electrical Diagnosis II (EDII)* e-learning piece is a rich example of the power of multistep tasks. The learner, placed in a problem-solving environment, given access to accurate simulated tools, and provided with a working representation of a faulty automotive electrical system, must determine the cause of the fault and make the necessary repairs without wasting time or resources.

The learner goes through a logical progression of context-setting steps prior to entering the actual problem-solving environment, in which the reported problem is analyzed at a conceptual level—systems relevant to the problem are selected and possible causes are identified. With this groundwork, the learner then is allowed to go about identifying the fault. When placed in the full simulation, the learner has access to a number of options: manually testing the operation of the physical components to verify the faulty behavior, using the provided diagnostic tools (such as a digital volt-ohm meter) and probing tool to take readings within the system, disconnecting the harnesses that connect the various components to each other, reading the original work order, repairing any of the parts, or simply reviewing the possible causes identified in the preparatory sequence (Figures 5.32 to 5.36).

In the real world, this analysis is a multistep process in which each test or decision point is based on what other information the technician has already discovered. Any single test cannot be measured as right or wrong without the context of the entire process. A step that may at first appear

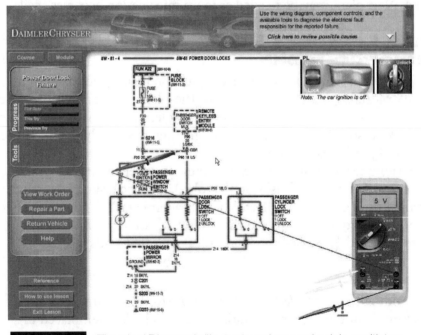

**FIGURE 5.32** *Electrical Diagnosis II* is centered around a rich, multistep problem-solving model.

*Figures 5.32 to 5.38 from* Electrical Diagnosis II. *Courtesy of DaimlerChrysler Corporation.*

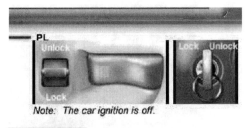

Note: The car ignition is off.

**FIGURE 5.33** The learner can test the system using simulated controls.

unrelated may actually be a critical step in an unexpected but powerful strategy for solving the problem at hand. The real measure is whether the tests and measures considered *as a group* lead to a solution of reasonable efficiency. There are often multiple paths to the same conclusion, a characteristic attested to by the fact that even expert technicians will not always use the exact same procedure, but will often rely on experience and intuition to determine the best approach.

An e-learning solution that eliminates the multistep strategizing from the learner's behavior will never be able to provide the practice necessary to develop these skills. It is important to note, however, that multistep tasks do not require that learners proceed blindly. The success of a multi-step approach emanates from meaningful feedback—not traditional "right" and "wrong" messages but useful intrinsic clues regarding the decisions made by the learner and the appropriateness of the information

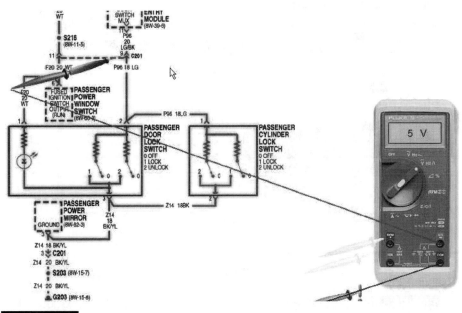

**FIGURE 5.34** Accurate simulated diagnostic tools facilitate multiple divergent strategies for each problem.

**FIGURE 5.35** Progress is shown only in terms of how this attempt compares to "flat-rate" or minimally acceptable efficiency.

**FIGURE 5.36** The learner determines when a solution is found by first repairing one or more parts and then returning the vehicle.

gained with each step. If the feedback indicates a fruitful course of action, then the learner proceeds; if not, it's time to back up or try a different strategy. It is this metaprocessing of the learner's own strategy made possible with multistep tasks that fosters the richest and most memorable understanding of a body of content.

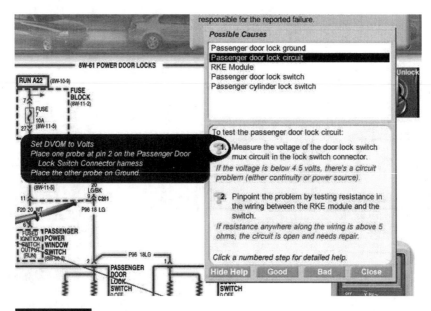

**FIGURE 5.37** Help screens provide clues at multiple levels; they suggest strategies and specific actions to guide learners who need some intermediate assistance.

Another important aspect of building multistep e-learning pieces is that a safety net must be provided in case a particular learner is stymied in a way that will prevent ever reaching the end point. In *EDII*, a help system provides this support (Figure 5.37). It can suggest the best strategies for testing the possible causes the learner identifies.

When the task is complete, it is important to give feedback on the specific steps the learner chose to do. This requires an advanced level of record keeping in the lesson to provide delayed feedback on specific steps the user should have taken, given the problem and the suggested strategy (Figure 5.38).

The final feedback provides general information about the sufficiency of the solution (here the learner solved the problem correctly) and also gives specific information about particular steps (here the learner neglected to test the system to verify the fault.)

Building instructional interactions incorporating multistep tasks usually requires abandoning traditional questioning. After all, answering a question but not getting any information about whether you were right is just frustrating. If the tasks are naturally built into an extended problem, the reverse becomes true. Arbitrary feedback statements seem intrusive; learners are much more attuned to gathering clues from the environment and self-assessing their actions when those actions all build cumulatively to arrive at a complete solution for a meaningful challenge.

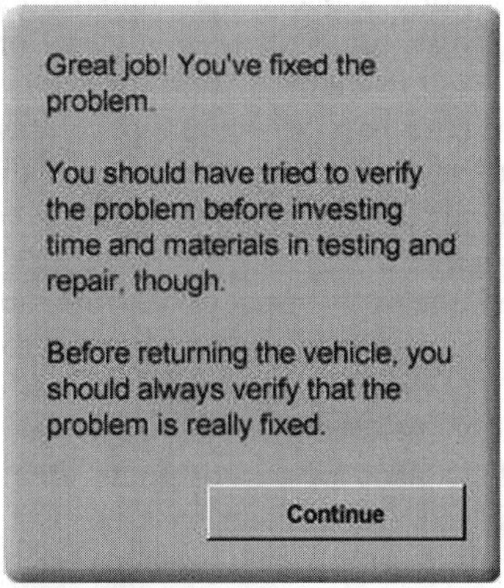

Great job! You've fixed the problem.

You should have tried to verify the problem before investing time and materials in testing and repair, though.

Before returning the vehicle, you should always verify that the problem is really fixed.

Continue

**FIGURE 5.38** Final feedback reinforces the lesson.

# Magic Key 6: Provide Intrinsic Feedback

Intrinsic feedback allows learners to see for themselves that their performance was good and effective or incorrect and ineffective. It doesn't rely on the usual instructor assessment and didactic comment. It doesn't misdirect learners' efforts toward pleasing the instructor, rather than learning essential skills. It doesn't suggest that learning is about getting a good grade or passing a test.

Intrinsic feedback allows learners to see how their correct performance is empowering to them and how, step by step, they are becoming more capable, powerful, valuable persons. As a result, learners are usually quite eager to learn more.

How does this work in e-learning? It requires a learning context in which learners can try different approaches and solutions and see the results. The concept is quite simple, but important and powerful. To make it more concrete, consider the contrasting feedback designs described in Table 5.8.

**Break the Rules**

## Don't Tell Learners If They Are Right or Wrong

Let learners see for themselves whether or not their performance works as well as it needs to. Some aspects of a simulation are needed, although not necessarily a complex or even visual one. The familiar story problem often used in mathematics, for example, provides the needed improvement over bare arithmatic problems. Intrinsic feedback responds within context, such as reporting where the train stopped, whether the apples overflowed the pie pan, or the corporation was fined for tax underpayment.

The feedback can be entirely visual to demonstrate outcomes of student performance. This is often best, but you need to be sure learners fully grasp the quality of their performance and in what way it needs to be improved. In fact, it may be wise to *ask learners* to rate their own performance and to state their plans for improvement. But *don't* give feedback, even if their plans will fail. Let learners try their plans and see the results. Provide hints if their next plans repeat previous errors.

Intrinsic feedback in e-learning typically causes a positive domino effect. Consider these likelihoods:

## TABLE 5.8 Examples of Extrinsic and Intrinsic Feedback

| Learning Behavior | Typical Extrinsic Feedback | Intrinsic Feedback |
|---|---|---|
| When learning structured management techniques, a learner provides clear objectives to employees. | "That's correct." | Key business indicators show increased profit margins and reduced employee complaints. Your boss compliments you on your work. |
| When learning subtraction, a learner deducts 166 from 1000 and gets 44. | "Not so good. Let's go through the rules of borrowing again." | Shopkeeper says, "This must be my lucky day. From your $1,000 you only want $44 in change after buying that $166 watch. Is that right?" |
| When learning electronics, a learner mistakenly connects a 400-volt lead to a 12-volt circuit. | "No, that's not the correct power source. What voltage do you need for the 12-volt circuit?" | Circuit graphically melts down with animation and sound. |
| When learning music composition, a learner puts only three quarter notes in a common time measure. | "No, that's not correct. Think how many quarter you need in 4/4 notes time and try again." | Music plays with unexpected consequences. |

- The design will probably speak to learning outcomes the learner will value.
- The context will relate strongly to actual work or performance conditions.
- Tasks are likely to be multistepped.

It's actually possible that all seven of the Magic Keys to motivating e-learning will be incorporated as a result of working toward intrinsic feedback. If you specify intrinsic feedback as a design requirement, you're likely to build very effective e-learning—and it won't be boring.

## Example

Another sequence from *What's the Secret?* provides an outstanding example of intrinsic feedback in action. This instructional sequence is intended to teach how honeybees communicate with each other about the location of pollen. It turns out that these seemingly simple creatures "talk" to each other through a dance; the shape of the dance, the direction of the dance, the degree and speed of waggling, and the length of the dance all communicate vital pieces of information about where the bee's coworkers might go to gather nectar.

We've been down this road before. You can imagine a typical tell-and-test presentation of this material. The rules for this communication could be presented and then the learner could answer factual questions regarding the content, earning typical feedback messages in response to errors. Boring and ineffective.

In "Do Bees Talk to Each Other?" the learner can study two experiments. In Experiment 1, the learner positions the beehive, the flower, and the sun and can manipulate attractiveness of the flowers to observe the bee dance that matches that situation (Figures 5.39 and 5.40).

In Experiment 2, the roles are reversed: The learner is presented with an arrangement of hive, sun, and flowers and must tell the bee how to

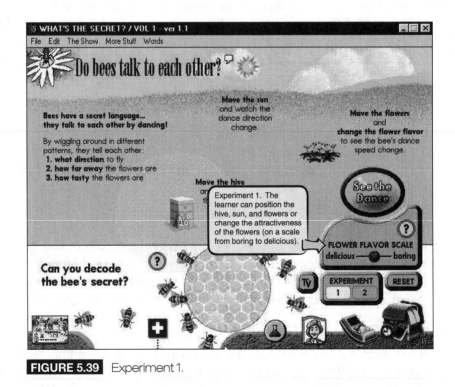

**FIGURE 5.39** Experiment 1.

*Figures 5.39 to 5.43 from* What's the Secret?, *Vol. 1. Courtesy of KCTA-TV, St. Paul, MN.*

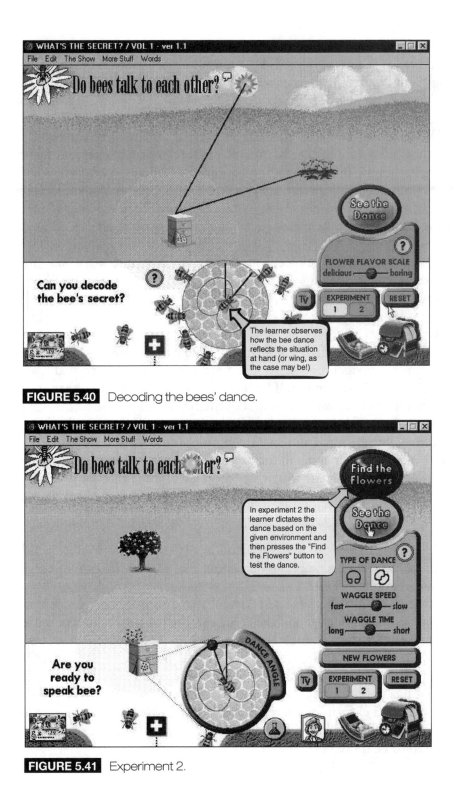

**FIGURE 5.40**  Decoding the bees' dance.

**FIGURE 5.41**  Experiment 2.

dance by choosing a dance pattern, the dance angle, the waggle speed, and the waggle time (Figure 5.41). Careful observation in Experiment 1 should have given the learner several theories about how the dance works. At any time, the learner can return to Experiment 1 to investigate some more.

What can we say about this learning environment? The learner is quickly made aware of the anticipated outcomes, accepts a level of game-like risk, sees the most interesting content immediately, works in an entertaining yet informative novel context, and must execute several steps in succession to achieve success. Wow! This already has all five of the Magic Keys previously discussed. How does intrinsic feedback come into play?

The power of intrinsic feedback is clear in Experiment 2 when the learner puts his or her theory to the test by sending the swarm of bees off in search of flowers (Figure 5.42). The only feedback the learner gets (or needs) is to see the bees head off to exactly the point indicated by the dance.

What makes this feedback intrinsic? The correctness of the learner's choices is made obvious without the need for any sort of external "No, that is incorrect" statement. The learner knows immediately that an error has been made because he or she sees the bee swarm move to the wrong place. There's nothing to distract the learner, even momentarily, from this engaging learning environment. Even more important, this intrinsic feedback provides richer clues about *how* the learner's response is wrong more quickly and fully than any extrinsic feedback statements could ever do. The learner sees immediately without extra words that the bees went too far, went in the wrong direction, or even found the flowers but had been misled regarding their flavor.

The learner then can make adjustments based on this feedback and continue to refine his or her understanding of this fascinating insect behavior (Figure 5.43).

Intrinsic feedback lends itself naturally to discovery environments; a process can be simulated and the results of the learner's actions can be demonstrated naturally. However, the principle is an extremely important one, even in situations in which it may not be possible to implement it as fully as in this example. Extrinsic feedback messages are rarely as helpful as we'd like in conveying useful information. Intrinsic feedback gives the learner both a clear message regarding the correctness of a response and also more meaningful information about how the response should be adjusted to be more correct.

**FIGURE 5.42**   The power of intrinsic feedback.

**FIGURE 5.43**   Further learning is encouraged through intrinsic feedback.

# Magic Key 7:
# Delay Judgment

In e-learning, it's possible to assess each gesture a learner makes and communicate its appropriateness to the learner. This capability is, in fact, one great advantage of computer-delivered instruction. Unfortunately, judgment of every step transfers responsibility for monitoring the validity of a course of action from the learner to the instructor or instructional application. Sometimes it's appropriate to give immediate feedback, but often it isn't.

Many e-learning designs that try to go beyond presentation of information use personal mentoring as a model of instruction. We feel greatly privileged to have an accomplished individual attend only to us and assist us in a course of learning, so it would seem that good emulation would create a welcome learning opportunity. Unfortunately, assumptions about what good mentors do are often faulty.

A good mentor allows learners to make mistakes and then helps them understand why the mistakes occurred and also their consequences. A good mentor knows when to keep quiet, when to present information, and when to ask questions. In many cases, it is much better to allow learners to evaluate their own performance than to immediately evaluate it for them. If judgment is immediately imposed on learners, they are robbed of a very beneficial activity, however grateful they may be. Discerning between good performance and poor performance is an important component of learning.

## A-ha!

When I ask instructional designers what constitutes good instructional design, I receive a wide range of answers. One frequent fascinating response is that good instructional applications invoke a steady stream of "A-ha!" experiences. Everyone agrees. Epiphany is a wondrous thing!

Great satisfaction comes from meeting a challenge successfully, even if the competency demonstrated is relatively useless. When the competency really means something, when it actually empowers us to do things we care about, the success—the "A-hah!"—can be prodigious. It is, in fact, this quality that we seek and should perhaps expect from a technology that has so few boundaries.

Too bad we so often get "Oh no!" instead of "A-ha!"

## Valuable U-Turns

If an assessment is given following each response, it's harder for learners to focus on the bigger context; they tend to focus only on the singular response at hand. There are occasions when what we are trying to teach is an isolated, single response, but most education and training challenges are far more complex. For these types of learning, delayed judgment is appropriate.

Suppose learners were working the following subtraction problem.

$$\begin{array}{r} 20 \\ -108 \\ \hline \end{array}$$

It wouldn't be surprising if a learner began by subtracting 8 from 20, getting 2:

$$\begin{array}{r} 20 \\ -108 \\ \hline 2 \end{array}$$

*Buzz!* You could make the e-learning application respond instantly, indicating that an error was made. You could tell the learner to reverse the numbers—to subtract 20 from 108, then use the sign of the larger number. But what if you waited? The learner might proceed with:

$$\begin{array}{r} 20 \\ -108 \\ \hline 12 \end{array}$$

And *then* realize that the approach wasn't working. The number 12 really doesn't describe any relationship between 108 and 20, regardless of sign. If the learner held the bigger concept of negative numbers and positive numbers lying on a continuum

$$-30 \quad -20 \quad -10 \quad 0 \quad +10 \quad +20 \quad +30$$

and therefore understood that the positive number (20) would push the negative number (108) back 20 notches toward 0, the learner might, *on his or her own*, decide to try an alternative approach, quite possibly constructing the correct one along the way:

$$-108$$
$$+\ \underline{20}$$
$$-\ \ 88$$

Of course, there are other things learners might do as well, such as getting +88. They might also get −128 or +128. Having time to evaluate is precious, important learning time. The software should not interrupt and intrude into it. It could silently monitor the learners' various attempts, respond to questions, and provide reminders when asked, but otherwise stay silent until the learners concluded they had reached the correct answer. A wonderful opportunity exists for an "A-ha!" realization at this point, and learners will need only the slightest confirming feedback to feel truly rewarded.

**Break the Rules**

## Resist Telling Learners If They Are Right or Wrong

Immediate feedback deprives learners of the opportunity to make U-turns—that is, the opportunity to correct themselves, to go back a few steps or start over to see if they are right or what might be going wrong. By evaluating a specific response within a meaningful context, learners begin to take responsibility for evaluating their behaviors. Just as important as having the basic skills is the ability to properly and habitually assess one's own work. It contributes greatly to success in real-world performance. Providing opportunities to build and rehearse these work habits, supported by e-learning software, provides a vastly more interesting, valuable, and effective learning experience. It's not boring, either.

It's important to remember that the appreciation and understanding of context may well be more important than any one skill and that developing each related skill will be much easier if the learner has a firm grasp of the big picture—of the context. Delayed judgment is an extremely helpful technique for keeping a proper orientation and avoiding the acquisition of detached skills and facts that tend to have value only for answering multiple-choice questions. Interestingly, e-learning is uniquely capable of giving both instantaneous judgment and delayed judgment. We need to use these capabilities wisely.

### Why, You Ask?

We can't see what learners are thinking, and neither can e-learning software, unless the learners communicate each step as they work toward an answer. Although one can consider requiring learners to declare each intermediate step, it sometimes makes more sense to ask afterward. In doing so, we might actually facilitate learning epiphanies.

The technique is reasonably simple. After learners have responded (answered a question, solved a problem, made a decision, etc.), you ask them, "Why is this the right thing to do?" "Why is this the correct answer?" (Figure 5.44).

There are then four possibilities—two when learners give the correct answer and two when they don't.

Even when giving the correct answer, learners may or may not be able to justify it—such as in the case of a lucky guess.

With an incorrect answer, learners may cite valid attributes about the answer given, but these attributes would not relate sufficiently to the problem and therefore wouldn't justify the answer. Alternatively, learners may give points that would actually justify another answer, perhaps even the correct answer, but not the one given.

## Delayed Judgment

Critical to the full effectiveness of this approach is the delay of judgment. Feedback is not given until learners have submitted justification for their answers (i.e., learners are not told whether they are correct immediately

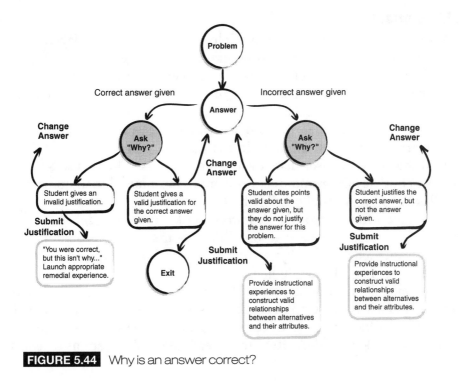

**FIGURE 5.44** Why is an answer correct?

after they answer). Further, they are not given such feedback until after they have submitted a justification for their answers. This delay is crucial, because while learners are working on justifying their answers, there is a high probability they will realize they have given the wrong answers. We therefore allow learners to back up and change their answers and to do so as many times as they desire until they have both answered correctly *and* justified their answers.

It's very rewarding for instructional designers to observe learners working through an implementation of this paradigm. Many learners cannot help muttering out loud as they realize they cannot justify their answers and that they were wrong. Learners can feel privileged by the ability to correct themselves. Combined with multistep tasks and opportunities to back up, delayed judgment can provide fascinating and effective learning experiences.

Many permutations of this design are possible. The approach can be articulated into sophisticated paradigms, including those effectively incorporating artificial intelligence. But the use of this design is quite practical once the basics have been implemented. The structure can be used over and over again with different content for cost-effective, rapidly implemented learning solutions.

## Example

We've already discussed a clear example of the strength of delayed judgment in the *Electrical Diagnosis II* program used as an example of Magic Key 5, multistep tasks. In that example, learners can explore, test, gather information, and suggest answers any number of times in trying to identify the fault in an electrical system. As each clue is discovered, the learner constantly reassesses the validity of early hypotheses and adjusts the strategy to arrive at the best solution. It isn't until the learner chooses to return the car to the user that any judgment occurs. The rich self-assessment that this promotes is vastly more meaningful than immediate feedback messages could possibly be.

It's straightforward to take a multistep task and delay feedback until many of the steps have been accomplished. Some situations do not fall as naturally into a delayed judgment environment, but can be just as powerful when the magic key is applied.

One module in a training program for a major insurance company was intended to teach new employees the uses and value of the different policies offered. One approach, of course, would be to treat this as a trivia contest: Provide the information to be read, then ask questions to assess how many details the learner can remember. Our example applied a delayed judgment scheme that forces the learner to continually assess the importance of various policies in a meaningful context.

The learner begins with a set level of wealth (indicated by the diamonds in reserve in the upper right corner of the display) and can spend those resources as life events are outlined (Figure 5.45).

For example, an early event might be a car purchase, at which time the learner can choose the best type of policy for the need and situation. Learners can quickly read the reference materials for each type of form to help them make the best decisions.

Learning interactions occur throughout an extended sequence of similar challenges over which the user has control. There is very little offered in the way of feedback, but as time passes and policies are purchased, events occur (some catastrophic) that will illustrate the adequacy of the chosen insurance portfolio (Figure 5.46).

The delayed judgment is especially effective here, because one is encouraged to make insurance decisions in a longer time frame than as a one-time decision. The events and the judgment of the learner's response

**Demo on CD**

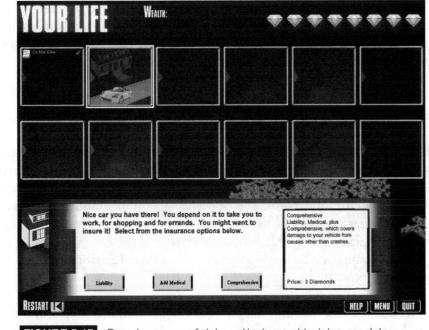

**FIGURE 5.45** Opening page of delayed judgment training module.

*Figures 5.45 and 5.46 from* Herman's House. *Courtesy of American Family Institute.*

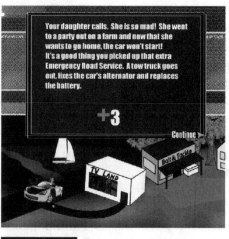

**FIGURE 5.46** Delayed event illuminates consequences of learner's selection.

to the events happen at points seemingly unrelated to the triggering activity. This is very powerful in encouraging the learners to verify their assumptions and, if necessary, to modify earlier decisions based on changing circumstances. This self-review is possible only in a supportive lesson structure that provides delayed rather than immediate feedback.

# Summary

I can't stress strongly enough the importance of considering motivational factors in instructional design. In many of my presentations, I do my best to make the following case: If you do nothing other than address learner motivation, you may have done the best and most important thing you can do. In a recent presentation to one of America's most prestigious corporations, I explained why this is so important and the effects of doing it well. I listed some specific ways you can do it, as are described in this chapter. I demonstrated examples.

The response?

"This was very interesting, but we really need practical help and direction on how to design e-learning applications. We have a lot of content and not a very big budget. What's the most cost-effective way to present a lot of content?" Sigh. Just shoot me.

Presenting a lot of content that has no chance of affecting behavior (or even of being recalled a few days after training) can never be cost-effective, *period*. It's a waste of money and a lot of time. With all apologies, no matter how politically correct and popular it may be, it remains a stupid thing to do.

Look: Dealing with motivation to learn *is* practical help. It is what you need to do. It will turn heads and engender questions—possibly skepticism. But you do it anyway. It's right, and it works—big time.

## CHAPTER SIX

# NAVIGATION

The two-dimensional world of the computer's display prohibits exploration of an e-learning application in the ways we naturally like to explore things. We can't evaluate an e-learning application by touching the screen, for example. When we touch the monitor, we feel only the monitor and nothing of the application. We can't lift the application to see how heavy it is or measure it to determine its size.

We can't run a finger over an e-learning application to feel its texture. We can't tell if it's smooth and refined, or rough and ill fitting. Taste and smell don't help. There are no telltale noises to suggest a well-engineered design or a cheap chassis. We're often stuck with only our sight to evaluate them.

Unfortunately, we can't see anything of an application other than what the designers and programmers chose to reveal. And although navigation is only one component of an e-learning application, it is the component that controls the learner's ability to size up an application. It is the component that determines the learner's ability to explore, and the ability to control the application for personal needs.

## Victim or Master?

Learners are sometimes so controlled by e-learning applications that they feel victimized. They have few options, if any, beyond how to answer questions. Learners can perform the next step put in front of them or quit—and that's it.

Good navigation does just the reverse. It provides learners as many controls as is reasonably possible, then does everything else possible to help learners feel that they have almost limitless control—or at least all the control they could realistically want, and certainly everything they need.

# Navigation Services

Where navigation stops and individual interactions start is sometimes a gray area. Navigation gets learners to the interactions and resource materials needed, but it also overlays all these components to allow learners sometimes to interrupt one activity with another and then return. An important learning activity can be deciding when to take control and use a navigation service versus continuing a current activity.

The list of learning services presented in the navigation overview in Chapter 3 is expanded here to identify the many things that navigation is. Navigation provides:

- Abilities to preview and personally assess:

    What can be learned

    How valuable it will be

    How much time it will take

    How difficult it will be

    The structure of the content

- Abilities to:

    List menus and submenus (if any)

    Select menu items

    Determine if any prerequisites exist and whether they have been met

    Go to selected items

    Determine where you are within the structure

    Back out of selected items

    Access help on using the application

Access instructional help, glossaries, reference material, or other resources

- Overall, abilities to:

    Back up and review

    Back up and try different answers or options

    Skip ahead, preview, and return

    Bookmark and return to points of interest or concern

    Call up services such as glossaries or examples

    Restart and resume where you left off

- Once learning has begun, abilities to determine:

    How much has been accomplished

    The scores or mastery levels earned

    How much remains to be learned

- Sometimes many performance details, such as:

    How much time was spent in each activity

    How many trials were necessary for the initial success

    How many practice sessions occurred

    What the scores on practice sessions were

In many ways, navigation ties together the structural components at many different levels, much like the trunk of a tree with all its limbs. Interactions are the essential leaves on the tree, fitting on the branches and giving the whole structure a reason to exist.

# Reusable Navigation

Because navigation can provide many valuable learning and interface functions, designing and developing good navigation structures can be difficult and costly. Fortunately, navigation is an area in which reusability can save e-learning design and development costs. Although custom-designed and -built navigation can build more strongly on unique aspects of the content, successful structures can often be used for a variety of applications. Once the user interface is refined and the underlying programming is perfected, navigational structures should need minimal testing. Larger portions of the budget can then be applied to building interactions that are specifically devised for the instructional content.

Developers commonly choose a solution between custom development and reapplication of existing navigation structures. After a number of e-learning applications have been developed, teams often find they can reuse many of the navigational structures with only moderate amounts of revision. The revisions allow better integration with the subject matter and the overall instructional context chosen for the application. To achieve appreciable savings from reapplication, it is important to carefully organize and structure navigation systems so that modification and reapplication is possible.

# Navigation Imperatives

There is much to navigation design, as you can deduce from the list of possible services given earlier. There are many successful approaches, but for each one there are many unfortunate paths. In order to provide practical guidance here, I have focused on essential navigation design concepts and those most frequently misapplied or overlooked in e-learning. The result is a list of simple imperatives—simple in concept if not implementation.

They aren't imperatives in the sense that failure to follow or implement them means certain failure. They are imperatives in the sense that e-learning is usually much, much more effective and able to provide the needed return on the investment when the imperatives are implemented. Whether you are buying, building, or contracting for the development of an e-learning solution, the imperatives should usually be included in the specifications.

## Imperative 1: Let Learners See the Boundaries of Their Universe

Children have their school day structured for them and make few decisions about time investments. In contrast, as adults in a much too hurried world, most of us are constantly verifying for ourselves that we are using our time wisely. Our time is valuable—we don't want to throw it away unless we choose to do so, and we guard against letting others waste it.

Even if we actually have only a few options, we don't like being treated as schoolchildren. We don't like someone else saying, "This is good for you. Do it now." We like to know how long something is likely to take, to have the option of doing things now or later, and to decide in what order we will do things.

As adults, we like to know the purpose of our activities. We like to get some perspective, consider options, and then decide whether to make the commitment or to search for other options.

Sure, adult learners can be forced into the schoolchild's role. Some adults snap right into it, having become quite accustomed to it and probably successful at it in their youth. But even those willing victims are likely to have a better experience if they have the means to survey the opportunity before the event launches in earnest. How long will it take? What does it cover? How hard will it be?

### Is It Bigger than a Breadbox?

In a content-focused trance, many designers launch right into instruction following a listing of learning objectives. If they follow my suggestions, they will often take some effort to sell the value of the pending learning experience before attempting to deliver it. But what they might not do is give learners any sense of how big this thing is, what shape it is, what kind of crust and filling it has.

You can size up a book fairly easily. You can assess some of its characteristics even as it sits on a shelf. Pick it up and you can quickly check to see how many pages it has, about how much is on a page, how it's divided up, how big the divisions are, what the illustrations are like, how useful

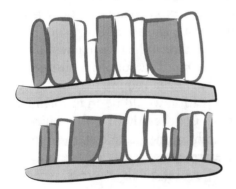

the index and glossaries appear to be, and so on. In just a few minutes standing in a bookstore, you can set some fairly reasonable expectations of what reading a book will be like. Of course, the book designer is doing everything possible to give you a positive impression quickly. But you have the option to jump directly to the meat of the offering if you want to.

### I Can't Tell

Not so with e-learning. Unless the means are provided to browse, play around, test features, and get to it at randomly selected points, many basic parameters of the product remain hidden. Learners need your help.

For example, with a book, you can quickly check to see if each chapter really is of about the same length, but with e-learning the amount of material to be presented, the number of interactions to be used, and the amount of time to be spent depend on each learner's performance. There isn't (or at least shouldn't be) a simple page count that can reflect all this.

Some applications provide time estimates for learners. The estimates might be inaccurate, because the actual time needed depends on the learner's readiness and abilities. But learners can understand this and appreciate the estimates even if they are somewhat inaccurate. Combined with a good browsing facility, time estimates can soothe many of the discomforts of e-learning and make adults feel more like adults.

## Imperative 2: Let Learners See How the Contents Are Organized

Navigation, by definition, builds on content organization. This creates an opportunity to let learners review the organization of the content, which can help learners not only get their bearings but also learn something about the content itself. If the content is organized from easy to hard, learners will gain a sense of what is easy and what is more difficult; if content is ordered according to a process, the structure will impart knowledge of the sequence; if content is ordered chronologically, learners can get a sense of precedent and consequent events; and so on.

There is often a necessary compromise between the efficiency of navigation and the information that navigational controls supply. A simple click to go to the next sequential topic doesn't even require presentation of a list of topics, but this streamlined navigation would be an unfortunate extreme of simplicity over informativeness. On the other hand, requiring learners to open layer upon layer of hierarchical menus in order to access the next topic would err at the opposite extreme.

Excellent designs are both efficient, allowing quick and easy access to content, and informative, allowing users to see the content organization clearly. And they do more: They also present multiple points of view to the organization. They might, for example, provide the following views:

- Sequence of topics in the order of recommended study
- Structured listing of topics by discipline, such as accounting, management, and communications

- List of topics by instructional activities provided, such as simulations, drill and practice, and problem solving
- List of topics by media, such as videos, animations, and narrated text

All these views and many other possible ones add potential value to the e-learning application. Of course, the design should also provide the convenience and functionality of taking learners to any displayed topic they want to investigate further.

## Imperative 3:  Let Learners See Where They Are

Once you've launched yourself into an e-learning experience as a learner, it can be difficult to know where you are. Again, the intangible nature of e-learning creates an uneasiness, so the design needs to compensate by providing a sense of orientation and position (Figure 6.1).

There are many creative ways to help learners see where they are. This is a good place to have fun with the design, but even a simple thermometer or a dot moving from one end of a line to another as a report of progress will become a meaningful display of information to be keenly observed. It's not unusual for the learner's vocabulary to reflect how important progress measures are: "My dot is halfway there!" "I'm in the last building!" "Only one more stone to complete my pyramid!" They even compare progress notes with each other: "How far did you get? Did you make it to the green level yet?"

Of course, we'd rather they were boasting about how much they have learned, but it's not often easy to put that in a short sentence.

## Imperative 4:  Let Learners Go Forward

"I don't want to back up to go forward," said Carl Philabaum, in one of his many profoundly insightful moments. Carl, one of my fellow cofounders of Authorware, Inc., often brought brilliant clarity to our dis-

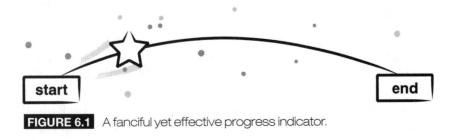

**FIGURE 6.1**  A fanciful yet effective progress indicator.

cussions about user interface. Once you saw his vision, you couldn't possibly go any other way. As usual, he was right on this point about going forward.

Why would you want to back up to go forward? Learners don't want to be forced to back up through a series of submenus, for example, in order to get to the next topic. Designers might justify such an annoying requirement by suggesting that it helps learners keep the structure in mind. But if learners want to see the structure, let them. If they want to go forward to the next logical item in their path, let them do that, too.

There's no reason you can't remind learners of the overall structure without forcing them to retreat first. You can do it with a graphical map, for example, showing learners where they have arrived with their command to go forward. If learners don't want to be where they've come so easily, they can just click another point on the map. With a single click they've gone forward again. Easy.

Thanks, Carl.

## Imperative 5:  Let Learners Back Up

It can be a programming challenge, especially if the learning experience is a complex simulation, but being able to back up is almost always essential to providing an optimal learning experience. We often think we understand something, only to find out a bit later that we really don't. Being able to back up at that moment of realization is very important, especially for adult learners who don't want to be constrained and may be taking responsibility for their own learning.

Not being able to back up raises anxiety, creates a helpless, lack-of-control feeling, precludes a potentially beneficial experience, and suggests to learners that:

> We're in charge here, not you. If you had been paying attention, you wouldn't need to back up. If we had thought people couldn't understand this in one pass, then, of course, we would have let you back up. Because we must take responsibility for your learning, and you didn't get what you needed, here's what's going to happen to you next. . . .

A bit dramatic, perhaps. But not providing a means for backing up is a regrettable constraint in many e-learning applications. It can severely limit their potential.

In simple page-turning applications, it is not difficult to back up. But with highly interactive e-learning, backing up can become complex—so complex, in fact, that development teams sometimes abandon efforts to build powerful learning experiences because they cannot devise a backup function. If the design requirement to allow learners to back up is established early in the design of each application, the team will find it isn't as difficult to build as it might seem, assuming the use of a powerful authoring tool. Programming the function is a bit harder, but making provisions for backing up isn't an unreasonable effort as long as it is anticipated at the start. It's almost impossible to retrofit a backup capability into a completed or nearly complete e-learning application, however, so it is essential to be clear about this early in the design process.

## Imperative 6:  Let Learners Correct Themselves

The experience of privately discovering you have made a mistake, fixing it, and finding satisfaction in your work describes the perfect learning experience. The outcome includes knowing what happens when you make the error and knowing what happens when you do the right thing. Instead of being told what to do, you find the path and appreciate it in all its nuances more than you ever could by simply following step-by-step instructions. The fidelity of your learning is at maximum. Why, then, don't we design learning experiences that enable and nourish such events?

Perhaps it's because some extra work is involved. It takes work to provide intrinsic feedback through which learners see the consequences of their choices directly, instead of hearing from you, "No, that's not correct. Try again." It takes work to allow learners to manipulate objects, make decisions, and collect information before they make those decisions. It takes cleverness to construct challenges that reveal important truths or fully present opposing points of view.

The learner-interface control for backing up may be only a very simple BACK button. However, helping learners know where they are, what their previous decisions or actions were, and the state of a simulated process or product will also be essential interface components. These can range from simple to very complex.

Yes, it takes some effort to reap the value effective e-learning can provide. And it takes more creativity than does the simple presentation of information. But once you've done the right things, the costs stop and the benefits will continue to accrue for each learner and the organization. If you don't, the *costs* just continue to accrue without the benefits.

Give learners the means to correct themselves. It's powerful.

## The Imperatives

There are always exceptions, but justifiable exceptions to the listed imperatives are rare. They pay off handsomely in the creation of successful learning events. Unless there are incontestable objections, insist that your learning applications follow the imperatives. Write them into the specifications whether you are buying, building, or contracting for e-learning solutions.

# Additional Learner-Interface Ideas

Table 6.1 shows some additional learner-interface features you should consider. These aren't imperatives, but you can expect them to pay back handsomely.

I have seen all these capabilities implemented at one time or another in various e-learning applications. They are much appreciated by learners, who often appreciate the ability to print notes and selected content elements for later reference. Once you have developed the software for these features, they can be dropped into applications at an acceptable expense. They resonate well with adult learners, many of whom remain skeptical that all this computer stuff is really an improvement over more traditional methods of instruction. They recognize the learner's desire for freedom and control and empower those who truly want to take responsibility for managing their own learning.

**TABLE 6.1   Handy Learner-Interface Features**

| Feature | Advantages |
|---|---|
| Bookmarking | Learners can mark and return to any marked point. |
| Personal index | An elaboration of bookmarking. Learners can essentially create a titled list of selected contents or interactions. They can use default titles provided by the application or use titles they find more meaningful. Each title is linked to a point of interaction, allowing learners to return to that point on demand. |
| Highlighting | Just as with a book and highlighting pen, learners can drag the cursor over items to mark them with a distinctive color. |
| Margin notes | Learners can type in the margins of screen displays. In some implementations, these notes are automatically assembled in an online notebook. Learners can then click any note to return to the screen and see the note in its original context. |
| Posted notes | Learner-created notes can be stuck anywhere on screen displays. |

# Examples

It always helps to see examples, so before we take up any other topic in navigation, let's take a look at a couple of very different approaches to navigation.

## *WorldTutor*

Originally designed for American Airlines for training across a variety of topics, including such diverse performance domains as ticketing and security procedures, this structure has proven valuable for many different content domains. It has been repeatedly reapplied without redevelopment.

The navigation structure provides a uniform framing device that presents all content consistently (Figure 6.2). (Because this discussion focuses only on navigation, the content areas in the illustrations are blank for clarity.)

The navigation controls are concentrated in a narrow band along the bottom of the screen, maximizing the screen real estate reserved for instructional and content purposes.

Let's look at this system in more detail in terms of the six imperatives.

**Demo on CD**

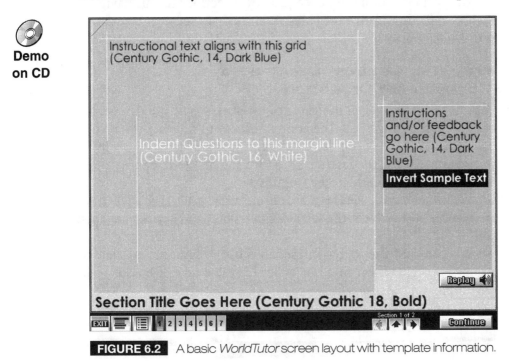

**FIGURE 6.2**   A basic *WorldTutor* screen layout with template information.

*Figures 6.2 to 6.8 from* WorldTutor. *Courtesy of Allen Interactions Inc.*

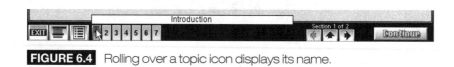

**FIGURE 6.3** The numbered rectangles represent topics with the current topic highlighted. The current section and the total number of sections in the current topic are displayed above the arrow buttons.

## Imperative 1: Let Learners See the Boundaries of Their Universe

The navigation system accommodates several levels of organization. A course is divided into topics. Each topic is organized into sections. Each section might be made up of one or more pages or challenges. This structure is displayed at all times, no matter where learners are in the course (Figure 6.3).

The navigation bar (Figure 6.3) shows the course structure in a very compact space. A numbered rectangle or topic icon represents each topic in the course. These icons are arranged in order from left to right. For each course, only the appropriate number of icons is displayed—there are no placeholder blank images. In addition to clearly showing the number of topics, it is also effective as a more general indicator of scope. For a learner who will be completing even just a few sections in this navigation framework, a fleeting glance provides an immediate sense of whether it is a long or short course.

## Imperative 2: Let Learners See How the Contents Are Organized

The topic icons give a visual indicator of the skeleton of the course, but do not convey anything about the content except to indicate the recommended order of study. More details about topics and sections are available in two ways. First, the learner can move the mouse over any topic icon to view the name of the topic (Figure 6.4).

For even more detail, the learner can select the TOPICS & OBJECTIVES button (second button from the left) to view topics and sections in a list (Figure 6.5).

Learners can view the topics and sections list without losing their place in the course. Detailed learning objectives for the course are also available from the topics and sections list.

**FIGURE 6.4** Rolling over a topic icon displays its name.

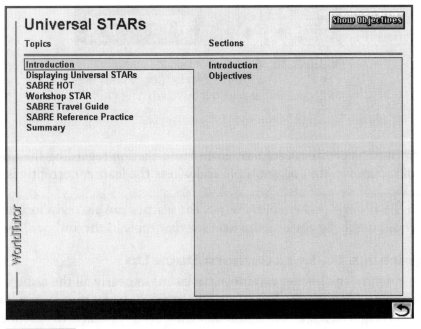

**FIGURE 6.5** A typical list of topics and sections.

## Imperative 3: Let Learners See Where They Are

The topic icons change status as the learner moves through the course. The current topic is highlighted, and completed topics are marked with a colored bar. Learners also have the ability to earmark pages for later review by clicking in the upper left corner of the screen. Earmarked pages are indicated at the upper left as well as on the topic icons (Figure 6.6).

**FIGURE 6.6** Topic icons showing progress. Topic 5 is the current topic. Topics 1, 2, and 4 have been completed. Topics 2 and 4 are earmarked for review.

## Imperative 4: Let Learners Go Forward

This navigation allows users to go forward in several ways. At the most basic level, the CONTINUE button takes the learner through the entire course in the suggested order (Figure 6.7). The continue function is disabled only during a challenge, when the learner must successfully complete an activity before being allowed to proceed.

The arrow buttons allow learners to move forward (and backward) on a section basis rather than just one page at a time. The notation above the

**FIGURE 6.7** The CONTINUE button provides default forward navigation through pages and partial pages. The arrow keys facilitate moving among sections.

arrow buttons provides useful orienting information regarding the number of sections in the current topic and where the learner currently is working.

In the context of the larger course, the learner can also skip forward to any topic simply by clicking the icon for that topic, if the author allows it.

### Imperative 5: Let Learners Back Up

Conveniently, the learner can move backward in nearly all the same ways as foreward. Clicking the left arrow button takes the learner to previous sections (Figure 6.7). Clicking the up arrow button restarts the section. Clicking the icon for a topic that has been studied previously takes the learner back to that topic.

### Imperative 6: Let Learners Correct Themselves

This navigation model is somewhat neutral in regard to making mistakes. However, it does allow corrections in that learners are generally one or two clicks away from any part of the content, so an unintended stray click can be corrected quickly and easily. The REPLAY button is available in case the learner missed or did not attend to the audio narration.

In addition to these imperatives, the *WorldTutor* structure also provides some other handy features. The options button reveals a set of buttons for other enhanced features (Figure 6.8).

The buttons include a glossary of definitions for specialized vocabulary; a help function to describe lesson features; a word finder that enables learners to search the course for keywords; a volume control; a flash-card system that allows learners to tag specific concept displays and review them as a drill later; and a comments section where the learners can write notes for themselves, their instructor, or the system administrator. For the

**FIGURE 6.8** *WorldTutor* option buttons.

most part, each of these special options operates within the same space occupied by the navigation controls, so it doesn't restrict the learner's view of the actual lesson content.

## What's the Secret?

Chapter 5 looked at two instructional pieces from *What's the Secret?* as examples of applying the Seven Magic Keys. Now let's take a look at how these hang together in a navigation system. This navigational structure differs in many ways from that of *WorldTutor* but provides many of the imperatives. Because the application is intended to encourage exploration, it uses creative visuals and is somewhat less oriented toward indicating specific progress than are many other navigation systems.

The main menu is a great example of combining playful and enticing visuals with effective navigation (Figure 6.9).

This doesn't look like a menu, but in the spirit of exploration, all graphic objects are actually hot menu choices. This is indicated by a cursor change when the learner moves the mouse pointer over each object (Figure 6.10).

**Demo on CD**

**FIGURE 6.9** Main menu of *What's the Secret?*

*Figures 6.9 to 6.15 from* What's the Secret?, *Vol. 1. Courtesy of KCTA-TV, St. Paul, MN.*

**FIGURE 6.10** The cursor changes when it's moved over an active menu item.

Each menu selection ultimately launches an extended exploration context, so it is helpful in this case to let the user confirm the menu choice. The first click shows the section title, and engaging narration asks leading questions that characterize what will be covered in that section (Figure 6.11). If the preview seems satisfactory, the learner chooses the LET'S GO button to enter the section.

Each section is focused on a central experiment or investigation with related supporting resources (Figure 6.12). Again, since we're focusing on navigation issues, we'll ignore the instructional interactions and just look at how the users can move around.

The navigation controls are clustered at the bottom of each screen. The image in the lower left is a thumbnail of the menu screen, and indeed will return to the menu when clicked. The other navigation buttons

**FIGURE 6.11** The menu provides a preview before launching each section.

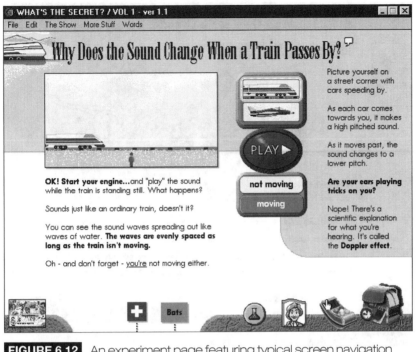

**FIGURE 6.12** An experiment page featuring typical screen navigation controls.

are divided into two groups: some placed in the white gap and others grounded to the solid surface to the right. This difference in position tells the learner what to expect. The elements in the gap represent excursions to a related topic. Taking one of these excursions takes the learner away from the current activity and moves to a related topic in a new context (Figure 6.13).

On the excursion page, all navigation disappears except for an option to go back to the experiment page. The GO BACK button is exactly parallel to the button that brought this section up and follows the same rule: The button is in the gap, so by choosing it, learners expect to go to a new screen.

In contrast, the "grounded" navigation buttons bring up additional resources on top of the current experiment screens (Figure 6.14). These resources typically represent additional experiments, puzzling questions pertaining directly to the experiment, or additional video resources. The original experiment remains in the background.

One final clever and powerful twist in the navigation is represented by the backpack on the navigation bar that is really a submenu for some important learning aids (Figure 6.15).

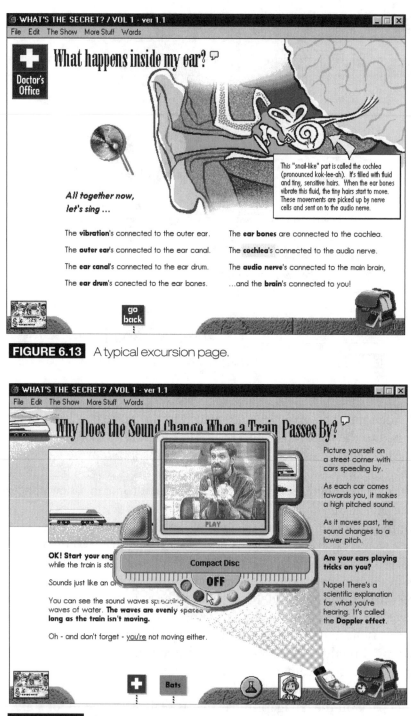

**FIGURE 6.13** A typical excursion page.

**FIGURE 6.14** Some resources, such as this video controller, float on top of the main display and disappear when finished.

**FIGURE 6.15** This backpack is a submenu to additional resources.

The backpack notepad is always available to record interesting facts or observations during the lessons. While this is very handy, the backpack has another more interesting function: While exploring an experiment, the learner can earn reward patches if some serious attention has been spent in the activity. The learner collects these patches by dragging them to the backpack. The payoff is that these patches provide access to fun games and exercises. So even though there is no mechanism to force learners through the whole program systematically, these patches accomplish the same thing in a much more motivating way. Very few learners are content until they know they have gathered all the patches—and the only way to do that is to be systematic and thorough in exploring the sections of the program.

*What's the Secret?* represents a very different structure from what is typical in corporate e-learning applications. Yet it still provides the things a navigation system must have, in a fresh, unorthodox context. We need to strive for this vitality of design for all audiences, instead of immediately thinking that this kind of creative solution is inappropriate or out of our grasp.

## Hypertext

Hypertext was hailed as a revolutionary user-interface construct for learning. Any word or sequence of words could be tagged and linked to another content element or location. Clicking tagged words would summon the linked information. The linked information might be laid over current screen contents so that learners could easily dismiss it and resume the previous activities, or the information could be linked so that learners could jump to the new location, entirely replacing their current screens.

With hypertext capabilities, content could be linked together in a vast network, so that learners could explore in multiple ways. Learners might, for example, browse at a high level, avoiding examples or extended discussions. At any point, they might decide to explore a selected topic in depth. Avoiding related notions, they could dig deeply into the foundations of a single concept until the content was exhausted or another interest took over. A great deal of power and freedom could be seen in such an environment. In many ways, this is what the World Wide Web is today—a very large multistructured hypertext network.

Because of the high cost of building such networks, rich with many links and great volumes of information for learner exploration, few are built. Although the World Wide Web itself is evolving into such a network it is insufficiently and inappropriately structured for most training and even educational needs, even with all the resources it offers.

Designers must ensure that learners are acquiring basic skills and undertaking reasonable challenges. Otherwise, learners are likely to flounder. Learners need some form of guidance and mentorship to effectively allocate their time. Although it can be a very valuable resource, simple access to information doesn't create an effective learning environment—just as a presentation of information does not equal teaching.

Hyperlinked resources are arguably richer in the breadth of the learning content they can provide and are more responsive to momentary learner interests than structured e-learning, but they're less efficient in leading learners to defined proficiencies. In the preparation of e-learning, designers find it important to focus much of their effort on chunking information into segments learners can handle. Designers work hard to provide needed overviews, reviews, examples, exercises, and elaborations at the right points, and they provide transitions to help learners structure the knowledge they are attempting to internalize. Unstructured linked resources just don't provide learners the support they need. It's just not that easy.

## Lost in Hyperspace

With no guide, learners can easily become lost in hyperspace and spend a good deal of time navigating without learning much. While experts may find the lack of restrictions refreshing and supportive of their objectives in traversing the knowledge domain, learners can easily lose sight of meaningful goals—if, indeed, they were able to formulate them at the start. After spending a good deal of time, learners often come away feeling they gained little or only incomplete knowledge.

## Hyperdisappointment

As with so many gizmos that purport to instantly transform learning into an entertaining, effortless, and self-gratifying adventure, hypertext has failed to introduce significant advances. The Internet, of course, has become a wonderful resource for learning research and exploration, but the work necessary to build focused, productive learning environments remains a complex undertaking. It's not readily simplified by any single invention, whether it's a new user-interface capability or even the availability of low-cost personal computers.

Hypertext is, of course, valuable, but it is more a branching or navigation mechanism than an instructional concept. It can be a very handy and effective alternative to more visually restrictive buttons.

### To Underline or Not to Underline

Hypertext is broadly used today simply as a way of branching—as an alternative to buttons linked to various displays. While conventional underlining marks clickable links quite effectively, many find underlined text to be visually unappealing. Unfortunately, conventions can have great utility, and supplanting them has its perils. Many interface designs today make rather unforgivable errors both when using conventional underlining and when attempting to create intuitively understandable alternatives:

- Using underlined hypertext links *and* underlining headings and other text that are not hyperactive

- Not underlining hypertext, and in the process making headings and other text that are not hyperactive look the same as hypertext

- Using color to demark links embedded within text—a problem of separating a series of links (three blue words in a row could be one, two, or three links)

### Helpful Hypertext

Hypertext can be a useful tool. It isn't the instructional technology revolution early proponents thought it might be. It doesn't make design and implementation of effective instructional applications much easier, if any easier, and it is easy to misuse. But hypertext can make applications easier (or harder) to use, depending on how it's applied. Check Figure 6.16 for some rules on using hypertext in learning applications.

# Navigational Metaphors

Metaphors are often used to impart instant familiarity to navigational structures. A building, for example, has analogies to the usual components of an interactive course of instruction: the building as a whole (the course of instruction), the reception area (a place to register or log on), the building directory (list of main topics), floors of the building (levels of skill and challenge advancing to the top), rooms (modules or subtopics), labs (places for experimentation), gym (place for practice), and so on.

Rules for using hypertext.

1. Establish a unique visual representation for active, linked objects.
2. Don't use the visual representation or anything similar to it for anything else.
3. Avoid jumping when the content to be accessed can be included easily on the base page or brought onto the page without actually leaving it.
4. Make it clear what you're linking to. Links to examples should have a different visual appearance than links to new content, for example.
5. Provide easy returns all the way back to the original linked item.
6. Mark links already taken.
7. If you circle back to the original item, make sure the learner understands this is happening.
8. Don't intentionally insert undefined hypertext words in the middle of a paragraph and force learners to click them for clarification.
9. Provide a visual guide or map to help learners orient themselves.

**In general, if there is an appealing alternative to hypertext, it's probably a better alternative.**

**FIGURE 6.16**  Rules for using hypertext.

Any structure with multiple parts can be used as an organizational and therefore navigational metaphor, such as a book, a car, a city, a train, or a camp. Consider also a road map, a treasure map, or a pyramid with all its hallways and vestibules.

Metaphors can be quite powerful, providing terminology, a familiar structure, and even visual representation. For a complex structure or for a very large application, they can provide some welcome orientation.

## Some Concerns

Although metaphors for navigation—or for any interactive controls for that matter—can be powerful, they're sometimes used to mask a lack of good instructional interactivity. It's very disappointing to begin an e-learning application with an extravagant rendering of a metaphor, only to find that once you've selected your topic of instruction, the metaphor has no further utility. Even worse is to find that the interactions are shallow and lacking in imagination because too much effort was spent devising the navigational window dressing.

To make it even worse yet, metaphors are sometimes forced into every nook and cranny of interactions, where they provide no benefit, become wearisome, and may actually distract or confuse learners.

Compounding all these problems, metaphors sometimes feel childish and demeaning. There's a fine line between gamelike metaphors—those that can provide energy and a helpful lightheartedness to otherwise taxing learning events—and silly metaphorical contexts that add no value and may impede learning. From my perspective, it's usually best to find interest and energy in the content and skills being taught.

## Simplicity is Best

In general, the simplest way to represent the structure and content of a course of instruction may be the best. Selecting a segment of content to study shouldn't involve learning the controls of a starship to fly through an alien sector to the next solar system. As fun as that might be, it seems more beneficial to put such talents and resources to work building meaningful learning experiences.

Consider giving navigational metaphors the boot!

# Summary

Navigation capabilities provide the backbone and many of the instructional services learners need for a successful learning experience. This chapter describes a number of very important but too seldom found navigational features. Because they are so valuable, they are dubbed *imperatives* to suggest that there should be immutable objections before any project decides to omit them.

Hypertext was once thought to be the solution to many impediments to the development of rich technologically delivered learning experiences. However, today we are finding it more valuable in noninstructional Web sites than in e-learning. While hypertext structures are indeed easy to implement and use, they are generally insufficient instructional mechanisms. More like a library than a learning event, hypertext can help learners probe for information, but much more is needed to construct most training applications.

Finally, a few comments are offered on navigational metaphors. While metaphors can help learners understand application structures more quickly, they can easily become overworked, too cute, too attention getting, and too annoying. If structures need a metaphor to be readily understood, they may be overly complex. However, metaphors are too often used to explain structures that are easily understood without them. My recommendation is that metaphors be kept to a minimum and navigational structures be kept simple so that maximum attention can be given to what really counts: the development of effective learning experiences.

## CHAPTER SEVEN

# INSTRUCTIONAL INTERACTIVITY

We come now to the truly fun and exciting point at which everything comes together as a creative blend of instructional design, subject matter, management vision and objectives, multimedia treatments, and technology. It comes together for the purpose of enabling specified behavioral changes to happen—the changes needed for performance success.

In this chapter, I have attempted to get at the heart of instructional interactivity. I've tried to separate the wheat from the chaff, as they say; to explore the differences between interactivity and *instructional* interactivity; to provide a framework for thinking about instructional interactivity that should help designers create the kind of interactivity that works to engage learners, builds needed competencies, and provides value in e-learning that fully justifies the investment.

Throughout this book, I've minimized theoretical discourse in favor of plain talk and practical prescriptions. It is especially appropriate to continue this approach here, as it seems to me that theory-based approaches have not resonated effectively with many designers. My attempt here is to clearly identify the essential components of instructional interactivity, flag some frequent misconceptions, and provide a number of successful models—all in a way that you will find meaningful and useful, whatever your goals for e-learning may be.

# Supernatural Powers

Interactivity is the supernatural power of e-learning. It has dual powers that together are capable of achieving the ultimate goal of success through behavioral change:

- *Thinking.* Used properly, interactivity makes us think. Thinking can lead to understanding. Understanding can lead to increased capabilities and a readiness for behavioral change.

- *Doing.* Interactivity requires us to do things—to perform. Rehearsed performance can build skills. Improved skills can lead to behavioral changes.

# Natural Learning Environments

From the moment we are born, we are learners. As infants, we love learning because almost everything we learn gives us a bit more power or comfort. Even before we can actually do anything to improve our lot, we gain satisfaction from recognizing signs and predicting. We predict that food is coming, that we are going to be picked up, or that we are about to hear an amusing sound. And we are happy to be right.

Learning environments that truly connect with us as learning individuals universally employ interactivity. We learn much of what we learn from attempting various solutions and observing their results. It's evident in children as they undertake the myriad skills they must conquer, from just holding up their heads to communicating differentially the needs of thirst and a diaper change. As we grow older and acquire the ability to understand language, we can be told how to do things and when to do them. But such learning can dissipate easily until we've actually performed successful behaviors ourselves and seen the results. Even then, rehearsal is important to fully ingrain new notions.

# e-Learning Environments and Rehearsal

Interactivity in e-learning provides an important opportunity for rehearsal without the risk of damaging equipment, hurting people's feelings, running up waste costs, or burning down buildings. Behaviors that help the learner avoid danger cannot be learned safely through experimental means except through very close mentoring or in simulated environments, such as those often possible in e-learning. And even if they could, setup time and costs would prevent needed repetition. Instruction of many people, who might be in many different locations, would present onerous problems.

Whether we are guided by a mentor or prompted by e-learning, interactivity is vital to effective learning events. As important as interactivity is for learning, however, *instructional* interactivity is a surprisingly difficult concept to define.

# Instructional Interactivity Defined

It is difficult to define and distinguish the salient attributes of instructional interactivity; perhaps because of this, we often mistakenly believe that true instructional interactivity is present when it is not. We can be deluded by all the buttons, graphics and animated effects of today's multimedia, or distracted by visual design and presentation technologies. It's common to mistakenly assume that instructional interactivity is present, and therefore expect more impact from an application than it can deliver.

Instructional interactivity is much more than a multimedia response to a learner's gesture, such as hearing a sound after clicking the mouse button; yet interactivity in e-learning definitely does involve multimedia responses to learner gestures. Chapter 3 offered the following working definition:

> **instructional interactivity**   Interaction that actively stimulates the learner's mind to do those things that improve ability and readiness to perform effectively.

There are many varieties of instructional interactivity. Sometimes interactivity simply entreats us to rehearse fledgling skills. At other times it puts forth a perplexity for us to untangle. It may even lead us to profound and original discoveries, not just the identification of preestablished "correct" answers.

The many types and purposes of instructional interactivity compound the problem of definition, but in each case, there are four essential components, integrated in instructionally purposeful ways (Figure 7.1):

- *Context*—the framework and conditions
- *Challenge*—a stimulus to action within the context
- *Activity*—a physical response to the challenge
- *Feedback*—reflection of the effectiveness of the learner's action

**FIGURE 7.1** Essential components of instructional interactivity.

# Examples

Let's look at a couple of e-learning designs to observe how they create effective interactivity. Then we will clarify the essential characteristics of each component of instructional interactivity.

## Example 1: *Supervisor Effectiveness*

In this example, supervisors learn to recognize signs of potential safety risks to employees, investigate recognized signs, determine if risks are genuine and warrant preventative action, and identify appropriate actions. Note each of the interaction components and how they work together to create a fascinating learning experience:

### Context

*An aerial view of a populated office work area.*

The depiction immediately provides an interesting visual context and creates an identifiable, real-world setting (Figure 7.2). It gives both visual and cognitive perspective to the subject, saying, in effect, "Let's step back

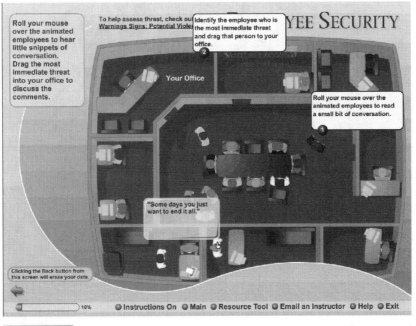

Roll your mouse over the animated employees to hear little snippets of conversation. Drag the most immediate threat into your office to discuss the comments.

To help assess threat, check ou[t] Warnings Signs: Potential Viole[nce]

Identify the employee who is the most immediate threat and drag that person to your office.

YEE SECURITY

Your Office

Roll your mouse over the animated employees to read a small bit of conversation.

"Some days you just want to end it all."

Clicking the Back button from this screen will erase your data.

10%    ● Instructions On  ● Main  ● Resource Tool  ● Email an Instructor  ● Help  ● Exit

**FIGURE 7.2**   Office context in *Supervisor Effectiveness* training.

and look at a typical work environment without being too involved in everyday business operations to think about what's really happening."

The context provides both an immediate sense of contextual familiarity for the supervisors being trained and a vantage point for objectivity and thoughtful decision making. No large blocks of text are needed to build this valuable rapport with the learner.

This is a permissive context. Learners can jump right into the activity without any guidance or background information, or they can first request information on assessing threats.

## Challenge

*Identify the most immediate safety threat.*

Employees make many comments during the day that reflect their frustrations, both trivial and serious, and they imagine remedies of all sorts (Figure 7.3). The "solutions" they contemplate may range from silly pranks to devastating violence. Most such fantasies are harmless. They provide a means for blowing off steam. But some reflect building hostility and forewarn aggression and possible injury to themselves or others.

*Figures 7.2 to 7.7 from* Supervisor Effectiveness. *Courtesy of Corning, Inc.*

**FIGURE 7.3** Viewing thoughts of employees.

The challenge for learners is to recognize potentially serious concerns among momentary exasperations.

### Activity

*Listen to conversations, and decide who's making the most concerning comments. Then move that employee into your office.*

Learners roll the mouse pointer over the image of each person appearing in the office complex to "listen" to what employees are saying to each other. Supervisors select the employee making the most concerning comments by dragging the person's image to the area labeled *Your Office* (Figure 7.4).

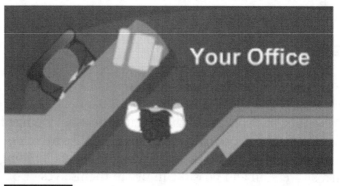

**FIGURE 7.4** Your Office area. Learners can drag the selected employee's icon into the office.

## Feedback

*At the gesture level, pop-up captions reward pointer placement with needed information, and at the decision level, correct/incorrect judgment is augmented with action-consequence information.*

As the learner moves the pointer over employees in conversation (indicated by waves animating around the speaking person), their comments appear in caption bubbles. When choosing the highest-level concern, the image of the selected employee appears in your office.

Selecting and placing an employee in your office represents a decision made by the learner. In this application, feedback at this point also includes an instructive evaluation (Figure 7.5).

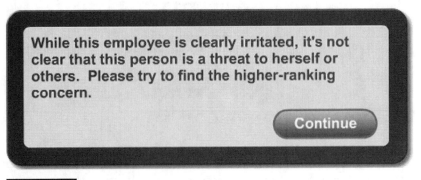

**FIGURE 7.5**  Feedback with instruction.

When the highest-level concern is identified, confirming feedback is given (Figure 7.6).

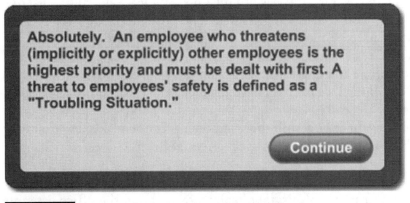

**FIGURE 7.6**  Feedback after correct threat identification.

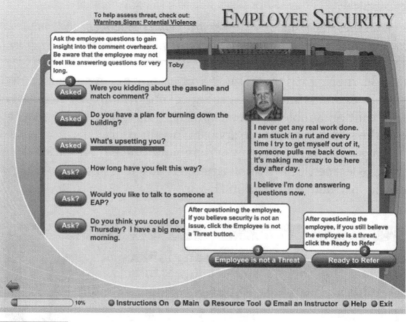

**FIGURE 7.7** Options for questioning the employee.

Identifying high-risk comments is only the first step of this learning sequence, of course. Learners are then asked to question the distressed employee to further determine the probability of risk and decide what to do about it (Figure 7.7).

## Analysis of Example 1

There is a lot to learn in this example, but it is fun and engaging to learn this way. In contrast, it is easy to imagine a typical e-learning design being used here. Lists of danger signs would be presented. After reading them, an explanation of appropriate preventative actions would be listed for the learner to read. Then learners would be given scenario questions that would require them to select an action or two from the multiple-choice list. No context, weak challenge, abstract activity, extrinsic feedback—*boring*.

Look again at how well the components in the preceding example integrate to make the learning experience effective:

- Learners not only go through comparative steps to rank the levels of concern; they also symbolically move around the office listening to employees. Good supervisors are good, active listeners. They must circulate through work areas, and they must spend time listening to their employees. The interaction leads learners to envision gathering information that is critical to their responsibility for ensuring safety.

- When a security problem is identified, face-to-face encounters with employees are necessary in order to probe further. Symbolically moving the image of an employee into the learner's office helps supervisors to imagine this encounter and to realize that preparation for it will make the task less daunting and more productive.

  When being asked probing questions, employees may feel relieved by the attention and therefore speak freely, but they may just as well feel uneasy, embarrassed, and guarded. It may be difficult to get information from them. The interactions in this example are designed so that employees will sometimes answer only a few questions, then stop. Experiencing this likely occurrence not only makes the learning more engaging, but also continues to reveal the value of the learning experience to participants.

- The focus is on actions and consequences. Although factual and conceptual information must be learned, it is offered within the context of task performance, stressing its relevance and making it more interesting, easier to learn, and easier to remember.

### No Design is Perfect

The feedback could be more intrinsic and possibly more effective. For example, if the learner mistakenly identified a lower-risk comment and took that individual to the office for investigation, the person representing a greater safety threat might actually carry out a violent act. Such a design might increase the learning impact and make it easier for supervisors to remember the consequences of certain decisions, but the design would have to be effected carefully so as not to trivialize an important responsibility and concern.

## Example 2: *Statistical Process Control (SPC)*

Sometimes the tasks being learned aren't so obviously performance tasks. It is sometimes necessary, for example, to work on subtasks or preparatory tasks, such as learning to differentiate between deciduous and coniferous trees, recalling and identifying the parts of a nerve cell, or defining the difference between sales and marketing. However, just a little bit of analysis reveals how almost all content to be learned can be put in an action-oriented context—even at stages preparatory to learning more complex and interesting tasks. This example is a case in point.

In DaimlerChrysler's *Statistical Process Control (SPC)* training, learners need to become aware of the many potential sources of variation that can cause process problems. Variations can come from any of five categories. In order to systematically search for potential variations, learners need to be constantly aware of the five categories and understand that each category represents a large number of variation sources.

## Context

*A hypothetical plastic fish manufacturing process is having problems controlling the variance in the length of the fish produced* (Figure 7.8).

**Demo on CD**

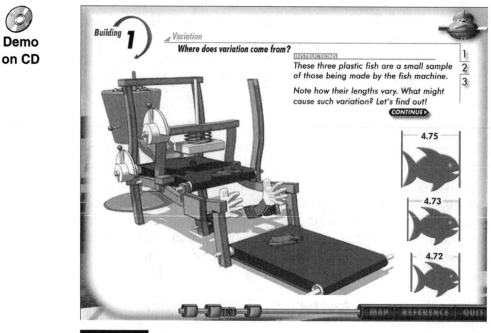

**FIGURE 7.8** Fish manufacturing machine.

*Figures 7.8 to 7.14 from* Statistical Process Control. *Courtesy of DaimlerChrysler Corporation, DaimlerChrysler Quality Institute.*

Plastic fish production was chosen for this project for two reasons:

- The automotive workers being trained needed to free themselves from the specific details of their work to look objectively at issues in manufacturing and quality control.
- A fishbone diagram is often drawn to show the many sources of variation that affect quality. The fish imagery was used repeatedly as a thematic memory aid.

## Challenges

1. *Select possible causes of variation that might affect the length of manufactured fish.*

2. *For each relevant variation, identify the appropriate group of variation sources.*

3. *Name the five groups of variation sources.*

The third and primary challenge is actually not presented to learners until the first two are completed. This is done to underscore that the value of learning the group names isn't just to be able to answer a test question. There are so many possible sources of variation for any manufacturing process, it's important to review each group to be sure nothing has been overlooked.

In subsequent interactions, the challenge rises to require learners to actually discover the causes of problematic variation. They'll find the task easier if they keep the five groups in mind.

## Activity 1

*Recognize variations that could cause problems* (Figure 7.9).

The learner has to consider each potential variation presented and decide if it is relevant to the process at hand. Worms, for example, probably would not contribute to variances in length, but variations in the density of the plastic might very well produce some longer and some shorter fish.

## Feedback 1

*Immediate narrated feedback is given when variances are classified as relevant or irrelevant* (Figure 7.10).

Short text and audio feedback is given when each item is classified as relevant or irrelevant.

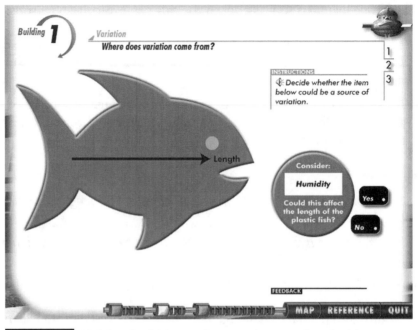

**FIGURE 7.9** Building the fishbone diagram—learners first decide whether a randomly chosen factor, such as humidity, is relevant.

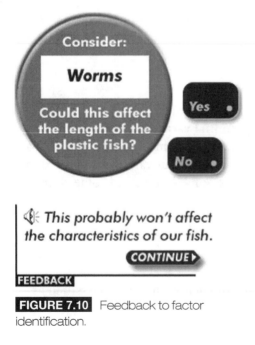

**FIGURE 7.10** Feedback to factor identification.

### Activity 2

*Build the SPC fishbone diagram* (Figures 7.11 and 7.12).

As the learner works, the fishbone diagram is constructed on top of the fish graphic. Initially, only one of the five groups is shown on the diagram. For each source of variation determined to be relevant, learners decide if it belongs to one of the groups of variation shown. If it does, they click the appropriate group name. If it doesn't, they must request additional groups, one at a time, until an appropriate group is available.

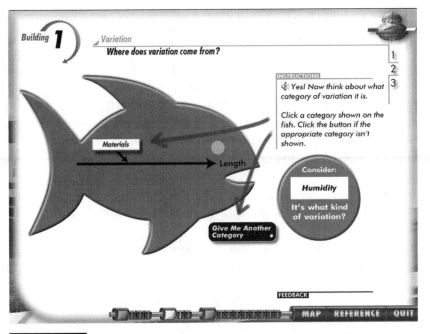

**FIGURE 7.11** Building the fishbone diagram—learners classify each relevant source of variation.

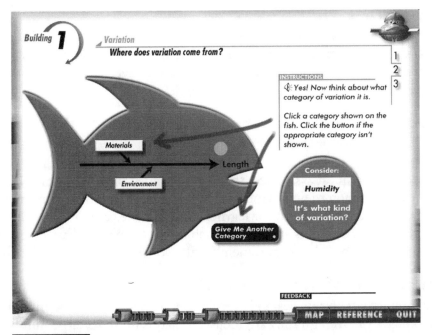

**FIGURE 7.12** The learner needed another category, because humidity isn't a manufacturing material.

As shown in Figure 7.11, the learner has properly identified *humidity* as a possible source of variation in the length of plastic fish produced. The learner is now confronted with a classification decision: Is humidity a type of *material?* If it is, the learner clicks MATERIALS. If not, the learner must request another category for consideration.

In Figure 7.12, the learner clicked GIVE ME ANOTHER CATEGORY, and the category Environment appeared. The learner must again reflect on whether the specific variation, humidity, is a variation in materials, environment, or some other group.

### Feedback 2

*Immediate feedback with sound effects is given when variances are classified as relevant or irrelevant.*

If the learner chooses an incorrect group, the group designation is removed from the screen (with a crashing sound), thus reducing the choices and also requiring the learner to bring it back later, as appropriate, by clicking the GIVE ME ANOTHER CATEGORY button. If the learner chooses the correct group, the cycle repeats with another specific variation candidate until the full diagram is built and many specific variations have been considered.

### Activity 3

*Recall the five categories of variation by typing their names* (Figure 7.13).

As shown in Figure 7.13, after the learner has practiced classifying many specific sources of variation, the *real* test is revealed: *Recall the five categories!*

### Feedback 3

*Immediate feedback confirms correct answers. After several incorrect answers (which almost never happens), learners have access to Help* (Figure 7.14).

If learners request assistance, they are reminded of some specific sources of variation they previously categorized. Seeing these items makes it easy, with a little thought, for learners to recall the categories. By the way, the software accepts synonyms, such as *people, crew,* and *work shift.* It's important that these learners remember the concepts, not specific terms.

## Analysis of Example 2

The interactivity in this design is very effective in achieving the intended outcomes. Even though they are focused on considering a large number of specific variations, learners can almost invariably list the five categories

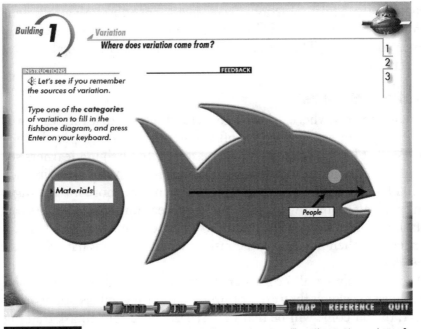

**FIGURE 7.13** Building the fishbone diagram—recalling the categories of variation.

**FIGURE 7.14** Help is available in the form of hints.

at the end. They almost chuckle at such an easy and unexpected question. They are visibly pleased with their ability. Through repetition, learners become fully aware that there can be large numbers of specific causes of variation within each of the categories (i.e., there are many potential challenges in maintaining the manufacturing quality desired).

Perhaps most important, the learning process itself is interesting and rewarding. It takes a certain amount of reasoning ability to select appropriate categories, yet almost everyone does quite well and appreciates the rewards. What's really fun is that learners are very often surprised to discover that they know the five categories at the end of the activity. The interactions foster persistence through a sufficient number of repetitions needed to learn, while repeated successes build learner confidence. The activity is enjoyable and seems effortless. Good interactivity.

## Learning Subtasks

As mentioned elsewhere, it's wise to start with tasks that interest learners. Admittedly, interesting tasks are often complex tasks, composed of many subtasks that learners may not have mastered, but helping learners see the relevance of mastering subtasks is an important learning event in and of itself. This can be done by initially introducing the more interesting tasks, then breaking them down into subtasks for learning as needed. As each subtask is mastered, focus should return to the primary task at hand. Learners can then be helped to consider whether additional subtasks need to be learned.

You might always allow learners to attempt tasks at their own volition, even those for which they are not prepared. If they fail, as you would expect, the outcome will be that they see the need for subtask training. This is a win. If they succeed, they will have demonstrated skills you didn't know they had. This is a win.

In any case, positioning subtasks as components of interesting primary tasks will, among other things, help to motivate learners to take on necessary subtasks that might otherwise seem irrelevant or uninteresting.

## Invented Tasks

Sometimes tasks need to be invented in order to maintain an effective perspective on the primary training objective, avoid overwhelming learners with too much complexity, and provide interesting and effective activity. Example 2 is just such a case.

The big task being learned is to identify sources of variation that can affect manufacturing quality in specific instances. While this might sound simple, manufacturers wouldn't have much trouble controlling quality if indeed it were so simple. The fact is, however, that problem variation is often very difficult to track down. It can elude manufacturers for years.

Without some aids, learners are likely to flounder unproductively in trying to discover problem sources of variation, such as those taken from real occurrence scenarios. Therefore, training gives learners a framework and some checklists to apply. The learning is accomplished through invented subtasks charged with the following two-part intent:

- Make manufacturing employees aware that there are many, many easily overlooked sources of potential variation
- Enable learners to name the five types of variation sources so they can keep them in mind as they work to ferret out problems:

>   Materials
>
>   Methods
>
>   Equipment
>
>   People
>
>   Environment

It would be easy to go through the mechanics of designing something that would look like instructional activity but would, in fact, be quite ineffective. For example, you could easily get everyone to answer the true/false question correctly:

> Are there many possible variations in a manufacturing process that can affect product quality?     TRUE     FALSE

A high percentage of people would answer this question correctly without really understanding how important the underlying fact is to quality control. Teaching people to consistently answer such a question correctly would be easy, boring for the learner, and of little consequence. In addition, teaching people to correctly list the five categories of variation sources would be a boring learning task of modest instructional challenge, of little consequence unless put in proper context.

## No Design Is Perfect

This design successfully integrates the context, challenge, activities, and feedback so that together they build the needed outcome. Each activity is interesting in and of itself, is suitable to the capabilities of learners (which, in this case, ranges greatly), and helps unfold important concepts about variation in almost a storytelling manner.

There is considerable excellence in this design; however, as with almost all designs, many improvements could be made if time and money were not a consideration. For example, judgment might be delayed. Instead of overriding the learner's acceptance of an unrelated variation, the learner could be asked to go ahead and classify the variation. When considering how to classify *worms*, for example, the learner might think:

Actually, worms wouldn't be one of the materials used in this process, or even related to any of them. They wouldn't be part of any of the other categories either. I'll bet I made a mistake and should have rejected worms as a relevant source of variation.

If the learner could then correct the answer and reject worms as a variation of concern, the context of the interactivity would have a greater effect.

# Anatomy of Good Interactions

Let's now reexamine each component of instructional interactivity.

### Context

*Context provides the framework and conditions which make the interaction meaningful.*

The media available in e-learning provide an important opportunity to make the interaction much more than a rhetorical or abstract event. Since we are often working to maximize the transfer of learning to performance on the job, the more realistic the context can be, the more likely the learner will be to imagine the proposed situation actually occurring. The learner is then likely to visualize taking alternative actions and visualize the outcomes—a mental exercise that will increase the probability of transferring learning to real behavior.

Some researchers believe humans do much, if not all, of their reasoning through the use of mental images. Images can communicate to us more rapidly and with more fidelity than verbal descriptions, while animations can impart a sense of urgency with unequaled force. Presenting traditional academic questions, such as multiple-choice, fill-in the blank, true/false, and matching questions without illustrations takes little advantage of the instructional capabilities present in e-learning.

### Challenge

*Challenge is a stimulus to exhibit effective behavior.*

Challenge focuses learners on specific aspects of the instructional content and tells them what they need to do.

In its simplest (and often least effective) form, the challenge is a question the learner is to answer. In more complex and probably more effective settings, the stimulus may be such things as:

- Indications of a problem on a control panel
- Customer service complaints
- A spreadsheet showing an unreconciled difference
- An animated production line producing poor quality
- Increasing business losses
- A simulated customer call
- A medical prescription to be filled
- A simulated electrical fault
- A client record to be updated

"Click NEXT to go on" is not a stimulus for instructional interactivity unless you are trying to teach people how to advance to the next screen.

## Activity

*Activity is the physical gesture in the learner's response to the context and challenge.*

Whether learning physical skills (such as typing) or mental skills (such as sentence construction), learners need ways to communicate decisions, demonstrate abilities, ask for assistance, test solutions, and state answers. The gestures learners can use for input to the computer should be natural and easy to use; they should readily and quickly represent the learner's intentions. The mechanisms with which learners express their questions, decisions, answers, and so on should not impede or bias the learner's ability to communicate.

Just making the learner do something, however, doesn't comprise an instructional interaction. Even if the computer responds specifically to what the learner does, a sequence of input and response doesn't necessarily constitute an instructional event.

The structure of the input tools (i.e., the recognized learner gestures) is a major design consideration. In many cases, they determine the extent of the cognitive processing the learner must perform. They may determine, for example, whether the learner needs to recognize an appropriate solution, recall it, and apply it.

Poorly constructed interactions require learners to translate what they know or can do into artificial gestures. The task may be so difficult that fully proficient learners fail to respond "acceptably," not because they are unable to perform the targeted tasks, but because they have trouble communicating their knowledge within the imposed interface constraints.

For example, learners may be able to perform long division on a notepad, but be unable to do it via keyboard input.

On the other hand, very good interfaces are themselves a delight to use; their value to the learning process goes beyond just efficiency and machine-recognized gestures. Not only can they create a more memorable experience, perhaps just by providing a happily recalled event; they also help learners see and understand more fully many kinds of relationships, such as "a part of," "an example of," or "a complement to."

Assembling the glassware for a chemistry experiment and sorting fruits, vegetables, dairy products, grains, and meats into appropriate storage containers, for example, underscore appropriate relationships. Learners might very well remember the process of moving displayed objects as a cognitive handle for recalling underlying relationships and concepts needed in on-the-job performance. Such kinesthetic association can enrich both understanding and recall, whereas having answered multiple-choice questions would give little aid.

## Feedback

*Feedback acknowledges learner activity and provides information about the effectiveness of learner decisions.*

When learning, we seek to make cognitive connections and construct relationships—a neurological cognitive map (Figure 7.15). The formation of meaning—creating understanding—is a process of drawing relationships, whereas the process of learning uses rehearsal to strengthen the forming relationships for later recall and application.

Feedback is essential in these processes to make sure learners construct effective relationships and deconstruct erroneous relationships. The instructional challenge is to devise feedback that will prove the most helpful to learners in their efforts to identify, clarify, and strengthen functional relationships.

It is often easier for learners to link specific actions to their consequences than it is to simply associate two objects with each other. For example, it's easier to recall that sticking your finger in a live electrical outlet is likely to result in a shock, even though you may never have done it, than it is to recall the capital city of Maine (Augusta) or the name of an enclosed object with seven equal sides (heptagon). Of course, if you travel

**FIGURE 7.15** A cognitive map.

to Augusta or do design work with heptagons, you will have an easier time remembering them. Why? Well, in part because of repeatedly hearing the names, but also because it's likely you would associate them with actions and consequences. You like to go to Augusta because you enjoy the views of the Kennebec River and the shops in the Water Street area. Actions and consequences, not just names.

It is extremely fortunate for us in training that action-consequence learning is easiest, because the objective of training is to improve performance. While performance is based on factual, conceptual, and procedural knowledge, learning the necessary facts, concepts, and procedures is easier if done in the context of building relationships between actions and their consequences.

High-impact feedback allows learners to determine the effectiveness of their actions, not just whether an answer was right or wrong. In fact, good feedback doesn't necessarily tell learners directly whether their actions are correct or incorrect; rather, it may help learners determine this for themselves.

Good feedback, therefore, is not necessarily judgment or evaluation, as most people think of it (although at times offering such judgment is critical). Rather, good feedback reflects the different outcomes of specific actions.

## Good and Bad Interactivity Components

Perhaps the primary challenge of creating effective learning experiences is designing great interactions. The simple presence of the four essential components—context, stimulus, activity, and feedback—doesn't create valuable interactions. It is the specific nuances of each component individually and the way that they integrate with and support the effectiveness of the other components that leads to success.

Table 7.1 contrasts the characteristics of good and poor interaction components.

**TABLE 7.1   Characteristics of Good and Poor Interaction Components**

| Component | Good | Poor |
|---|---|---|
| Context | Focuses on applicable action/performance relationships<br>Reinforces the relationship of subtasks to target outcomes<br><br>Simulates performance environments | Focuses on learning abstract bodies of knowledge<br>Uses a generalized, content-independent screen layout<br><br>Simulates a traditional classroom environment or no identifiable environment at all |
| Challenge | Requires learner to apply information and skills to meaningful and interesting problems<br><br>Progresses from single-step performance to requiring learners to perform multiple steps | Presents traditional questions (multiple-choice, true/false, matching) which at best require cognitive processing but not in an applied setting, and typically require little cognitive processing in an abstracted, rhetorical setting<br><br>Requires (and allows) separate, single-step performance only |

| Component | Good | Poor |
|---|---|---|
| | Puts learners at some risk, such as having to start over if they make too many mistakes | Presents little or no risk by either revealing the correct answer after a mistake is made or using such structures as, "No. Try again." |
| Activity | Builds on the context to stimulate meaningful performance | Uses artificial, question-answering activities such as choosing a, b, c, none of the above, all of the above |
| | Provides an opportunity to back up and correct suspected mistakes or explore alternatives | Allows only one chance to answer |
| | Asks learners to justify their decisions before feedback is given; learners are allowed to back up and change responses at any point | Facilitates lucky guesses (and makes no effort to differentiate between lucky guesses and well-reasoned decisions) |
| Feedback | Provides instructive information in response to either learner requests for it or repeated learner errors | Relies on content presentations (given prior to performance opportunities) |
| | Helps learner see the negative consequences of poor performance and the positive consequences of good performance | Immediately judges every response as correct or incorrect |
| | Delays judgment, giving learners information needed to determine for themselves if they are performing well or not | Focuses learners on earning points or passing tests, rather than on building proficiencies |
| | Provides frank and honest assessments; says so if and when learners begin making thoughtless errors | Babies learners; always assumes learners are doing their best |

# The Elusive Essence of Good Interactivity

It's clear that not all interactions are of equal value. Nobody wants bad interactions; they're boring, ineffective, and wasteful of everyone's time, interest, and energy. And they're quite easy to build. Good interactions are, of course, just the opposite. They intrigue, involve, challenge, inform, reward, and provide recognizable value to the learner. And they require more design consideration.

The essence of good interactivity seems quite elusive. It would be helpful if all the necessary attributes of good interactions could be boiled down to a single guiding principle, or even a simple checklist. Even if imperfect, if the essence were easily communicated and widely understood, e-learning would be far better than it is today. For this reason, I have kept searching for that guiding principle for quite some time. I offer the checklist in Table 7.2 as a tool that's surely better than nothing.

### TABLE 7.2   Good Instructional Interactions— A Three-Point Checklist

| | |
|---|---|
| ✔ Good interactions are purposeful in the mind of the learner. | Learners understand what they can accomplish through participation in the interaction. To be of greatest value for an individual, the learner needs to see value in the potential accomplishment and each learning step. |
| ✔ The learner must apply genuine, authentic skills and knowledge. | It should not be possible to feign proficiency through good guesses. Challenges must be appropriately calibrated to the learner's abilities, readiness, and needs. Activities should become as similar to needed on-the-job performance as possible. |
| ✔ Feedback is intrinsic. | The feedback demonstrates to learners the ineffectiveness (even risks) of poor responses and the value of good responses. |

# Interactivity's Mistaken Identities

Confusions abound in e-learning. They derive from the multifaceted natures of instruction, technology, art, and science. And they have been exacerbated by the recent enthusiasm for e-learning and fanaticism about all things Internet, with the result that form is often prized over function. Identified delivery technologies are mandated, while instructional effectiveness is neither defined nor measured. Although there are signs of a backlash effect, there has been a tendency to believe that instruction delivered via technology has credibility just because of the delivery medium. This surely is as wrong as believing that all things in print are true or that because a course of instruction is delivered by a living, breathing instructor, it is better than the alternatives.

Nothing in e-learning has been more confused than the design and application of interactivity. Its nature, too, is sufficiently multifaceted to be inherently confusing, yet we've been investigating technology-supported instructional interactivity far too long to continue such confusion without embarrassment and impatience.

People confuse instructional interactivity with various multimedia components at both the detail and aggregate levels. At the detail level, very important design nuances separate highly effective interactivity from that which just goes through the motions. At the aggregate level, presentations, navigation, and questioning are wholly mistaken for instructional interactivity. To be clear that these are quite different entities with very different applications and outcomes, let's round out our examination of instructional interactivity with some final differentiations—that is, classifications of what is not instructional interactivity.

## Presentation versus Instruction

It's easy to be deceived by appealing design. From book covers to automobile fenders, designers work endlessly to attract our attention, provide an appeal, paint a fantasy. The appeal they strive for is one that will create an enthusiasm and a desire to buy, regardless of other factors that should be taken into account. They are often successful in getting us to disregard practicality, quality, and expense and to pursue a desire, to buy into a dream, but most important, to *buy*. Just because it's attractive, of course, doesn't mean it is a good product, good for us, or a smart buy.

A beautiful presentation is certainly worth more than an ugly one, but even superb presentation aesthetics don't convert a presentation into instruction or pronouncements into interactivity. These very different solutions should not be confused, just as the differing needs they address should not be confused.

Sometimes merely the presentation of needed information *is* sufficient. Persons who are capable of the desired performance and need only some guiding information neither need nor would benefit from instruction. They need only the information. Because instruction takes time and is much more expensive to prepare and deliver, it is important not to confuse a need for information with a need for instruction; see Table 7.3.

**TABLE 7.3   Presentations versus Interactivity**

| Choose Presentations When . . . | Choose Interactivity When . . . |
|---|---|
| Content is readily understood by targeted learners. | Content is complex and takes considerable thought to comprehend. |
| Learner differences are minimal. | Learners are diverse in their ability to understand the content. |
| Errors are harmless. | Errors are injurious, costly, or difficult to remedy. |
| Information is readily available for later retrieval and reference. | Information needs to be internalized. |
| Desired change to existing skill is minor and can be achieved without practice. | Behavioral changes will require practice. |
| Learners can easily differentiate between good and inadequate performance. | Learners need guidance to differentiate between good and poor performance. |
| Mentorship is inexpensive and will follow. | Mentorship is costly, limited, or unavailable. |

# Navigation versus Interactivity

Navigation is the means learners have of getting from place to place—of getting to information. It includes such simple things as controls to back up, go forward, replay, pause, quit, and bring up such tools as a glossary, help function, calculator, hints, and progress records.

Because navigation involves input from the learner and provides a response from the computer, people frequently confuse navigation with interactivity. Further, interactive systems need good navigation capabilities. They depend on good, supportive, integrated navigation and suffer when it's weak. But navigation and instructional interactivity are very different in terms of what they are, the learning support provided, and where they are appropriate. As before, good navigation doesn't turn presentations into interactivity, although it can certainly improve the ability of learners to retrieve and review information when needed.

Good navigation systems are valuable. They are neither easy to design nor easy to build. To be highly responsive to user requests and to provide intuitive controls is much more difficult than it would seem, and failed attempts repeatedly attest to the level of challenge involved.

Nevertheless, with good navigation, content, and presentation components, performers can be aided to the point that their performance is hard to differentiate from that of an expert.

# Electronic Performance Support Systems (EPSSs) versus Instructional Interactivity

Closely related to navigation are applications that provide prompts, guidelines, questions, and information in real time. They depend on very responsive navigation to keep in step with people throughout the performance of their tasks.

Electronic performance support systems (EPSSs) attempt to skip over the expensive, time-consuming efforts of taking people to high levels of proficiency. The EPSS takes advantage of circumstances in which computers can communicate with people as they perform, prompting many tasks in real time without the need of prior or extensive training. There are many benefits, even beyond the obvious benefit of avoided training costs:

- People can rotate into different positions on demand as workloads change from season to season, day to day, or even hour to hour.
- New hires can become instantly productive.
- Errors caused by memory lapses, poor habits, and distractions can be greatly reduced, possibly even eliminated.
- Infrequently performed tasks can be performed with the same level of thoroughness and competency as frequent tasks.

In short, an EPSS is an economical solution when training is *not* needed. It is an inappropriate and ineffective solution, however, when training *is* needed. We need to be careful to be clear about both the need and the fitting solution.

The navigational components of an EPSS can look much like instructional interactivity when they are designed to respond to observations made by users. If, for example, in making a payment-collection call to a person leasing a sports car, it is discovered that the payments have ceased because the car has been stolen, the EPSS's prompts on what to say will instantly change to appropriately address the unexpected context. The caller might not have learned how to handle such situations and might not have any background in missing property circumstances, but the caller can still work through an instance successfully. The caller doesn't know—and doesn't need to know—what different behaviors might have been appropriate if the leased vehicle had been stolen before the payments fell behind rather than afterward. But with the computer's support present, it doesn't matter. The employee isn't really a learner, just a performer successfully carrying out on-screen instructions.

Although the conditional programming necessary to help performers in real time can range from quite simple to extremely complex, even including components of artificial intelligence, the interactions built into these applications serve navigational needs more than instructional ones. Repetitive performance with EPSS aid should impart some useful internalized knowledge and skills, but EPSS applications are designed to optimize the effectiveness of the supported transactions rather than the building of new cognitive and performance skills (see Table 7.4).

## TABLE 7.4   EPSS versus Interactivity

| Choose EPSS When . . . | Choose Interactivity When . . . |
| --- | --- |
| The task or job changes often. | The tasks are relatively stable. |
| Staff turnover is high. | Workers hold same responsibilities for a long time. |
| Performers do not need to know why each task step is important and whether it is appropriate in a specific circumstance. | Performers need to evaluate the appropriateness of each step and vigilantly monitor whether the process as a whole continues to be appropriate. |
| Tasks are systematic but complex and difficult to learn or remember. | Tasks may require unique, resourceful, and imaginative approaches. |
| Tasks are performed infrequently. | Tasks are performed frequently. |
| Tasks allow time for performance support. | Tasks are time critical and prohibit consulting a performance guide. |
| Supervision of employees on the job is limited or unavailable. | Supervision is expensive or impractical. |
| Mistakes in performance are costly. | Mistakes are easily rectified. |
| Learners are motivated to seek a solution. | Learners don't appreciate the value of good performance. |

## Hybrid Applications: Using an EPSS for Instruction

Some applications both assist new learners to perform well immediately and teach operations so that they can be done either without computer support or more quickly with reduced support. That is, the techniques used for teaching and those that support performance are not mutually exclusive.

In fact, the early work of B. F. Skinner (1968) used a technique of *fading*, which had learners perform tasks, such as reading a poem. After learners read a poem to be memorized, some words were deleted from the text of the poem. Learners were generally able to continue reciting the poem, filling in the missing words as they read. Successively, more and more words were deleted until the whole poem could be recited with no assistance.

A similar approach can be used with EPSS applications, although considerably more learning support can be provided to learners than simply removing support steps. Instructive feedback, for example, can show learners the potential consequences of an error, while the EPSS application intervenes to prevent that error from actually occurring.

## Questioning versus Interactivity

Question-answering activity is just question-answering activity, regardless of whether it is done with paper and pencil or a computer. If the learner doesn't have to apply higher-order mental processes, the learning impact is the same, whether learners drag objects, type letters, or click numbers. Just because the learner's gestures are more sophisticated doesn't mean that more learning is going on.

The screens in Figures 7.16 to 7.20 show five interaction styles, but the differences among the instructional impacts of each style are insignificant.

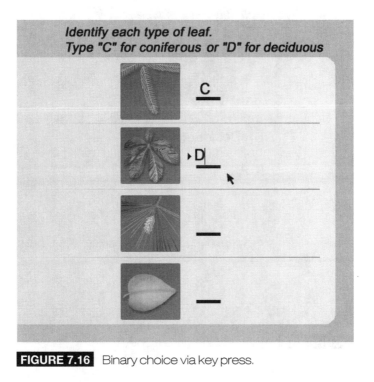

**FIGURE 7.16** Binary choice via key press.

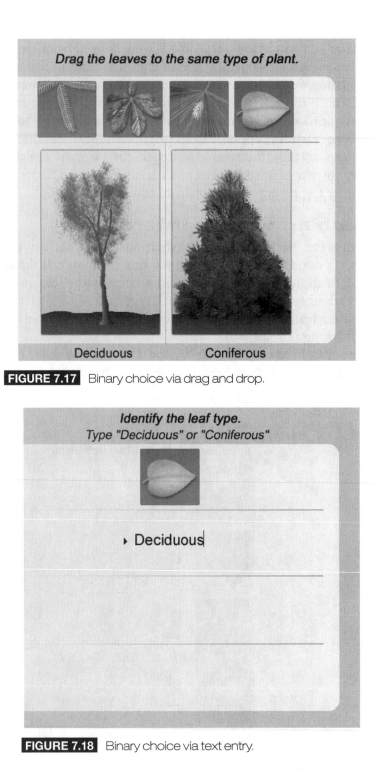

**FIGURE 7.17**    Binary choice via drag and drop.

**FIGURE 7.18**    Binary choice via text entry.

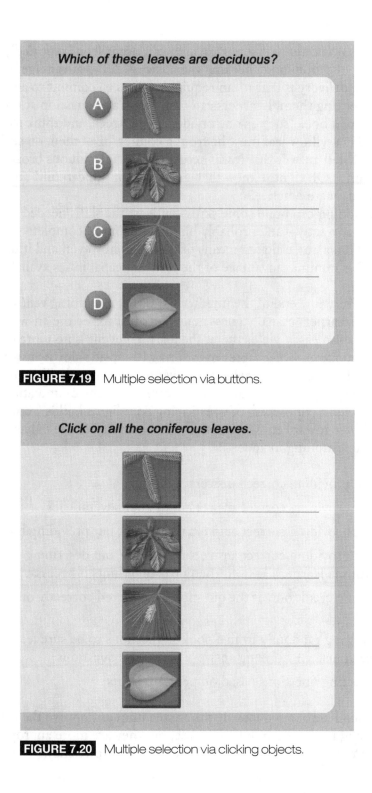

**FIGURE 7.19** Multiple selection via buttons.

**FIGURE 7.20** Multiple selection via clicking objects.

There's no doubt that some learning can occur from repeatedly answering questions and checking the answers. A big advantage of e-learning delivery is that it can require learners to commit to answers before checking them. Learners can easily look at a question at the end of a chapter of a book, such as one on identifying trees, and think to themselves, "That willow leaf must be from a conifer." But then, on seeing from the listed answer that it was actually from a deciduous broadleaf, they'll think "Oh right. I knew that. Should be more careful," and go on without adequate practice.

Questioning can build some skills—at least the skills needed to answer questions correctly—and probably builds some more complete understanding. It isn't an efficient means of doing so, however, and it unfortunately takes minimal advantage of the learning capabilities available in e-learning.

At the very low end of the interactivity scale, e-learning relies on questioning. If learners casually guess at answers just to see the answers, and the application easily yields them, the learning event is no more effective than the book's end-of-chapter questions with upside-down answers. This structure does not create memorable events and is mostly likely to result in "test learning," which is quickly forgotten after the examination.

Of course, a continuum of questioning paradigms builds from this low-end base toward true instructional interactivity. Some enhancements on basic questioning include:

- Not providing correct answers
- Not providing correct answers until after several tries
- Not providing correct answers right away, but providing hints first
- Not providing correct answers right away, but describing the fault with the learner's answer, then providing hints if necessary
- Giving credit only if the question is answered correctly on the first try
- Drawing randomly from a pool of questions to be sure learners aren't just memorizing answers to specific questions
- Selecting questions based on previous faults

And so on. There's no doubt that these techniques improve the value of questioning for instruction to a degree, but they are more appropriately used to improve techniques of assessing learner proficiency.

Remember, to hit an instructional home run we need to create meaningful and memorable experiences. Unless the training is specifically designed only to teach learners to pass a test, there are much more efficient and *effective* methods than drilling through sample questions.

# Interactivity Paradigms That Work

Interactivity in e-learning might so frequently be weak because application builders aren't aware of more effective models. Or it might be that the more effective models people have seen were judged too difficult, too time-consuming, or too expensive to build.

With proper preparation, including some advance tool building, and a thorough understanding of interactivity instruction, these frequent excuses for noninteractive e-learning melt away. As mentioned in Part 1, there really aren't any rational justifications for spending good money to build ineffective instruction. *It if isn't going to work, it's too expensive—no matter how little it costs.*

Let's look at a few specific models that have been very successful in multiple applications. They range from easy and very inexpensive to build, to challenging work requiring substantial investment. All of them, however, have been very successful (getting people to do the right thing at the right time) and have been used with different content. Once built, their repeated use has made them very affordable—even more affordable than much more simplistic approaches that are typically rebuilt from scratch each and every time.

## Trapdoor Hints

Sometimes complex tasks have to be overlearned so as to become almost automatic—so that they can be performed accurately with little thought even under stressful or distracting circumstances. Airline ticket agents, for example, often have to work their computers to locate and enter information while people are talking to them, reciting numbers and information not yet part of the transaction or making friendly but nevertheless divergent conversation.

Reservation and ticketing operations can be complex, requiring multiple steps, interpreting codes, responding to restrictions, looking for options, and so forth. Interfaces vary from more prompted and helpful designs to those that originated years ago, when a tightly coded, invariant syntax was used, such as:

A quick explanation of the system: * indicates a display operation, 122 is the flight number, 17SEP is the date (September 17), and the passenger is THAYER. Ticket agents need to be able to make these entries quickly and without error.

## Context

This is a case in which repetition is important. Many commands can be formed from the syntax; but with few exceptions, if elements are out of order or missing, the command will have to be reentered, costing precious time.

## Challenge

Beginning learners were given a basic overview of command structures and rules. Then, in drills, they were given information about a customer and asked to retrieve records related to the customer's travel.

## Activity

Learners had to type a syntactically correct command to complete each exercise, just as they would have to do on the job.

## Feedback

Parsing software analyzed each command entered and detected specific faults. It was possible to tell learners exactly what was wrong with each command they entered, both in the general sense of format and in the specific sense of whether they had entered the correct command and information for the exercise at hand.

Two levels of feedback were given to learners:

- A general statement of the error (or of the first error) found was given.
- To require learners to think and internalize information, rather than floundering around guessing or simply parroting back correct commands that had been revealed, hints were written to help learners make corrections. A succession of hints was devised, beginning with general principles and eventually revealing the correct command using information specific to the exercise.

Hints were hidden beneath a spring-loaded trapdoor. Learners had to look for hints by sliding a hint door open (Figure 7.21). To do this, they would click the mouse pointer on the door and drag it to the side. As they

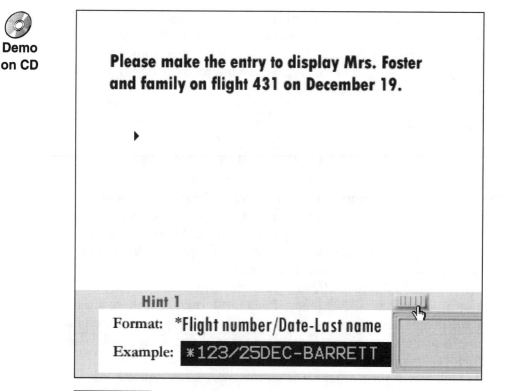

**Please make the entry to display Mrs. Foster and family on flight 431 on December 19.**

▶

Hint 1

Format:   *Flight number/Date-Last name

Example:   *123/25DEC-BARRETT

**FIGURE 7.21**   Sliding door hints.

held the door open, they could read the hint, but the moment they released the mouse button to type a revised command, the door slid shut.

Each time they reopened the hint door, a different and more specific hint would appear. Learners quickly realized that they needed to concentrate carefully on the message of the hint, because it wasn't going to stay on the screen. Further, even though the last and final hint would reveal the correct command verbatim, it took more effort to repeatedly obtain hints than it did to simply learn the principles of command construction. Learners are often interested in the shortest, easiest path. If it's easier to learn than to ask for help, they'll try harder to succeed without asking for help. Hey!

## Reusability

The trapdoor hints mechanism is very easy to program and is widely applicable where repetition of moderately varying exercises is appropriate. Although it can be embellished with scoring systems, such that each retrieval of a hint costs some penalty points, the design is amazingly effective even in its simplest form. Perhaps asking for help, even from a machine, is enough of a psychological expense to motivate concentration and learning. Perhaps we unacceptably disappoint ourselves if we need to repeatedly ask for the same help. I'm sure there are explanations and many opportunities for research here. What we can see from simple observation, however, is that this is a simple interactivity design that works and has many applications.

## Task Model

Much training is developed to teach people to follow procedures. As many tasks become more information based and systems become more complex, the number of procedures to be learned increases dramatically. When there are many procedures to be learned, learners can be overwhelmed if we try to teach all procedures individually and specifically. Learners are often better served by learning how to learn new tasks on their own. They need to learn some general skills, practice learning specific skills, do some analysis, and experiment.

Learners need to have confidence that they can figure out new processes with reasonable efficiency. They need to know if there are risks of making dangerous errors and how to avoid them, especially when they must perform a task never specifically taught to them. They need to know what kinds of errors can be corrected and what kinds can't.

All in all, this is quite different from the approaches typically used to teach new procedures, such as using a new software application. Yet when people are taught only as many selected procedures as fit into a class of reasonable length, there is often much left untaught and unlearned. A different approach truly is needed.

### Context

A simulation of the Microsoft Windows 95 operating system.

### Challenge

From the very beginning, learners are asked to perform operations without having been told how to do so. After learners choose an operation they want to learn from a menu, the challenge is on: See if you can do it (Figure 7.22).

### Activity

With the tools currently available, it's often possible to simulate applications at a very high level of fidelity without extravagant costs, especially in the limited form needed for this paradigm. Learners operate the software application exactly as they would the real application.

**Demo on CD**

**FIGURE 7.22** Challenging task presented.

As in this example application, if there are multiple methods or sequences that can be used to complete a task, all paths should be active in the simulation as much as possible, to avoid artificial constraints. Dead end paths may also be active, if budget allows; if the cost of simulating all dead-end paths is high, you might simulate just the most common ones.

A variety of learning aids are provided (Figure 7.23). These help to:

- Enumerate the steps that result in successful performance.
- Specify actions needed to complete each step.
- Demonstrate any selected step.
- Demonstrate the whole task.

It is important that learners actually perform tasks themselves. Although demonstrations are constantly available, each demonstration resets the simulation at the point of the learner's last activity. Learners must perform each step themselves in order to be given credit for task completion.

*Figures 7.22 and 7.23 from* Breeze Thru Windows 95 Basics. *Courtesy of Allen Interactions Inc.*

**FIGURE 7.23** Learner options for help.

## Feedback

The simulation itself provides intrinsic feedback—the most valuable feedback for learning. If learners are changing the color scheme, for example, the simulated Windows environment will reflect the change. To be sure new users see that they have succeeded, additional intrinsic feedback can point out evidence of the accomplishment and enumerate the value of the completed task.

Progress information is also shown. For example, as learners accomplish each step, the step number changes color. In some instances of this design, different colors provide extensive status information, such as:

- Current step
- Not attempted
- Completed, but with errors
- Completed, but with assistance
- Completed with no errors or assistance

## Reusability

This very successful interactive model has been used to teach a wide range of procedural tasks. It is applicable to almost any process-oriented environment, such as electrical and mechanical systems, in addition to the obvious computer and information systems, where a number of specific operations will be carried out to perform tasks. The operations taught might include operation of a system, problem diagnosis, maintenance, or repair.

The capabilities of this design not only teach defined operations but also build a general competency with the software application and its conventions. Learners finish with a heightened probability of being able to complete untaught operations, as well. They practice thinking about the logical location of options. They have a sense of what is possible—of what features are likely to be discovered with sufficient effort. They know how to reverse actions, if possible. They have a sense of what may be dangerous and what is probably open for exploration.

The model can be adapted in a number of ways, depending on the level of mastery required and the complexity of procedures being taught. Adaptation possibilities include:

- Requiring completion of an entire task from beginning to end without viewing a demonstration along the way
- Requiring completion of an entire task without demonstrations or using other aids such as hints or step outlines
- Requiring completion of each step without any errors or help
- Using scoring systems to reward good performance
- Setting speed criteria

Once again, the wide applicability of the general model makes it worth the programming effort to accept content stored in files or a database. This approach allows the designer to edit, maintain, and expand the content without additional programming. In addition, each new application can be built rapidly and at low cost.

## Drill and Practice

The drill-and-practice method was once thought to be appropriate only for rehearsing and strengthening acquired skills. As such, it was thought to be of less value than other forms of instruction designed to teach new skills and considered to be a less sophisticated approach over all.

Today, however, we see that drill and practice can be one of the most effective instructional techniques, even for teaching new concepts. With performance-sensitive algorithms, it becomes quite sophisticated in its ability to adapt to the learner's skill and readiness levels, adjusting both practice repetitions and new content introduction in the process.

### Corrective Feedback Paradigm

One very effective drill-and-practice approach is called the *corrective feedback paradigm* (CFP). This approach sets an effective pattern for the rehearsal of failed problems. When the learner fails to complete a problem correctly, it is presented again after one or two other problems are worked. If the learner succeeds, the problem will be presented again a bit later, perhaps after four to six other problems. The technique works to keep learners reworking problem areas until their performance reliability strengthens. Rehearsal is then gradually distributed more broadly over time until problems no longer need practice.

In Figure 7.24, *a* through *k* represent a list of items to practice. When the second item *B* is missed, it is inserted in the list several times, each time with more intervening items (first two items later, then four, then six). As the items are answered correctly, they are removed from the list. This is precisely the review schedule that will best facilitate establishing new information in long-term memory. When additional items are missed, it is easy to see how complicated the review schedule for items can become. Complicated, that is, for a human to track. It's not at all difficult for a computer program to track such information. The power of this technique in achieving lasting results, even without addressing issues of interactivity, has been demonstrated a number of times.

**FIGURE 7.24** Corrective feedback paradigm example.

A fascinating illustration is found in a project undertaken by the National Food Services Management Institute to teach school food service workers the differences between types of flour. While the final objective was to help cooks understand the appropriateness of different types of flour for various recipes, an intermediate step required learners to know what is in each type of flour.

An invented subtask took the form of a game, Who Wants to Be a Miller?, which demonstrates interactivity and corrective feedback to build engaging interactivity.

## Context

A conveyor belt presents empty flour sacks to be filled with the ingredients necessary to match the sack label, such as all-purpose flour, cake flour, and bread flour. The milling plant has wheat supply hoppers, supplies of other ingredients necessary to make a variety of flour products, and, of course, a wheat-grinding mill (Figure 7.25).

## Challenge

Learners must fill each bag with exactly the right ingredients for each type of flour and demonstrate the ability to do so reliably. The CFP design integrates multiple instructional functions:

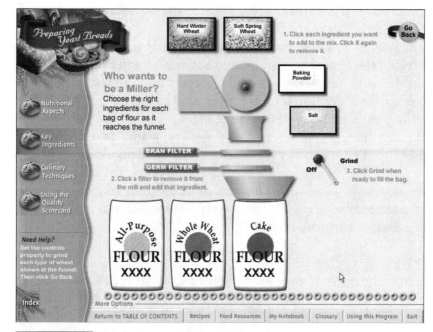

**FIGURE 7.25**  Context screen of Who Wants to Be a Miller?

- Sequencing
- Building on guesses and good thinking
- Assessment
- Practice
- Feedback and reinforcement

A short list of only three types of grain begins the challenge. For learners who have little background and may have decided to jump into the activity without any prior study (which is fine), differentiating the ingredients of three different products provides enough of a challenge.

If the learner correctly identifies the ingredients for the first sack, either by knowledge or by luck, the learner will have to repeat this performance a bit later to confirm the knowledge. However, the learner will be directed to a few different tasks before being challenged to repeat this

*Figures 7.25 to 7.28 from* Cooking with Flair: Preparing Yeast Breads, Quick Breads, Cakes, Pasta, Rice & Grains. *Courtesy of National Food Service Management Institute, University of Mississippi.*

initial success. If the learner succeeds three times without error, the challenge is retired.

If the learner makes an error, the same type of flour sack will reappear at the left of the conveyor belt, behind any sacks currently there. Learners see that they will have to compose the correct mixture after a delay of filling intermediate sacks, so they are motivated to mentally rehearse the correct ingredients specified in the feedback.

Failed challenges repeat frequently, generally after two intervening exercises, until a correct answer is given. The challenge continues to repeat, but if the learner continues to respond correctly, spacing increases—that is, increasing numbers of intervening exercises appear—until the learner has satisfied the mastery criterion, often set at three consecutive perfect performances.

### Activity

An intuitive interface allows learners to control the feed from supply hoppers that contain such things as hard winter wheat, soft winter wheat, salt, and baking powder through very simple interfaces (Figure 7.26). Clicking the supply bins once opens them. Clicking again closes them.

Similarly, learners click filters for bran and germ to deactivate or reactivate them, then click the GRIND lever (Figure 7.25) to begin the process of grinding the wheat and mixing the ingredients. Note the use of delayed judgment here—the learner can adjust the ingredients any number of

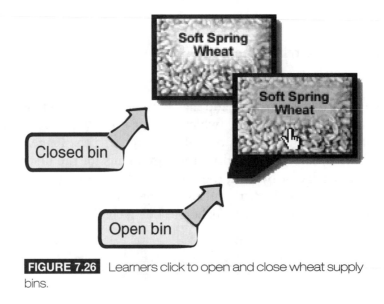

**FIGURE 7.26** Learners click to open and close wheat supply bins.

times with no penalty when considering the correct choices. It isn't until the GRIND lever is pressed that any judging begins.

At their option, learners can access information describing the composition of various special-purpose and general-purpose flours (Figure 7.27). Those learners who want to avoid all risk of making an error may prefer to study first, rather than guess. However, to confirm mastery, learners must eventually complete the exercise on their own, without having reference information displayed.

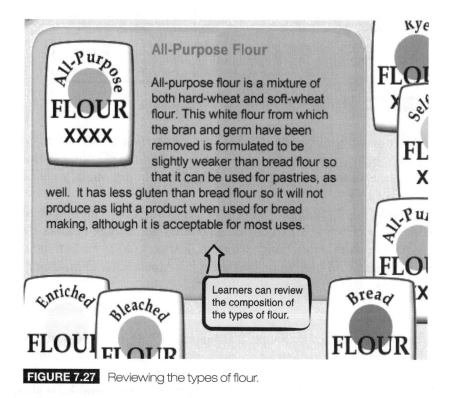

**FIGURE 7.27** Reviewing the types of flour.

## Feedback

Animation and sounds confirm every gesture, making the interaction pleasant and building anticipation as learners watch to see if their selected ingredients are correct. When the process is complete, the bag is sealed, and the conveyor belt advances the sacks, bringing the next item to the filling hopper. A correct sack closes and moves along the belt; an improperly filled sack is rejected (Figure 7.28). (CFP aside, this animation makes for a remarkably entertaining activity.)

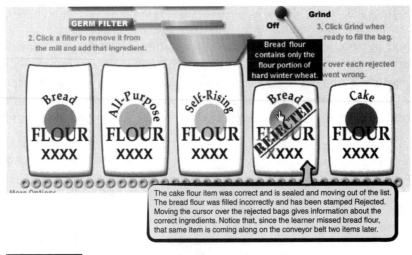

The cake flour item was correct and is sealed and moving out of the list. The bread flour was filled incorrectly and has been stamped Rejected. Moving the cursor over the rejected bags gives information about the correct ingredients. Notice that, since the learner missed bread flour, that same item is coming along on the conveyor belt two items later.

**FIGURE 7.28**  Learner errors trigger repeated practice.

To learn what went wrong, learners can move the cursor over rejected bags to see the proper ingredients. They must do this, of course, before they have filled enough sacks to move the rejected ones out of sight on the conveyor belt.

After successfully filling all bags of all types correctly and repeatedly, the conveyor belt stops. Learners are told what percentage of sacks they filled correctly. Almost without exception, learners scoring less than 100 percent opt to try all over again, with the full expectation of making no errors. Their expectations are usually met.

## Reusability

CFP, based on research by Siegel and Misselt (1984), and its interactivity have been shown to be effective across a wide array of tasks, content areas, and learner populations. CFP keeps interest and involvement high for both adult learners and children (Figure 7.29). Learners who have already developed strong skills merely have those skills confirmed and exit the sequence quickly. Those who are completely new to the content see its breadth unveiled slowly and at varying speeds, commensurate with their growing abilities.

Because of the paradigm's many positive attributes, it is very much worth programming the central logic in a generalized way so that a variety of user interfaces and content can be supported. As always, once this is done, this outstanding learning experience becomes very quick and inexpensive to implement.

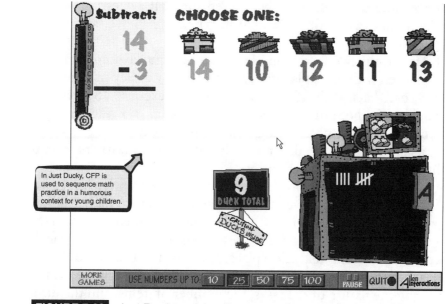

**Demo on CD**

**FIGURE 7.29** Just Ducky subtraction game demonstrates reuse of corrective feedback paradigm. (*From* Drill Bits Just Ducky. *Courtesy of Allen Interactions Inc.*)

## Not for All Instructional Needs

As energetic and popular as CFP is with learners, it is tempting to use it quite frequently. It would be a mistake to apply it to all learning needs, of course, at least without careful adaptation. While other situations would warrant caution, CFP is particularly appropriate for:

- Paired-associate learning, such as the names, sizes, colors, purpose, or locations of things

- Learning foreign language vocabulary (a form of paired-associate learning)

- Concept classification activities

- Short-process practice, such as arithmetic skills

When helping my children study for school, I have often used the CFP approach, even without computer involvement. It works for so many school learning tasks. When the kids got a question right, I'd ask it again later for verification, then retire it if they answered correctly. If they got it wrong, I'd ask it again one or two items later, then four or five items later, then once more for verification before retiring it. If a question were missed anywhere along the line, we'd start its cycle all over again, beginning after the next question or two.

CFP is extremely effective and fun. Learners quickly understand the paradigm even without explanation and know that if they miss an item, it's going to come back again after one or two other exercises. Sometimes my kids would recite both the problem and the answer, knowing exactly what I was about to ask them. Knowing how the paradigm works doesn't inhibit its effectiveness at all; it probably enhances it. Learners seem to delight in anticipating the repetition.

You may be wondering how to determine the appropriate parameters. Luckily, experience has proved that the paradigm is extremely resilient to minor differences in the review schedule. The retirement criterion (how many consecutive corrects indicate mastery) is most responsible for the degree of overlearning that takes place. A 1-3-5, a 2-4-6, or a different review schedule will have similar results. The choice should be made by considering the nature of the tasks, the number of items, and the degree of confusion between them. As long as the increasing ratio review pattern is maintained, the learning gains will be significant.

## Problem-Solving Investigation

Everyone loves a mystery. Storytelling is a wonderful way to establish a context for communication and learning, and mystery stories hold special interest. As luck would have it, mysteries provide just the right context for learning.

We've previously discussed the value of challenging learners before we start telling them all we want them to know. We put the challenge first because, among other things, there's a good chance learners will ask for the very information we wanted to tell them. When learners ask for help in the face of a challenge they can't meet, there's a specific and meaningful context for the information. They attend to and value the help being provided in a very concrete way.

Mysteries (problem-solving exercises) provide a natural context for putting the challenge up front. In this context, learners don't feel ill at ease, as if being tested will lead to an inevitable humiliation (perhaps just to demonstrate how much they need the training). Rather, learners realize it's part of the game, and they're into it easily. They know they'll have to be on their toes to figure things out—not a bad thing. And they even *expect* delayed judgment! Can't beat that.

For an example, I've chosen another lesson from *Statistical Process Control* (SPC). The need here is for learners to put together all the information they've learned from a series of lessons dealing with the facts, concepts, and procedures of SPC. It's done as a simulated investigation, because solving problems in real life isn't just answering some test questions correctly. It's asking around, searching for information, and putting two and two together. It is likely the problem you are facing isn't exactly like one in any textbook. You will need all the specialized facts, skills, and processes learned—but it will be an adventure rather than a class.

## Context

A manufacturing environment in which SPC is used is presented, including control charts and logs for the past two weeks and access to responsible individuals, such as the operator, supervisor, engineer, and maintenance staff (Figure 7.30).

**Demo on CD**

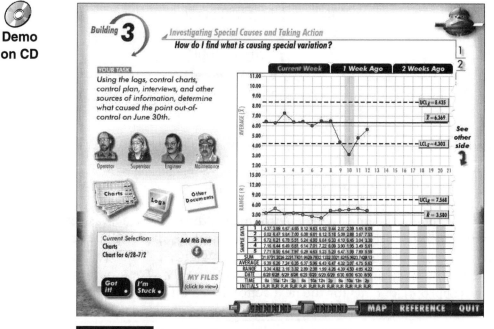

**FIGURE 7.30** Investigating control charts in SPC.

*Figures 7.30 to 7.38 from* Statistical Process Control. *Courtesy of DaimlerChrysler Corporation, DaimlerChrysler Quality Institute.*

## Challenge

Learners are presented with an out-of-control point on the control chart and charged with determining the cause (Figure 7.31). This sort of analysis activity is exactly what SPC is all about.

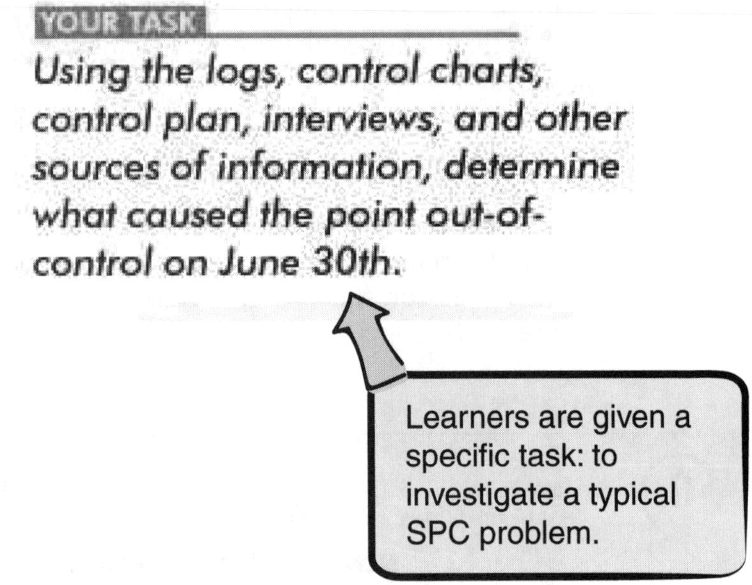

YOUR TASK

*Using the logs, control charts, control plan, interviews, and other sources of information, determine what caused the point out-of-control on June 30th.*

Learners are given a specific task: to investigate a typical SPC problem.

**FIGURE 7.31** Task challenge in SPC.

## Activity

Learners have a number of resources at hand to fuel their investigations. They can click coworkers to interview them regarding the evidence at hand (Figures 7.32 to 7.36).

Like all good problem-solving environments, the environment is very open, with many sources of information, only some of which will be productive in generating a solution. Some learners will need additional guidance if a promising path does not become clear. The I'M STUCK button provides appropriate hints for the next action based on what the learner has already discovered (Figure 7.37).

## Feedback

The learner indicates that the mystery is solved by clicking the GOT IT! button. Then the learner must identify the cause of the problem. Interestingly, the feedback for answering is an additional challenge to the learner.

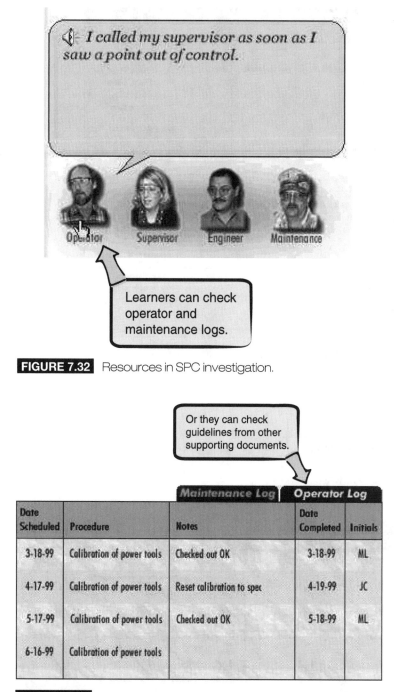

**FIGURE 7.32**   Resources in SPC investigation.

**FIGURE 7.33**   Maintenance log and operator log are available for inspection.

| Function | Potential Failure Mode | Potential Effects | Cause | Process Controls |
|---|---|---|---|---|
| Fender hanging process on BIW<br><br>- Hang right front fender<br><br>- Hang left front fender<br><br>- Gap door to fender at 5mm +/- 1.5mm | Improperly aligned door | Door to fender gap out of spec | Misaligned screws | Visual check of placement before fastening. Remove and refasten per work procedure |
| | | | Over/under torque of screws | Calibration of power tool at 30 day interval |
| | Improperly installed fender | Door to fender gap out of spec | Operator failed to locate fender to locating holes | Locate fender to locating holes during loose assembly |
| | | | Fender fixture out of spec | Recalibrate to master monthly |

**FIGURE 7.34**  FMEA document contains important clues for problem solving.

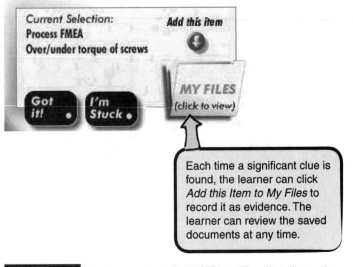

Each time a significant clue is found, the learner can click *Add this Item to My Files* to record it as evidence. The learner can review the saved documents at any time.

**FIGURE 7.35**  Learners can collect information they'll need later to support their conclusions.

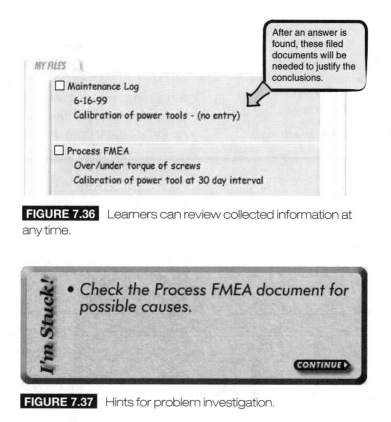

**FIGURE 7.36**  Learners can review collected information at any time.

**FIGURE 7.37**  Hints for problem investigation.

Now, the learner must indicate which specific pieces of evidence support the conclusion drawn (Figure 7.38).

If learners make the wrong conclusion, or have not collected appropriate evidence to support their conclusions, they have to go back and continue gathering evidence on which to build a solid argument.

### Reusability

This investigation model provides an excellent design for any situation in which the learner must analyze a problem by observation and research and then identify a solution. This design can be generalized to other situations quite directly, but the actual implementation may require some effort, simply because the data representations and learner gestures should match the context and desired learning outcomes.

Facing a problem with specific meaning and value to the learner rarely fails to enhance the motivation and value of the e-learning experience. Success in these interactions usually does two things for the learner: it

*What was the cause for the June 30th point out-of-control on the X-bar and R chart?*

**A** Misaligned screws

**B** Fender setter machine out of spec

**C** Under torque of fastening screws

**D** Bent measurement gage

**E** I don't know. Let me look some more.

🔊 *OK, you've made your choice. Now, put a check in the box by the clues in your Investigation File that support your conclusion. Click Done when you are finished.*

 Done •

FEEDBACK

**FIGURE 7.38** Identifying and substantiating the cause of the problem.

encourages exploration and a deeper understanding of the resources that lead to a solution, and it instills an enthusiasm to solve more problems—both in the e-learning context and also in the real work environment.

## Discovery

Discovery learning is one of the most effective of all learning models when done right. Ideally, the learner experiences a problem or phenomenon, then, through self-directed study and investigation, identifies and assimilates the underlying facts, rules, and concepts that describe the problem or phenomenon. Discovery may require the mastery of many facts and concepts and motivate learners to develop higher-level thinking skills and understand relationships.

Much has been said for and against discovery in the context of e-learning. When it works, discovery works very well. Learners who take responsibility for their own learning are generally motivated to discover everything they can about a problem, usually doing research that goes far beyond the specific needs of the moment. However, it can be slow and unreliable. Some learners may never realize the importance of experimenting with some key factor, for example.

In the training context, discovery models almost always veer toward a *guided* discovery approach. This combines the richness of a discovery environment and its attendant outcomes with the deliberate nature of more traditional task-based training. Goals are made clear, which helps direct everyone in fruitful directions, so time is used efficiently; but learners are still given considerable flexibility in manipulating and exploring the environment, and the intent is to develop a thorough, high-level understanding through learner-directed exploration.

A limited example of this can be found in the National Food Service Management Institute *Culinary Techniques* program in the section about yeast called "Bringing Up Baby."

## Context

The environment is a hypothetical laboratory with a petri dish for growing yeast colonies, a chart indicating ideal yeast growth, and various indicators describing the growth environment (Figure 7.39).

## Challenge

Learners are invited simply to experiment with various factors that affect yeast growth (temperature, availability of food, concentration of salt, and yeast age) to grow a yeast colony whose growth chart matches the target growth.

**Demo on CD**

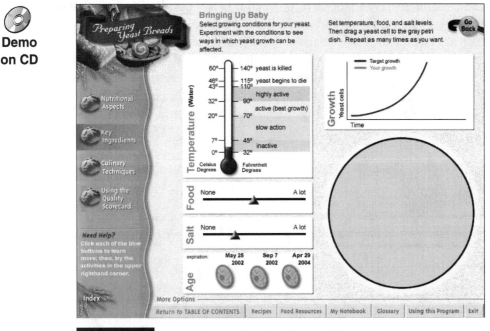

**FIGURE 7.39** Interactive yeast lab with petri dish.

*Figures 7.39 to 7.41 from* Cooking with Flair: Preparing Yeast Breads, Quick Breads, Cakes, Pasta, Rice & Grains. *Courtesy of National Food Service Management Institute, University of Mississippi.*

## Activity

The interface is simple: Sliders control relative availability of food and salt; clicking the thermometer resets the temperature. To start a colony in any given conditions, the learner grabs a yeast cell and drops it in the petri dish (Figure 7.40).

## Feedback

After starting the cell in the petri dish, the learner watches the colony thrive (or not) in the given conditions. A graph line is added to the growth chart so the learner can compare the growth achieved in the current conditions with ideal growth. Because this is guided discovery, messages in the petri dish offer additional guidance about how the conditions might be altered to achieve ideal growth (Figure 7.41).

That's it! The learner can repeat the experiment as many times as desired. There's no performance requirement regarding the activity whatsoever. Seems odd? Maybe, but just a few moments working in an environment like this reveals immediately that our traditional reliance on identifying behavior as right or wrong would not add much here. The attempt that kills all the yeast is just as useful and informative to the learner as the attempt that grows yeast perfectly. In fact, the learner who makes only the correct attempt and nothing more will know far less than the learner who makes lots of errors. In discovery, they're not errors, though. Each experiment and trial is a valuable activity in helping the learner understand the content.

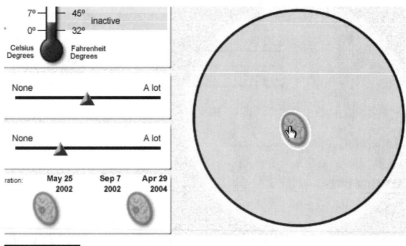

**FIGURE 7.40** Sliders control growing conditions.

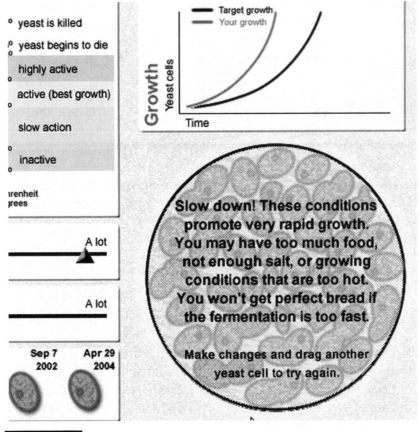

**FIGURE 7.41** Feedback clarifies the results of learners' experiments.

## Reusability

The effectiveness of discovery learning depends on the specificity of the behavioral objectives and the ability of the e-learning piece to effectively represent all parameters related to the target content. If the desired behavior is a sophisticated but general understanding of an environment in which learners must deal with unpredictable problems and challenges, discovery learning is unsurpassed, provided the parameters of the e-learning are reasonably true to the target environment. Unfortunately, in some cases when an attempt is made to design a discovery-based e-learning module, technical, budget, or other constraints compromise the relevance of the invented learning situation. Extended discovery learning in an unrepresentative environment can actually be far worse than a simple, more traditional approach. If the behavioral objectives for an e-learning project call for specific mastery of a body of knowledge or skills, discovery will probably not be terribly successful. It can often be a slow process, and unless exploration is carefully guided, it is difficult to guarantee that any specific content-based objective will be met.

## Storytelling

Another effective strategy for teaching a wide range of content is through the use of stories or scenarios. Stories provide an organizing structure that makes the subject matter more relevant to learners and can maintain learners' interest throughout a lengthy module or course; the stories lend personal importance that can be lost when dealing with abstract facts and rules.

This approach has two major strengths:

- The subject matter is embedded in a realistic context that learners find authentic and credible, making it easier for them to see the relevance of the new information and how they might use it on the job. This promotes transfer of learning.

- Learners remember the facts and concepts they have learned in terms of the stories and characters they encounter during the learning activities. They don't have to recreate abstract constructs; they can simply recall what specific people did in specific situations. This promotes retention of the new knowledge and skills.

An example of scenario-driven instruction can be found in an e-learning project done for a large financial corporation. This course was designed to teach employees about Individual Retirement Accounts (IRAs), and we used scenarios as a way of revealing a rather large body of very detailed subject matter.

### Context

A telephone conversation between a company representative and a customer or broker is presented on the screen. The actual conversation is presented via text in speech bubbles rather than via audio. The learner is able to listen in on these conversations and participate in their decisions regarding IRAs. During the scenarios, learners have to answer questions requiring knowledge and understanding of IRAs—with the help of a number of resource materials.

Each scenario is carefully constructed to illustrate the questions that ordinary people might have about IRAs over their lifetimes. For example, young professionals might have questions about what types of IRAs they are eligible for or what the tax advantages are, while those in their middle years might be concerned about moving one retirement fund into another or the penalty of early withdrawal, and retired individuals might have questions about how to get the funds out of their IRA accounts. The scenarios follow a set of characters through their lives, listening in on the events that cause questions about retirement planning and teaching the concepts and rules related to IRAs.

From time to time during the scenarios, learners can break away from the conversation and take an excursion, to delve more deeply into essential concepts and rules. They can then return to the scenario and apply what they have learned in the excursion to the questions that pop up in the conversations (Figures 7.42 and 7.43).

In Figure 7.43, the sequence of events begins when Taressa states that she has no retirement plan. Next, the learner sees both the question— "Why is an IRA a good idea for Taressa?"—and the possible answers. Once the learner selects an answer, feedback appears to the right of the answer selected. Finally, the expert (Ted) responds to Taressa's remark.

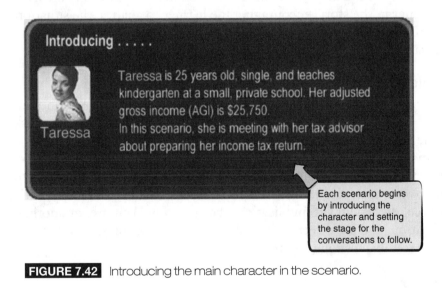

**FIGURE 7.42**  Introducing the main character in the scenario.

*Figures 7.42 to 7.45 courtesy of Allen Interactions Inc.*

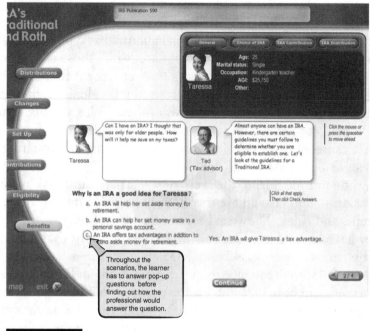

**FIGURE 7.43** Questions in the scenario.

The pop-up question (Why is an IRA a good idea for Taressa?) involves the learner in the story, encouraging the learner to analyze the situation and anticipate the expert's response. Then the conversation between Taressa and Ted continues.

### Challenge

Learners are presented with questions that get at the rules and concepts related to IRAs. These are usually the questions that the customer is asking the company representative, but may include other relevant pieces of information that should be considered when making recommendations to the customer. Throughout the scenarios, learners are asked questions that they haven't been told the answers to. They are referred to an appropriate resource, such as an IRS publication, the company Web site, or another publication, and are directed to read the relevant section to find the answer to the question (Figure 7.44).

### Activity

Learners choose from a limited number of options, which represent not only the correct answer but also common misconceptions that learners may have (Figure 7.43).

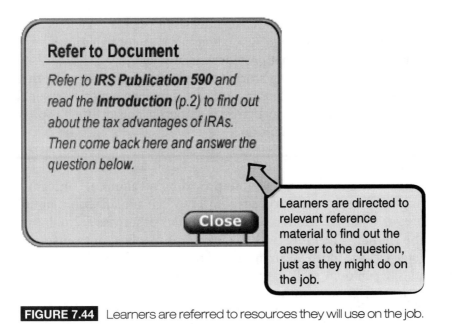

**Refer to Document**

*Refer to IRS Publication 590 and read the Introduction (p.2) to find out about the tax advantages of IRAs. Then come back here and answer the question below.*

Close

Learners are directed to relevant reference material to find out the answer to the question, just as they might do on the job.

**FIGURE 7.44** Learners are referred to resources they will use on the job.

## Feedback

After making a choice, learners receive immediate feedback about whether they made the best choice (Figure 7.45); they can then see how the company representative presents this information to the customer.

Here is another example of an effective instructional paradigm that doesn't tell learners everything they need to know up front, then tests to see whether they remember everything. Instead, all of the concepts, rules, and procedures to be learned are put in a work context. The situations stimulate the learner's need to know. This approach gives learners a rea-

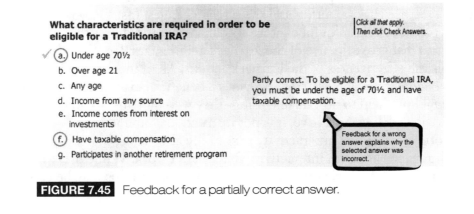

**What characteristics are required in order to be eligible for a Traditional IRA?**

*Click all that apply. Then click Check Answers.*

√ (a.) Under age 70½
  b. Over age 21
  c. Any age
  d. Income from any source
  e. Income comes from interest on investments
(f.) Have taxable compensation
  g. Participates in another retirement program

Partly correct. To be eligible for a Traditional IRA, you must be under the age of 70½ and have taxable compensation.

Feedback for a wrong answer explains why the selected answer was incorrect.

**FIGURE 7.45** Feedback for a partially correct answer.

son to want to find out the answer to a question (such as "Who is eligible for a Roth IRA?" or "Can Vanessa deduct her IRA contribution?") as well as the information source that provides the answer.

The customers' continuing stories provide a common unifying thread through several hours of online instruction. The stories put a personal face on the content and give it a more memorable context than is possible in a typical fact-based presentation.

### Reusability

Story structures can be very useful in providing meaningful context to what might otherwise seem to be trivia. They can add affection, humor, suspense, or other emotions to a topic that may otherwise seem distant from the learner. The more fully the learner is involved in an instructional episode, the more meaningful and memorable it will be. Continuing storylines, when done well, carry meaning and bring an established and automatic interest and motivation to each new topic.

Unfortunately, this storytelling technique is really difficult to achieve, as evidenced by the few good examples of it. Learners see through inadequate stories quickly. The stories may seem a contrivance that is more of a nuisance than an aid to learning. But when storytelling is done well, the continuity and personal meaning that it can add to disjointed content are exceptionally effective.

# Summary

The extraordinary power of interactivity is to get people thinking through doing and doing well by thinking. That power is not realized without careful and purposeful design. Instructional interactivity does not happen every time a learner clicks a button and the screen changes. Instructional interactivity provides a meaningful context, a challenge that requires thinking, activities that give evidence of the learner's abilities, and feedback that reveals the effectiveness of the learner's actions. All of these components must be integrated in a way that provides a beneficial experience for learners, enabling them to do valuable things they were not able to do before. Otherwise, whatever we have, it is not instructional interactivity.

Good instructional interactivity is not only affordable, but considerably less expensive than interactivity that doesn't work. While presentations, information navigators, and questioning applications may be easier to design and less expensive to build, they serve different purposes and are poor substitutes for effective interactivity when training is really needed.

Good instructional interactions have three essential characteristics:

- They are purposeful in the mind of the learner.
- The learner must apply genuine skills and knowledge.
- Feedback is intrinsic.

A number of strong instructional paradigms have broad applicability, such as the trapdoor hint, task model, corrective feedback paradigm, problem-solving investigation, and discovery designs presented in this chapter. If developed with externalized content and appropriate user-interface independence, these sophisticated models can be deployed very quickly and at reasonable cost.

# References

## Chapter 1

American Society for Training and Development. 2001. *E-learning Glossary*. Alexandria, VA: www.learningcircuits.org/glossary.html.

Andersen, David, Robert Cavalier, and Preston Covey. 1996. *The Dax Cowart Case*. New York: Routledge.

Bonk, C. J. 2002. *Online Training in an Online World*. Bloomington, IN: CourseShare.com.

Horton, William. 2000. *Designing Web-Based Training*. New York: John Wiley & Sons.

IDC. 2001. *Worldwide Corporate e-Learning Market Forecast and Analysis, 1999–2004*. Framingham, MA: IDC.

Korn, Errol R., and Anees A. Sheikh (eds.). 1994. *Imagery in Sports and Physical Performance*. Amityville, NY: Baywood.

Sandweiss, Jack H., and Steven L. Wolf (eds.). 1985. *Biofeedback and Sports Science*. New York: Plenum Press.

Werner, Tom. 2001. *Getting up to Speed on E-Learning*. Sunnyvale, CA: www.Brandon-Hall.com

## Chapter 2

Alessi, S. M., and S. R. Trollip. 2001. *Multimedia for Learning: Methods and Development*. Needham Heights, MA: Allyn & Bacon.

Carlzon, J. 1987. *Moments of Truth*. New York: Harper & Row.

Duffy, T. M., and D. H. Jonassen. 1992. *Constructivism and the Technology of Instruction: A Conversation*. Hillsdale, NJ: Erlbaum.

## Chapter 3

Atkins, R. C., and R. M. Schiffrin. 1971. The Control of Short-Term Memory. *Scientific American*, 225(2):82–90.

Gelernter, D. 1998. *Machine Beauty: Elegance and the Heart of Technology.* New York: Basic Books.

Johnson, J. 2000. *GUI Bloopers: Don'ts and Do's for Software Developers and Web Designers.* San Francisco: Morgan Kaufmann.

Keller, J. M., and K. Suzuki. 1988. Use of the ARCS Motivation Model in Courseware Design. In D. H. Jonassen (ed.), *Instructional Designs for Microcomputer Courseware*, pp. 401–434. Hillsdale, NJ: Lawrence Erlbaum.

Lenker, J. 2002. *Train of Thoughts: Designing the Effective Web Experience.* Indianapolis, IN: New Riders Publishing.

Malone, T. W. 1981. Towards a Theory of Intrinsically Motivating Instruction. *Cognitive Science*, 5:333–369.

Norman, D. A. 1999. *The Invisible Computer.* Cambridge, MA: MIT Press.

Pressey, S. L. 1926. A Simple Apparatus Which Gives Tests and Scores— and Teaches. *School and Society*, 23:373–376.

Pressey, S. L. 1927. A Machine for Automatic Teaching of Drill Material. *School and Society*, 25:549–552.

Shneiderman, B. 1987. *Designing the User Interface: Strategies for Effective Human-Computer Interaction.* Reading, MA: Addison-Wesley.

Skinner, B. F. 1987. Programmed Instruction Revisited. *The Education Digest*, 52:12–16.

## Chapter 4

Robinson, James: Quote from Quotation Dictionary, "Reason." In *The New Lexicon Webster's Dictionary of the English Language, Deluxe Encyclopedic Edition*, p. QD-79. Lexicon, 1987.

Rossett, A. 1999. *First Things Fast: A Handbook for Performance Analysis.* San Francisco: Jossey-Bass Pfeiffer.

## Chapter 5

Islam, K. 2002. Is E-Learning Floundering? *e-learning Magazine*, May 1.

Jonassen, David. 1991. "Thinking Technology: Context Is Everything." *Educational Technology*, June, p. 36.

Mager, R. F. 1997a. *Goal Analysis.* 3d ed. Atlanta, GA: Center for Effective Performance.

Mager, R. F. 1997b. *Measuring Instructional Results.* 3d ed. Atlanta, GA: Center for Effective Performance.

Mager, R. F. 1997c. *Preparing Instructional Objectives*. 3d ed. Atlanta, GA: Center for Effective Performance.

Reeves, B., and Clifford Nass. 1999. *The Media Equation: How People Treat Computers, Television, and New Media Like Real People and Places*. New York: Cambridge University Press.

## Chapter 7

Skinner, B. F. 1968. *The Technology of Teaching*. New York: Appleton-Century-Crofts.

Siegel, M., and A. L. Misselt. 1984. Adaptive Feedback and Review Paradigm for Computer-Based Drills. *Journal of Educational Psychology*, 76(2):310–317.

# Index

Just Ducky application, 140
Just-in-time training, 200

Kinesthetic association, as learning device, 272
Knowledge sharing:
    haphazard, 11, 248
    versus instruction, 277
    at start of design process, 126

Learner interface:
    design of, 68–75, 238
    as e-learning application component, 62, 198
    feedback about, 133
    function of, 272
    hypertext as tool of, 247–250
Learner motivation:
    in common instruction, 181–182
    as design issue, 226
    as e-learning application component, 62
    keys to (*see* Magic Keys to learner motivation)
    levels of, 153–155
    stimulating, 63–68, 150–153, 156–158,
        193–208
Learners:
    application control exercised by, 229–230
    content focus on, 77–91, 190
    creating experiences for, 60–62
    degree of participation by, 54, 150
    design role of, 22–23, 44, 45, 125, 131–135,
        137
    and failure, 172, 184
    feedback from, 128, 129
    guidance needed by, 220, 248
    input gestures made by, 271–272
    judging competency of, 96–97, 166–169, 185,
        186, 220–226, 275
    orientation within application, 235, 250
    time estimates for, 234
Learning content management systems
        (LCMSs), 187
Learning environments:
    effective, 248
    electronic interactivity in, 254–255 (*see also*
        Instructional interactivity)
    natural interactivity in, 254
    private versus social, 171
Learning experiences:
    action-consequence, 272–273
    designing, 60, 84, 86, 99–100, 274
    versus information presentations, 76–78, 98,
        248, 277–278
    initial impression of, 233–234
    navigation as component of, 93
    novelty factor in, 196, 197, 204–208

from question-answer activities, 284–285
    through repetition, 175–176
    teachers as providers of, 65
    and user interface, 75
Learning management systems (LMSs), 101,
    127, 187

*Machine Beauty* (Gelernter), 73
Macromedia, Inc., 118
Mager, Robert, 158
Magic Keys to learner motivation:
    anticipated outcomes, 158–169
    content, 179–193
    context, 193–208
    intrinsic feedback, 214–219
    judgment, 220–226
    multistep tasks, 209–213
    risk, 169–179
Management:
    decision making by, 28
    role in e-learning, 20–21, 23, 39, 43
    successive approximation used by, 122, 123
*Measuring Instructional Results* (Mager), 158
Mental images, versus verbal description, 270
Mentoring, 220, 248, 254
Metaphor, as navigational device, 249–252
Mistakes:
    learning from, 97, 172, 199, 237, 308
    mentor handling of, 220
    role in design process, 22, 55
    timely correction of, 133, 275
Models:
    for content, 130
    in design production, 139–141
    inappropriate use of, 141–142
    for instructional interactivity, 285–313
*Moments of Truth* (Carlzon), 36
Motivation. *See also* Learner motivation
    competition as, 170–171
    function of, 63–64, 66
    incentives as, 38–41
    influences on, 67–68, 151–152
    to learn, 59, 64
    learned versus instinctive, 158
    levels of, 67
    sources of, 65
Multimedia, interactive, 28, 39, 95, 161–169

National Food Service Management Institute
    (NFSMI), 174, 176–179, 189, 292, 305
Navigation:
    design imperatives for, 232–238, 251
    as e-learning application component, 62
    in e-learning application evaluation, 229

# Credits

Illustrations by Corey Stern. Screen captures by Allen Interactions Inc. unless noted.

Figures 3.9 to 3.16 from material codeveloped by Allen Interactions Inc. and the Multimedia Group at Lifescape, Sean York, director.

Figures 5.3 to 5.8 from *Breeze Thru Windows 95 Basics*. Courtesy of Allen Interactions Inc.

Figures 5.9 to 5.11 from *Internet Readiness Quiz*. Courtesy of Fallon Worldwide.

Figures 5.13 to 5.19 from *Cooking with Flair: Preparing Yeast Breads, Quick Breads, Cakes, Pasta, Rice & Grains*. Courtesy of National Food Service Management Institute, University of Mississippi.

Figures 5.20 to 5.23 from *Cooking with Flair: Preparing Fruits, Salads, and Vegetables*. Courtesy of National Food Service Management Institute, University of Mississippi.

Figures 5.27 to 5.31 from *What's the Secret?*, Vol. 2. Courtesy of KCTA-TV, St. Paul, MN.

Figures 5.32 to 5.38 from *Electrical Diagnosis II*. Courtesy of Daimler-Chrysler Corporation.

Figures 5.39 to 5.43 from *What's the Secret?*, Vol. 1. Courtesy of KCTA-TV, St. Paul, MN.

Figures 5.45 and 5.46 from *Herman's House*. Courtesy of American Family Institute.

Figures 6.2 to 6.8 from *WorldTutor*. Courtesy of Allen Interactions Inc.

Figures 6.9 to 6.15 from *What's the Secret?*, Vol. 1. Courtesy of KCTA-TV, St. Paul, MN.

# About the Author

**Michael W. Allen** is the primary architect of Authorware, the founder and former chairman of Authorware, Inc. (which merged with Macromind/Paracomp to form Macromedia, Inc.), and the chairman and CEO of Allen Interactions. Previously, he was a principal tools architect and systems designer of Control Data's PLATO computer-based education system, used around the world. He is widely respected for his abilities to define, design, and build tools which allow creative individuals to harness the potential of evolving interactive multimedia technologies. In recent years, he has concentrated on creative application design and defining unique methods for developing meaningful and memorable learning applications which fully engage the mind.

He holds PhD and MA degrees in educational psychology from the Ohio State University and a BA degree in psychology from Cornell College. He was twice elected president of the Association for the Development of Computer-Based Instructional Systems and is editor emeritus of the *Journal of Computer-Based Instruction*.

A frequent keynote speaker and widely consulted expert, he explains and demonstrates how interactive multimedia can be far more effective than it typically is. "It's time for a reinterpretation of the literature and an evolution of common practice."

# FREE CD-ROM

Whenever you see this icon, a portion of the application being discussed is provided on the free *Guide to e-Learning* CD-ROM, available on request. (The CD-ROM is PC-compatible.)

In some ways, describing an e-learning application is like describing a good movie. Just as there's no substitute for seeing the photography, witnessing the acting, and hearing the music and sound effects all combined, *experiencing* the e-learning examples discussed in the book will make some of my points clearer than any written description can.

Intrigued? I hope so! Here's how to get your *Guide to e-Learning* CD-ROM.

## What we need from you
Please communicate the following information to us:

Your Name
The name of your company or organization (if applicable)
Your mailing address, including zip code (or postal code)
Your telephone number (in case we can't read your address!)
Your e-mail address (in case you don't answer your telephone!)

## Request your free CD-ROM by mail, e-mail, or Internet
By mail, please write to:

*Guide to e-Learning* CD-ROM Offer
Allen Interactions Inc.
8000 West 78th Street, Suite 450
Minneapolis, MN 55439

By e-mail, address your message to:

books@alleni.com

Through the Internet, go to our Web site:

www.alleninteractions.com/books